Finance Fundamentals for Nonfinancial Managers Series
UNDERSTANDING CASH FLOW

UNDERSTANDING

FINANCE FUNDAMENTALS FOR

JOHN WILEY & SONS, INC.

NEW YORK   CHICHESTER   BRISBANE

CASH FLOW

NONFINANCIAL MANAGERS SERIES

FRANKLIN J. PLEWA, JR., AND GEORGE T. FRIEDLOB

TORONTO   SINGAPORE

Library of Congress Cataloging in Publication Data:
Plewa, Franklin James
    Understanding cash flow / Franklin Plewa and George T. Friedlob.
      p.   cm. — (Finance fundamentals for nonfinancial managers series)
    Includes bibliographical references.
    ISBN 0-471-10385-3. — ISBN 0-471-10386-1 (paper)
    1. Corporations—Cash position.   2. Cash flow—Accounting.
I. Friedlob, G. Thomas. II. Title. III. Series.
HG4028.C45P59 1995   94-45407
658.15'244—dc20   CIP

Printed in the United States of America

10 9 8 7 6 5 4 3 2 1

ACKNOWLEDGMENTS

We appreciate the patience of our families and the help of two graduate assistants, Trisa Starnes and Lynn Carter.

PREFACE

Because understanding cash flows is important for all managers and investors, this work contains sophisticated explanations written for unsophisticated readers. Our discussions contain hands-on directions and use real-life examples wherever possible.

Companies must budget cash flows in order to operate. They must deal with banks to collect cash, do business, or borrow money, and they must invest funds not used in operations. Companies must understand fraud and embezzlement and the controls that make them less likely to occur. To choose among investments in stock or to evaluate the efficiency of cash management, investors and managers must know how to evaluate the quality of earnings and analyze cash flow activity.

An income statement is a change statement that explains the changes that occur in the financial position of a company during a certain period. But the income statement does not explain all changes in financial position. Changes in working capital accounts, such as inventory or accounts receivable, affect both a company's liquidity and its cash flow from operations, but are not included on an income statement. Financial position can be altered drastically if a mortgage is paid off or stock is issued in exchange for land—activities that do not affect the income statement.

For this reason, the Financial Accounting Standards Board requires companies that publish financial statements to include a statement of cash flows. A statement of cash flows does show how changes in working capital or other accounts affect cash from operations or financial position. Therefore, we include two chapters discussing the statement of cash flows in a step-by-step, easy to understand presentation.

This book discusses both the philosophy and the mechanics of cash budgeting. It shows how to budget receivables and payables both for point estimates or in ranges using probabilities. It shows how to budget the investment of idle cash and how to evaluate a manager's skill in marshalling idle cash and investing the maximum amount for the longest times. All these techniques can be used to develop accounting spreadsheets, should you wish to, and the budgeting illustrations are prepared on accounting spreadsheets.

Managing cash inflows from sales requires knowing how to grant credit and then how to collect the cash due so that it can be used wisely. This book explains the four C's of credit and explains how to concentrate collections and speed them to the bank so that the company can use the cash as long as possible. The chapters on cash management explain the banking system and the different types of float a company might exploit.

Business bank accounts are different from personal accounts. This book explains these differences and tells how to deal with the bank. It tells how to read a business account activity analysis and explains in detail how to balance a monthly statement.

Four chapters are devoted to controlling fraud and embezzlement. We give examples from materials developed by Deloitte & Touche and KPMG Peat Marwick, two of the world's largest public accounting firms. We tell you how to recognize control weaknesses that allow fraud to occur and how to design controls that will make it less likely to occur. We devote a whole chapter to the kinds of controls that work best in small companies.

In one chapter we discuss quality of earnings, and then spend three more chapters explaining how to understand and analyze cash flows so that you can judge for yourself. One chapter contains the most complete compilation of cash flow analysis ratios yet printed and another explains step-by-step how to apply common-size and vertical analysis techniques to cash flows. These techniques have been used for decades to analyze income statements and balance sheets, but are new to cash flow analysis.

Our intention is to create a working reference. We hope this book helps you understand and manage cash flows. We hope you make good decisions—and lots of money!

CONTENTS

1

INTRODUCTION TO CASH MANAGEMENT:
Fundamentals of Cash Flow

Cash management is one aspect of the treasury function. At one time this meant that the cash manager was solely responsible for maintaining a company's liquidity. The cash manager's primary duty was to make sure enough cash was on hand to pay the company's debts as they came due. If a company had a cash reserve, the cash manager had done a good job. Excessive cash balances were not seen as a symptom of inefficiency.

This is not the case today. Cash management now is as important as the management of any other company resource and has developed into a full-fledged financial profession. Today's cash managers deal with the traditional areas of collection, disbursement, and concentration, but, in addition, they are also involved in the company's banking relationships, investment decisions, and forecasting. While cash managers are concerned about liquidity, they are now also judged by how well they manage the earnings potential of the company's cash. Effective cash managers know that cash is a scarce resource that must be conserved and invested to earn the maximum rate of return.

Cash Management Functions

Companies must have enough cash to purchase inventory for resale to customers, and to pay debts and operating expenses. In managing cash to meet these needs, cash management is divided into six functions:

1. Accelerating cash receipts and concentrating funds

2. Planning and delaying disbursements

3. Forecasting cash inflows and outflows

4. Investing idle cash

5. Reporting cash balances

6. Monitoring the cash flow system

Accelerating Cash Receipts and Concentrating Funds

Effective cash management involves speeding up the billing and collection process in order to move cash into the company's account so it can be used effectively. A company can reduce the time it takes to have cash available through several methods, including billing faster, using lockboxes, offering cash discounts, and using electronic funds transfers. Companies continually review and analyze their current systems to look for areas of improvement.

Concentrating cash involves moving cash from one place to another in the shortest time at the least cost. This means mobilizing funds inexpensively from banks at various locations throughout the country to a central location or locations. Concentration of cash can be in a single bank or in a number of regional locations.

Planning and Delaying Disbursements

The objective in planning and delaying disbursements is to gain the maximum use of cash, consistent with a company's goals and to have cash on hand when it is needed. In their strategy companies use such systems as a centralized accounts payable function, remote disbursing, controlled disbursement accounts, and payments by draft. Unlike collections, in which the credit manager plays an important role, disbursements is an area wherein the cash manager has complete control over the disbursement method, release date of funds, funding method, and other factors.

Forecasting Cash Inflows and Outflows

Forecasting cash inflows and outflows may be the most difficult task a company faces in managing its cash. Forecasting involves coordinating the cash inflows and outflows from the providers and users of cash throughout the company. Without an adequate cash forecasting system, the company could experience problems involving overdrafts, deficiencies, late payments, and reduced levels of earnings from invested idle cash. The company would be unable to assemble any overall cash plan. A forecast allows the company to know its cash position and make the necessary expenditures for such items as debt repayment, acquisitions, and payment of expenses. A company uses qualitative as well as quantitative analysis in forecasting cash flows.

Cash managers use both short-term and long-term forecasts. Short-term forecasts are more reliable and more specific than long-term cash forecasts.

Investing Idle Cash

Through efficient forecasting, a good cash manager can often generate excess cash for investing. Short-term investing has become an increasingly important activity for the cash manager. The process involves converting excess cash into short-term investments, then converting those investments back into cash when it is needed. Short-term investments include such items as money market funds, Treasury bills, commercial paper, certificates of deposits, and repurchase agreements.

Another option for the cash manager investing idle cash is to pay off short-term debt and reduce interest expense.

Reporting Cash Balances

Cash balances are normally reported on a daily basis to make it easy for a manager to determine and monitor the company's cash position. Daily management decisions are so affected by a company's cash position that information about cash is required for all operating units. Reporting cash balances includes gathering information from bank reconciliations, account analyses, and available funds reports.

Quarterly and annually, the company reports its changes in cash for the period of its published financial statements. The financial statement that contains this information is the statement of cash flows.

Monitoring the Cash Flow System

The purpose of monitoring the cash flow system is to determine whether the system is operating as designed and whether the company's goals are being met. Monitoring includes assessing how cash management affects other areas of the company. For example, how does the goal of accelerating cash receipts coincide with the lenient credit terms offered by the company's credit manager?

The monitoring process includes managing float and the costs and benefits of using specific banking tools. For example, a company may want to know if it is financially advantageous to reduce collection float by installing a lockbox system. (See Chapter 10 for a discussion of collection float.)

Influences on Cash Management

A company's cash management practices involve all of its overall goals and objectives. While the basic objectives of cash management are to receive cash as soon as possible and delay payment for as long as possible, other considerations confront the cash manager as he or she addresses the question of how to manage cash effectively as it flows through the system.

Other Operating Units

Cash management is directly related to manufacturing, marketing, credit, purchasing, and information systems, as well as the accounting function. The input of these operating units must be solicited, because they are an integral part of the overall cash planning process. The manufacturing and marketing personnel provide information useful in evaluating the amount and timing of cash inflows and outflows of cash for such items as sales, raw material purchases, labor, and advertising. The credit department can give insight into the effect on cash flows of alternative credit terms, customer billing, and collection procedures. The effect on cash of alternative payment practices by vendors can be estimated by the purchasing department, and information system and accounting personnel can provide support for collection and disbursement practices and help to analyze the effects of changes in those practices.

Upper Management

The involvement of upper management is important, because intercompany participation sometimes requires trade-offs. For example, upon examination of its accounting records a plastics manufacturing company found that it was making monthly royalty payments to an oil production company 10 days ahead of industry practice. When the production department was notified by accounting that this was happening, they resisted the accounting department's request to change the payment schedule because of their excellent working relationship with the oil production company. They were concerned that delaying the payments might jeopardize that relationship. Upper management intervened and consulted with all parties involved. The result was that the royalty checks were processed approximately 10 days later. The company experienced a significant cash savings because it had use of the funds for the 10 extra days each month.

Internal Factors

Internal factors that affect the cash position and cash management function can include the size of the company, degree of decentralization of cash management, and the makeup of the company's business. The size of the company, in terms of resources and breadth of operations, dictates the ability of the company to respond to changes in its economic environment. Large companies having numerous operating locations and extensive banking relationships tend to require a much more specialized cash management system than smaller companies. This type of cash management can justify the cost of a sophisticated cash management system, so that changes in cash management practices can be made more readily than in a small company.

The degree of decentralization of the cash management system plays an active role in the scope and structure of a company's cash management. As discussed in later chapters, centralizing the cash management function can be very effective. However, the more decentralized a company and its cash management practices, the more difficult it is to implement changes, because local operating units may be unwilling to give up control.

The makeup of a company's business can also impact its cash management practices and policies. Some companies generate amounts of cash that require more cash concentration and investment activity than needed in other companies. For example, the cash management problems of a large national grocery chain are not the same as those of General Motors Corporation, whose major business is the manufacture and marketing of automobiles. The grocery chain is more cash-intensive than General Motors and requires more cash concentration and investment activity.

Company characteristics include its scope of operations. For example, if a company needs to move funds to and from foreign locations, its cash management activities and organization will be different from those of a company that moves cash only domestically.

External Factors

Two external factors that affect the cash management function are (1) the local, state, and federal banking system and (2) float. The banking system, at all levels, exerts some influence on cash management activities because of its substantial influence on the check-clearing process and the availability of funds. The check-clearing process is discussed in Chapter 7.

The various types of float are discussed in Chapter 10. Float affects cash managers in two ways: first, by delaying the clearing of checks mailed out to creditors and vendors; second, by slowing the collection of checks deposited by the company.

Other Factors

Other factors that influence a company's cash management practices include the desired rate of return on assets employed, economic conditions, debt repayment and maturity dates, ability to borrow and at what terms, and expected short-term cash flows. A company must also evaluate its acceptable risk level, liquidity, financial strength, and the nature, amount, and timing of its sources and uses of cash.

2

LIQUIDITY, SOLVENCY, AND CASH FLOW

Liquidity, solvency, and cash flow are fundamentally related, and a manager should view these three factors as a composite rather than individually. This perspective should include an assessment of the adequacy (poor, good, or excellent) and trend (increasing, decreasing, or stable) of each of the three factors.

We will use the financial statements from the 1993 annual report of Texaco, Inc. in our discussion. These financial statements are presented in Exhibit 2-1.

EXHIBIT 2-1 FINANCIAL STATEMENTS—TEXACO, INC.

Consolidated Balance Sheet—Texaco Inc. and Subsidiary Companies

		Millions of dollars	
As of December 31		**1993**	1992
Assets	**Current Assets**		
	Cash and cash equivalents	$ 488	$ 461
	Short-term investments—1993 at fair value 1992 at cost, which approximates market	48	21
	Accounts and notes receivable (includes receivables from significant affiliates of $199 million in 1993 and $259 million in 1992), less allowance for doubtful accounts of $28 million in 1993 and $24 million in 1992	3,529	3,390
	Inventories	1,298	1,461
	Net assets of discontinued operations (see Note 3)	1,180	—
	Deferred income taxes and other current assets	322	278
	Total current assets	6,865	5,611
	Investments and Advances	4,984	4,533
	Net Properties, Plant and Equipment	14,171	15,226
	Deferred Charges	606	622
	Total	$26,626	$25,992

	Millions of dollars	
As of December 31	**1993**	1992
Liabilities and Stockholders' Equity		
Current Liabilities		
Notes payable, commercial paper and current portion of long-term debt	$ 669	$ 140
Accounts payable and accrued liabilities (includes payables to significant affiliates of $81 million in 1993 and $80 million in 1992)	3,324	3,177
Estimated income and other taxes	763	908
Total current liabilities	4,756	4,225
Long-Term Debt and Capital Lease Obligations	6,157	6,441
Deferred Income Taxes	1,162	1,370
Employee Retirement Benefits	1,104	1,102
Deferred Credits and Other Noncurrent Liabilities	2,636	2,693
Minority Interest in Subsidiary Companies	532	188
Total	16,347	16,019
Stockholders' Equity		
Variable Rate Cumulative Preferred Stock	648	648
Market Auction Preferred Shares	300	300
ESOP Convertible Preferred Stock	536	543
Unearned employee compensation	(337)	(385)
Common stock—274,293,417 shares issued	1,714	1,714
Paid-in capital in excess of par value	655	654
Retained earnings	7,463	7,312
Currency translation adjustment	18	(24)
Unrealized net gain on investments	58	—
	11,055	10,762
Less—Common stock held in treasury, at cost—15,273,372 shares in 1993 and 15,545,777 shares in 1992	776	789
Total stockholders' equity	10,279	9.973
Total	$26,626	$25,992

EXHIBIT 2-1   *(continued)*

Statement at Consolidated Cash Flows—Texaco Inc. and Subsidiary Companies

For the years ended December 31	Millions of dollars				For the years ended December 31	Millions of dollars		
	1993	1992	1991			**1993**	1992	1991
Operating Activities					**Financing Activities**			
Net income	**$1,068**	$ 712	$1,294		Borrowings having original terms in excess of three months			
Reconciliation to net cash provided by (used in) operating activities					Proceeds	**821**	1,707	1,883
Loss on disposal of discontinued operations	**223**	—	—		Repayments	**(796)**	(1,529)	(1,022)
Cumulative effect of accounting changes	**—**	300	—		Net increase (decrease) in other borrowings	**296**	(49)	(319)
Depreciation, depletion and amortization	**1,631**	1,627	1,560		Issuance of preferred stock	**—**	300	—
Deferred income taxes	**(283)**	67	35		Issuance of preferred stock by subsidiaries	**425**	—	—
Exploratory expenses	**352**	349	436		Dividends paid to the company's stockholders			
Minority interest in net income	**17**	18	16		Common	**(828)**	(828)	(827)
Dividends from affiliates, less than equity in income	**(227)**	(149)	288		Preferred	**(101)**	(99)	(103)
Changes in operating working capital					Dividends paid to minority shareholders	**(84)**	(8)	(21)
Accounts and notes receivable	**(275)**	650	786		Other-net	**(11)**	—	—
Inventories	**26**	45	(125)		Net cash used in financing activities	**(278)**	(506)	(409)
Accounts payable and accrued liabilities	**(215)**	(529)	(1,061)		**Effect of Exchange Rate Changes on Cash and Cash Equivalents**	**(13)**	(38)	(25)
Other-mainly estimated income and other taxes	**(108)**	(184)	156		**Increase (Decrease) in Cash and Cash Equivalents**	**27**	(382)	150
Other-net	**153**	(231)	157		**Cash and Cash Equivalents at Beginning of Year**	**461**	843	693
Net cash provided by operating activities	**2,362**	2,675	2,966		**Cash and Cash Equivalents at End of Year**	**$488**	$461	$843
Investing Activities								
Capital and exploratory expenditures	**(2,326)**	(2,533)	(2,795)					
Proceeds from sales of assets	**373**	176	221					
Purchases of investment instruments	**(1,342)**	(1,457)	(860)					
Sales of investment instruments	**1,258**	1,303	982					
Other-net	**(7)**	(2)	70					
Net cash used in investing activities	**(2,044)**	(2,513)	(2,382)					

(continued)

EXHIBIT 2-1 *(continued)*

Statements of Consolidated Income and Retained Earnings

For the years ended December 31	1993	1992	1991
Revenues			
Sales and services (includes transactions with significant affiliates of $3,027 million in 1993, $3,672 million in 1992, and $4,124 milion in 1991)	$33,245	$35,687	$36,112
Equity in income of affiliates, income from dividends, interest, asset sales, and other	826	843	1,050
	34,071	36,530	37,162
Deductions			
Purchases and other costs (includes transactions with significant affiliates of $1,709 million in 1993, $1,838 million in 1992, and $2,062 million in 1991)	24,667	29,961	27,070
Operating expenses	3,086	3,072	3,306
Selling, general and administrative expenses	1,783	1,792	1,841
Maintenance and repairs	418	446	466
Exploratory expenses	352	349	436
Depreciation, depletion and amortization	1,568	1,536	1,496
Interest expense	459	477	558
Taxes other than income taxes	549	530	551
Minority interest	17	18	16
	32,899	35,181	35,740
Income from continuing operations, before income taxes and cumulative effect of accounting changes	1,172	1,349	1,422
Provision for (benefit from) income taxes (see Note 13)	(87)	311	130
Net income from continuing operations, before cumulative effect of accounting changes	1,259	1,038	1,292
Discontinued operations			
Net income (loss) from operations	(17)	(26)	2
Net loss on disposal	(174)	—	—
	(191)	(26)	2
Cumulative effect of accounting changes	—	(300)	—

Of the years ended December 31	1993	1992	1991
Net Income	$ 1,068	$ 712	$ 1,294
Preferred stock dividend requirements	$ 101	$ 99	$ 103
Net income available for common stock	$ 967	$ 613	$ 1,191
Net Income Per Common Share (dollars)			
Net income (loss) before cumulative effect of accounting changes			
Continuing operations	$ 4.47	$ 3.63	$ 4.60
Discontinued operations	(.73)	(.10)	01
Cumulative effect of accounting changes	—	(1.16)	—
Net income	$ 3.74	$ 2.37	$ 4.61
Average Number of Common Shares Outstanding (thousands)	258,923	258,656	258,410
Retained Earnings			
Balance at beginning of year	$ 7,312	$ 7,514	$ 7,150
Add: Net income	1,068	712	1,294
Tax benefit on unallocated ESOP Convertible Preferred Stock dividends	13	13	—
Deduct: Dividends declared on			
Common stock ($3.20 per share in 1993, 1992, and 1991)	828	828	827
Preferred stock	102	99	103
Balance at end of year	$ 7,463	$ 7,312	$ 7,514

Results for 1992 and 1991 have been reclassified to separately identify discontinued operations (see Note 3).

Liquidity and Cash Flow

Liquidity refers to a company's ability to pay its short-term obligations. Accountants measure a company's liquidity by looking at its cash flow and the timeliness of asset conversion. To ascertain how liquid a company is, we generally focus on a company's current assets and current liabilities. *Current assets* are short-term assets that either are cash, will be converted into cash, or will be used in operations within one year. Examples include (1) accounts receivable that will be collected in 60 days, (2) inventory that will be sold in the current period, and (3) prepaid insurance for coverage that will expire at the end of the year. *Current liabilities* are debts that will be paid in one year or less. Examples of current liabilities include (1) accounts payable, (2) bank loans payable due in six months, and (3) the current portion of long-term debt due in the next accounting period.

Measures of Liquidity

The measures of liquidity used by managers and others are as follows:

1. Working capital
2. Current ratio
3. Acid-test ratio
4. Accounts receivable turnover
5. Inventory turnover
6. Operating cycle

All of these measures use amounts from current assets and current liabilities. In general, they help to identify liquidity problems so that a company can take corrective action to prevent a cash crisis.

Working Capital—*Working capital* is the difference between current assets and current liabilities and is a crude measure of liquidity. For example, Texaco, Inc. had the following amounts of working capital at the ends of 1992 and 1993 (all amounts are in millions).

	1993	1992
Current Assets	$6,865	$5,611
Current Liabilities	4,756	4,225
Working Capital	$2,109	$1,386

An increase in working capital may not be a sign of increased liquidity, depending on the composition of the current assets and liabilities. That is, we do not know the makeup of current assets and liabilities and, therefore, cannot tell whether the company is truly more liquid. In addition, different inventory cost flow assumptions (such as FIFO or LIFO) result in differing inventory amounts on the balance sheet, thus hindering intercompany comparisons. A better measure of liquidity uses ratio trend analysis.

Current Ratio—The *current ratio* is:

$$\frac{\text{Current Assets}}{\text{Current Liabilities}}$$

The ratio gives us an indication of the ability of the company to use its current assets to extinguish its current liabilities. What should the current ratio be? Some managers and financial analysts use a rule of thumb of 2 to 1. Generally, the higher the current ratio, the better, but there is no definite answer because the ratio needs to be evaluated in relation to a benchmark, such as the industry norm. The ratio must also be analyzed as part of a trend. Exhibit 2-2 displays industry norms excerpted from a 1994 Dun & Bradstreet report.

EXHIBIT 2-2   INDUSTRY NORMS AND KEY BUSINESS RATIOS—DUN & BRADSTREET, INC. 1994

Industry	Quick Ratio (Times)	Current Ratio (Times)	Debt to Stockholers' Equity
Agricultural Production	.9	1.8	63.9
General Building Contractors	1.3	1.7	99.7
Newspapers	1.6	2.2	57.0
Petroleum Refining	.7	1.3	166.3
Public Relations	1.7	2.1	73.4
Surveying Services	2.1	2.5	48.7
General Medical and Surgical	1.5	2.0	88.4
Amusement Parks	.4	.8	158.6
Real Estate Agencies	1.3	2.0	55.7
Jewelry Stores	.7	3.2	58.5
Musical Instrument Stores	.4	2.3	97.5
General Merchandise Stores	.9	3.9	47.4
Natural Gas Distribution	.7	1.0	170.9
Electric Service	.8	1.5	162.6
Trucking and Warehousing	1.2	1.5	97.7

The current ratio suffers from the same problem as working capital, in that the use of the total amount of current assets or current liabilities might obscure information about the individual components. When we look at total amounts, we do not know how soon the current assets will be converted into cash nor when current liabilities will be paid. Obviously, then, we must look closer into the composition of these totals if we are to determine whether current assets are relatively liquid (such as cash and receivables) or not (inventory and prepaids), and to ascertain when current debt payments will be made.

The current ratios for Texaco, Inc. are:

$$\frac{\$6,865}{\$4,756} = 1.4 \qquad \frac{\$5,611}{\$4,225} = 1.3$$

1993   1992

Quick (or Acid-Test) Ratio—The acid-test ratio is quick assets divided by current liabilities. Quick assets are cash, near-cash assets such as temporary investments, and accounts receivable. The quick, or acid-test, ratio is a more stringent test of liquidity than the current ratio, hence the term "acid-test." The ratio indicates whether a company could pay its current liabilities should they become due in a rather short period of time. Both the current ratio and the quick ratio are called "coverage" ratios, because they measure the company's ability to "cover" the payment of current liabilities. Activity ratios, such as accounts receivable and inventory turnover, tell us how quickly receivables and inventory will be turned into cash.

The quick ratios for Texaco, Inc. are:

$$\frac{\$488 + \$48 + \$3,529}{\$4,756} = .85 \qquad \frac{\$461 + \$21 + \$3,390}{\$4,225} = .92$$

1993   1992

Accounts Receivable Turnover—*Accounts receivable turnover* measures how quickly a company collects (or turns over) its receivables. The ratio is:

$$\text{Accounts Receivable Turnover} = \frac{\text{Net Sales}}{\text{Average Accounts Receivable}}$$

Texaco includes notes receivable with its accounts receivable. This should not pose a problem as long as the ratio is computed consistently from period to period. Texaco's accounts receivable turnover for 1993 is:

$$\frac{\$33,245}{(\$3,529 + \$3,390)/2} = 9.6 \text{ times}$$

The numerator should be net credit sales, but in most cases a user does not have access to this information. Instead, total net sales (cash and credit) is used as the numerator. Average accounts receivable is computed by adding the beginning balance and the ending balance and dividing by 2. As an alternative, the ending balance of accounts receivable is sometimes used as the denominator.

The accounts receivable turnover tells us the number of times during the year that the average accounts receivable balance was converted into cash. As a general rule, the higher the turnover, the better. That is, a high turnover ratio indicates that cash is not tied up in receivables and is therefore available for other purposes. Note, however, that a high turnover ratio might also indicate that a company's credit policies are too strict. The result of such a policy might be reduced sales and profits.

Texaco's net sales amounted to $33,245,000 and the average accounts receivable is $3,460,000, resulting in an accounts receivable turnover ratio of 9.6 times. If accounts receivable turns over 9.6 times in a year, then the average collection period is 42.4 days (365 days/9.6 times). This tells us that funds are tied up in accounts receivable for approximately 42 days; that is, it took the company 42 days to collect the money owed to it. This measure is useful because it tells you whether customers are paying within the agreed-upon credit terms that the company has offered. If a company's credit terms for sales are payment within 60 days and the average collection period is 90 days, the implication is that the company has a problem. One possible explanation might be that the company is selling to risky customers, potentially resulting in uncollectible accounts. A reexamination of the company's credit terms may be necessary.

Inventory Turnover   A similar analysis can be used with inventory. *Inventory turnover* is calculated as follows:

$$\text{Inventory Turnover} = \frac{\text{Cost of Goods Sold}}{\text{Average Inventory}}$$

Texaco uses the term "purchases and other costs" instead of cost of goods sold. Texaco's inventory turnover for 1993 is:

$$\frac{\$24,667}{(\$1,298 + \$1,461)/2} = 17.9 \text{ times}$$

This ratio is very important, because the quicker the inventory is sold (or turned over), the faster the company converts its cash investment in inventory back into cash. Like accounts receivable turnover, average inventory is the beginning balance plus the ending balance divided by 2. Again, the ending balance in inventory is sometimes substituted for the average balance. Cost of goods sold from the income statement is the numerator. You can see that Texaco's turnover ratio is 17.9 times. Similar to accounts receivable turnover, we can determine the number of days cash is tied up in inventory by dividing 365 days by the inventory turnover ratio. The number of days is the *average age of the inventory*. The average age of Texaco's inventory is 20.4 days (365 days/17.9). An increase in the average age of inventory could indicate that the company has an obsolescence problem. This may eventually lead to cash shortages, because assets are tied up in noncash assets.

Inventory turnover measures the efficiency with which the firm moves its inventory, and, as in accounts receivable turnover, generally the higher the ratio, the better. High turnover improves cash flow and minimizes inventory holding costs. Still, we should caution that high turnover can also mean that a company is experiencing stockouts by not maintaining enough inventory. In contrast, decreasing inventory turnover can mean that the company is building up inventory levels, which will result in higher holding costs. A possible explanation might be that some inventory items are not selling very well. The company would then proceed to determine why this is so.

Inventory turnover is also affected by profit margins. That is, discount stores and grocery stores generally have a low profit margin and need high turnover to generate an acceptable rate of return. In contrast, car dealerships and jewelry stores have high profit margins and, consequently, require only low turnover.

Operating Cycle—The operating cycle is important in determining a company's liquidity. The *operating cycle* is the number of days from the purchase of inventory for cash, to the selling of inventory on account, to the collection of cash. Sometimes the operating cycle is referred to as the time it takes to go from cash to cash. The operating cycle is equal to the average collection period of accounts receivable plus the average age of the inventory. Texaco, Inc. had an operating cycle of almost 63 days (42.4 + 20.4). If all things are equal, the shorter the operating cycle, the better. That is, the shorter the cycle, the greater the profit earned and the higher the cash flow. Exhibit 2-3 depicts the operating cycle.

EXHIBIT 2-3   OPERATING CYCLE

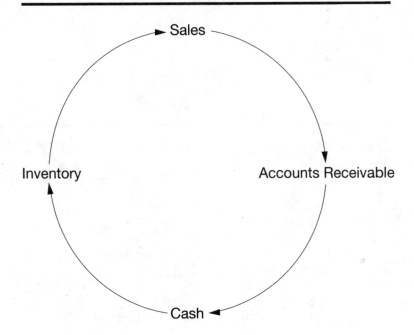

Solvency and Cash Flow

Solvency relates to a company's ability to meet its long-term commitments. Long-term creditors (such as bondholders) are interested in solvency because they receive interest payments and expect to have principal repaid. Stockholders are concerned about a company's solvency because even if the company is successful, dividends can be paid only if the company is solvent.

Measures of Solvency

Solvency ratios help determine the relative size of the claims of long-term creditors as compared with the claims (equity) of the owners. The best measures of solvency are:

1. Debt Ratio

2. Debt-to-Equity Ratio

3. Times Interest Earned and Fixed-Charge Coverage

Debt Ratio—The *debt ratio* is a common measure of solvency and is calculated as follows:

$$\text{Debt Ratio} = \frac{\text{Total Liabilities}}{\text{Total Assets}}$$

Texaco's debt ratios are 61% and 62% for 1993 and 1992, respectively.

1993	1992
$\dfrac{\$16,347}{\$26,626} = .61$	$\dfrac{\$16,019}{\$25,992} = .62$

Alternatively, the debt ratio can be calculated as the debt-to-equity ratio:

$$\frac{\text{Debt-to-Equity}}{\text{Ratio}} = \frac{\text{Total Liabilities}}{\text{Total Liabilities} + \text{Stockholders' Equity}}$$

Some prefer the *debt-to-stockholders' equity ratio:*

$$\frac{\text{Debt-to-Stockholders'}}{\text{Equity Ratio}} = \frac{\text{Total Liabilities}}{\text{Total Stockholders' Equity}}$$

The debt-to-stockholders' equity ratios for Texaco are:

1993	1992
$\dfrac{\$16,347}{\$10,279} = 159\%$	$\dfrac{\$16,019}{\$9,973} = 161\%$

As you can see, there are many variations of the debt ratio, but all variations attempt to answer the same question: Is the company too deeply in debt? All things being equal, the higher the debt ratio, the riskier the company. Too much debt places limitations on management's actions and increases the risk to stockholders. This is because the fixed charges associated with the debt must be paid by the company each period, thus reducing income and cash flow.

High levels of debt also have another effect. Because of the added risk to creditors, they may be unwilling to continue to lend the company more money. Funds may not be available, or may be available only at exceedingly higher interest rates, thus reducing cash flow.

However the debt ratio is computed, it is subject to essentially the same rule of thumb whereby an individual's house payment generally should not exceed a certain percentage of the individual's income. A company's debt ratio should be compared with a benchmark, such as the industry average debt ratio. From Exhibit 2-2 we see that Texaco's industry average debt ratio is 166.3%, indicating that Texaco's debt-to-stockholders' equity ratio is close to its industry average. A company's debt ratio should also be examined to see whether it is increasing or decreasing.

Times Interest Earned and Fixed-Charge Coverage— Additional information relating to a company's debt level is gained by calculating the times interest earned (interest coverage) and the fixed-charge coverage ratios. Both ratios assist in evaluating the burden of interest and other fixed charges, such as lease or insurance payments, on the company. The proportion of interest or other fixed charges that a company bears should be evaluated carefully, as it varies by industry. However,

in general, the higher the ratio, the more likely that the company will be able to continue meeting the interest and fixed-charge payments.

The ratios are calculated as follows:

$$\text{Times Interest Earned} = \frac{\text{Income Before Interest and Taxes (Operating Income)}}{\text{Interest Expense}}$$

$$\text{Fixed-Charge Coverage} = \frac{\text{Income Before Interest and Taxes (Operating Income)}}{\text{Interest Expense} + \text{Lease Payments (or other Fixed Charges)}}$$

Operating income is the numerator in both of the ratios, because interest is tax deductible and the numerator is a surrogate for cash flow from operations. A variation is to approximate cash flow in the numerator by also adding back depreciation or using cash flow from operations, which is taken from the company's statement of cash flows.

Texaco's times interest earned ratios are:

$$
\begin{array}{cc}
1993 & 1992 \\
\dfrac{\$1{,}259 + (\$87) + \$459}{\$459} = 3.55 & \dfrac{\$1{,}038 + \$311 + \$477}{\$477} = 3.83
\end{array}
$$

We start with income from continuing operations and add back income taxes and interest expense to arrive at operating income. We have subtracted the $87 million figure in the numerator for 1993 because Texaco had a tax benefit, mainly resulting from sales of interests in a subsidiary and changes in the tax law in the United States and the United Kingdom.

A Note on Debt—Do not get the idea that too much debt is bad because of its claim on a company's earnings and cash flow. Managers use long-term borrowings to increase returns (dividends) to stockholders through the use of financial leverage. *Leverage* is the use of debt to increase return on investment for stockholders. Companies can increase return on equity by using debt, provided that the return they receive on their assets is greater than the interest rate it pays to creditors. Therefore, long-term debt is not bad as long as it is not excessive.

The measures of liquidity and solvency are summarized in Exhibit 2-4.

EXHIBIT 2-4   MEASURES OF LIQUIDITY AND SOLVENCY

Liquidity

$$\text{Working Capital} = \text{Current Assets} - \text{Current Liabilities}$$

$$\text{Current Ratio} = \frac{\text{Current Assets}}{\text{Current Liabilities}}$$

$$\text{Quick (Acid-Test) Ratio} = \frac{\text{Quick Assets}}{\text{Current Liabilities}}$$

$$\text{Accounts Receivable Turnover} = \frac{\text{Net Sales}}{\text{Average Accounts Receivable}}$$

$$\text{Average Accounts Receivable Collection Period} = \frac{365 \text{ days}}{\text{Accounts Receivable Turnover}}$$

$$\text{Inventory Turnover} = \frac{\text{Cost of Goods Sold}}{\text{Average Inventory}}$$

$$\text{Average Age of Inventory} = \frac{365 \text{ days}}{\text{Average Inventory}}$$

$$\text{Operating Cycle} = \text{Average Accounts Receivable Collection Period} + \text{Average Age of Inventory}$$

Solvency

$$\text{Debt Ratio} = \frac{\text{Total Liabilities}}{\text{Total Assets}}$$

$$\text{Debt-to-Equity Ratio} = \frac{\text{Total Liabilities}}{\text{Total Liabilities} + \text{Stockholders' Equity}}$$

$$\text{Debt-to-Stockholders' Equity Ratio} = \frac{\text{Total Liabilities}}{\text{Total Stockholders' Equity}}$$

$$\text{Times Interest Earned} = \frac{\text{Income Before Interest and Taxes (Operating Income)}}{\text{Interest Expense}}$$

$$\text{Fixed-Charge Coverage} = \frac{\text{Income Before Interest and Taxes (Operating Income)}}{\text{Interest Expense} + \text{Lease Payments (or Other Fixed Charges)}}$$

3

THE IMPACT OF BUDGETING
ON CASH FLOWS:
Effects of Budgeting on Cash Flows

Budgets are used for both planning and control. Because of this dual role, an understanding of budgets is vitally important. It is essential to understand both the mechanics of the budgeting process and the goals management hopes to achieve. Budgets are the most formal and operational statements of objectives that most companies prepare. Budgets coordinate the plans of many different managers performing many different business activities, and each business activity will, in some way, affect cash flows: employees must be paid, equipment purchased and maintained, raw materials purchased and converted, sales collected, and so on. A "cash budget" compiles cash inflows and outflows, but all budgets (purchasing, sales, production, expansion) impact those flows.

Why Budget?

There is often a general resistance to budgeting among managers. Their resistance stems from two factors. First, managers often do not want to invest the time and effort needed to create a budget. Second, they may be afraid of the consequences of preparing a budget and having actual operating results differ unfavorably from those budgeted.

Many managers argue: "My operations are so stable there is no need to budget—they require very little planning"; or they may say, "My business is completely chaotic. Things are always changing. There is no sense in budgeting when conditions, costs, customers (and so forth) change frequently and unexpectedly."

Neither argument—stability nor chaos—is a valid reason not to budget. When operations are stable, careful budgeting enables managers to take maximum advantage of such stability. Idle cash may be invested to generate additional interest revenue. Inventory or accounts receivable might be examined to reduce the investment in these areas. Purchases may be altered to take advantage of bulk rates or seasonal price variations.

The chaos argument is even less credible. When business is not stable, there is an even greater need to budget, or plan operations. Failing to budget because the business environment is chaotic is analogous to refusing to chart a course for an ocean voyage because the sea is rough. A captain who must sail across rough water has an even greater need of a chart than one navigating when the sea is smooth. A manager who fails to budget is like a sea captain who releases the tiller when a storm comes up. When the water is rough, the captain needs to steer constantly and continually correct the course, checking each time with the charts.

When business conditions are unstable, managers must not only budget, they must budget carefully; not only for the most likely or preferred outcome, but also for the many other outcomes that might be encountered. If it is possible that the costs of raw materials will double, or that sales volumes will decline, these contingencies must be considered before they happen.

For each variable—materials cost, sales level, union negotiations—the budget often considers the high, low, and most likely outcome. This is what the military does: it plans for all contingencies. Because of the ease with which budgets can be changed on accounting spreadsheets, it is no problem to make multiple budgets once the template for the original budget is written.

Budget Games

The use of budgets as planning and control devices may generate apprehension in some managers. Once managers realize that the plans made before the year begins will return next year in their annual evaluations as benchmarks against which they are measured, they begin to budget differently. Frequently, a manager's participation in the budget process becomes entirely a game of "beat the budget."

"If I budget $150,000 for maintenance expense and actually end up spending more, I'll look bad," the manager may rationalize. "Even though I believe maintenance will cost $150,000 next year, I'll budget $175,000 so I can be sure I won't exceed my budget."

And so the budget becomes inflated.

The manager may be subject to another pressure to inflate budgeted costs or to reduce budgeted collections. The manager's supervisor may insist on cutting whatever amount is budgeted for costs or on increasing any amount budgeted for collections. That is another version of the same game.

Upper management may take the position: "I know they're inflating their budgets; I know they can do better, so I'll adjust the budgeted amount, whatever it is."

Knowing this, the middle manager preparing the budget will have a strong incentive to inflate budgeted costs and reduce budgeted revenues.

Budgetary Slack

The slack in a budget is the amount by which managers intentionally overbudget resource outflows and underbudget resource inflows. Budget slack is important in running a modern business. Even managers in businesses that are not chaotic are faced with many uncertainties and must make many decisions regarding unanticipated events in each budget period. If there were no slack in the budget, managers could not function. Budget slack gives managers the elbow room they often need to operate.

Types of Budgets

There are many types of budgets. The types are generally not mutually exclusive, however, and often tend to be budgeting approaches used by managers, more than actual separate types. We include a discussion of these approaches so that you will be literate in discussing budgeting with people who use such terms.

Continuous Budgets

The annual budget is often segmented into quarters, months, or weeks. When budgeting is by quarters, the first quarter is often broken down into weeks, the second into months, and the last two quarters prepared only as quarterly totals. As time passes and more information becomes available, budget data is updated. Each quarter eventually becomes the "second" quarter and is rebudgeted on a monthly basis. Then this budget period becomes the "first" quarter and is recalculated to show weekly activities. As each quarter passes, a new quarter is budgeted so that the budget is always for one year.

Continuous budgets, or rolling budgets, constantly add a new quarter as the current quarter has passed so that management is continuously refining its budgetary time frame. This practice forces managers to constantly look forward.

Static Budget

A static, or fixed, budget is based on a single reference level of activity. It quantifies sales, production, net income, or some other activity at a specific level specified by management. The activity level can be an actual historical or current level of operations, or an expected future activity level.

The significant feature of this type of budget is that it is for one level of activity and no other. If a company expects to produce 40,000 units in June, and so prepares a static budget for the cost of 40,000 units, the budget cannot be used as a target or benchmark if the company ultimately manufactures 42,480 units. To evaluate the company's performance in producing 42,480 units, a new static budget must be prepared at that level.

Master Budget

Most companies have a master, or comprehensive, budget that combines all the budgets for all activities in the company. Each separate budget must coordinate with the budgets of all the activities that interface with it. Shipping cannot budget without knowing how many units will be produced, sold, and shipped. Purchasing cannot budget without knowing the production levels budgeted for each month. Production cannot budget without knowing how many units are expected to be sold each month.

A master budget contains the budgeted financial statements that result from the budgets of all the company's individually budgeted activities. Master budgets are usually static budgets.

A master budget is composed of two parts, an operating budget and a financial budget. The operating budget shows how management expects all the components of operations to proceed. The operating budget contains detailed budgets for each of the different operating activities:

Sales budget
Production budget
Raw materials budget
Labor budget
Factory overhead budget
Selling expense budget
Administrative expense budget
Budgeted income statement

The financial budget portion of the master budget consists of:

The cash budget
The capital budget
The budgeted balance sheet

The relationship between the component budgets in the master budget is shown in Exhibit 3-1.

EXHIBIT 3-1   THE MASTER BUDGET

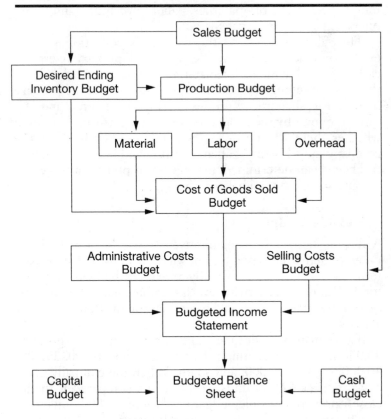

Preparation of the master budget usually begins with a sales forecast. The sales forecast and the anticipated inventory levels required to support the forecasted sales determine the production that must be budgeted. Once production is determined, the costs of materials, labor, overhead, and other operating costs can be calculated.

The sales forecast and the company's collection policies (and experience) determine the company's primary operating cash inflows. Payments for materials, labor, and overhead and the costs of selling and administration determine the primary operating cash outflows. By examining these flows and any flows required by the capital budget, managers can determine whether there will be excess cash to invest or whether the company must borrow. When investing and borrowing activities have been determined, managers can prepare a projected income statement and balance sheet.

Flexible Budget

A flexible budget is a quantitative expression of goals for a range of activities, based on knowledge of cost behavior patterns. A flexible budget is really a series of budgets prepared for several possible activity levels. Flexible budgets are used to determine what costs should have been for an attained level of activity.

If a company uses flexible budgeting and expects to produce 40,000 units, budgets might be prepared for 38,000, 39,000, 40,000, 41,000, 42,000, and so on. When the company actually produces 42,480 units, costs can be compared with the closest prepared flexible budget level (here, 42,000 units) or a new flexible budget can be prepared for precisely 42,480 units. Because the company has prepared a series of budgets, man-

agers know how costs change (or do not change) as activity changes and are prepared to quickly determine operating costs for any level of activity.

Often, flexible budgets express each cost or cost category as an equation. An equation for machine maintenance cost might be as follows:

$$Y = a + bX$$

Y is the total machine maintenance cost.

a is the portion of maintenance cost that does not change with activity, such as supervisory salaries or equipment leases. This cost is called a fixed cost.

b is the cost per unit of activity, such as the cost of wages and supplies per work order. This cost is called a variable cost.

x is the activity that drives or causes maintenance cost to change, such as work orders performed.

If the month-to-month fixed costs of machine maintenance (designated as a) total $80,000 and work orders each cost (designated as b) an average of $400, the equation for monthly maintenance cost (Y) is as follows:

$$Y = \$80,000 + \$400X$$

If 100 maintenance work orders (X) are expected next month, the budget for next month's machine maintenance cost (Y) is as follows:

$$Y = \$80,000 + (\$400)(100)$$
$$Y = \$80,000 + \$40,000$$
$$Y = \$120,000$$

Maintenance costs can be either out-of-pocket cash costs (as salaries paid) or the cost of consuming previously acquired items (such as wearing out tools). Both are costs, and, either way, cash flows are eventually affected (by paying salaries or by replacing tools).

Incremental Budgeting

The most popular and laziest way to budget is to think, "Well, what did we spend on machine maintenance last year? Oh, yes: $100,000. Well, let's just raise it 5% for inflation, plus 10% for sales growth, and let that be our new budget."

That is incremental budgeting. Each year is increased by an "increment" to capture whatever change management thinks next year will bring. Incremental budgeting is not very accurate and may result in careless allocation of scarce cash resources.

Zero-Based Budgeting

Zero-based budgeting begins the budget process by casting out all old assumptions and preparing the budget as if the function had not existed. To continue with machine mainte-nance, the department manager might first determine the recommended maintenance schedule for the machines, decide how many maintenance people of what skill levels are required to carry out the schedule, what tools and supplies will be needed, and so forth.

Incremental budgeting starts with last year's budget and builds. Zero-based budgeting starts with zero. This type of budgeting is too time-consuming to use every year, but it is wise for managers to examine their budget requests in this fashion from time to time. Zero-based budgeting makes a manager justify and defend a budget request, beginning with the need for the manager's department.

Participative Budgeting

Modern theory supports participative management. The premise is that employees who participate in setting operating standards or determining operating budgets will work harder to meet the standards or to hold costs within budget. Frequently, however, participative budgeting is just another budget game. Management asks for participation, but ignores the employees' contributions. When employees realize that their input is ignored, they may become demoralized.

Standard Costs

Standard costs are budgets for one unit of activity. In a manufacturing operation, standards are generally developed for one unit or one batch of product. Exhibit 3-2 shows a bill of materials, or standard cost, for a 410-B housing unit. In a retail or service operation, standards may be given for one activity, such as the standard cost of typing a letter or changing a tire.

EXHIBIT 3-2   BILL OF MATERIALS FOR A 410-B HOUSING UNIT

1	Q35 shaft assembly	@	$34.33
3	St-2 shaft primary seals	@	1.23
2	Primary pin connector stems	@	5.56
4	Primary pin connector stem nuts	@	.44
2	Half-size steel Cudoule flask	@	52.88
8	10 mm section pins	@	16.32
8	Section pin washers	@	4.00
8	Section pin locks	@	2.88

When standard costs are used, standards are set to represent efficient, effective, economical service. When the actual work is done, variations in efficiency, effectiveness, or economy can be determined from the difference between the standard cost and the actual cost incurred. Exhibit 3-3 shows the variances between actual and standard materials usage encountered in manufacturing 100 410-B housing units.

EXHIBIT 3-3   MATERIALS USAGE VARIANCES FOR 100 410-B HOUSING UNITS

Q35 shaft assembly	$68.66	Unfavorable
St-2 shaft primary seals	4.92	Unfavorable
Primary pin connector stems	55.60	Unfavorable
Primary pin connector stem nuts	4.84	Unfavorable
Half-size steel Cudoule flasks	0.00	
10 mm section pins	8.16	Unfavorable
Section pin washers	12.00	Unfavorable
Section pin locks	0.00	

Cash flows are affected by all wasteful actions, but certain variances key in on budget or price differences from standard. These variances and the significance of each are discussed in the following paragraphs.

Materials Purchase Price Variance

When raw materials are purchased, variances from price are isolated and included in the purchasing officer's performance report with an explanation as to why the variance occurred. Events that might cause an unfavorable materials purchase price variance include:

A general raw materials price increase.

A small-lot purchase from an alternate supplier to keep that supplier's product on an approved supplier list.

A small-lot purchase from a regular supplier because of an unexpected shortage resulting from a big order.

An emergency purchase that required special handling or shipping.

A favorable materials purchase price variance might result from a general reduction in materials prices, a reduced contract price negotiated by the purchasing officer, or an increase in buying volume that results in a quantity discount or reduced shipping cost.

A materials purchase price variance is calculated as follows:

$$\text{Materials Purchase Price Variance} = \text{Change in Price from Standard} \times \text{The Actual Quantity Purchased}$$

Labor Rate Variance

Because certain workers are generally used for the same activities each day, labor rate variances are not common. A labor rate variance occurs when wage rates change or a different worker is used for a particular job; for example, there may be a standard requiring an apprentice to drill holes that are actually drilled by a master craftsman. A labor rate variance is calculated as follows:

$$\text{Labor Rate Variance} = \text{Change in Rate from Standard} \times \text{Actual Hours Worked}$$

Overhead Variance

Often, the overhead charged to a product is tied to the labor used; such as overhead charged to products at a rate of $50 per labor hour. An overhead variance might be caused by such things as an increase in the cost of energy, lease payments, or maintenance. The overhead variance is calculated as follows:

$$\text{Overhead Variance} = \text{Budgeted Overhead} - \text{Actual Overhead}$$

Sales Collection Variance

Cash from sales is affected by changes in either the price or quantity of goods or services sold. But sales are also affected by the inability of a company to collect all its credit sales. Uncollectible credit sales are shown as bad debts expense. It is often useful also to reconcile budgeted sales to actual cash collected from sales, rather than only to credit sales. In companies in which collection is a problem, isolating a sales collection variance helps keep management and others focused on collections as equal in importance to sales volume or selling prices.

A collection variance is calculated as follows:

$$\text{Collection Variance} =$$

$$\left[\begin{array}{c}(\text{Actual \% of Sales} \\ \text{Uncollected})\end{array} - \begin{array}{c}(\text{Budgeted \% of Sales} \\ \text{Uncollected})\end{array}\right] \times \text{Actual Credit Sales}$$

If a company budgets uncollectible sales of 4% but actually has uncollectible sales of 7% of $100,000 of actual credit sales, the unfavorable sales variance is $(.07 - .04) \times \$100,000 = \$3,000$.

In the variance that follows, the company had a very small reduction ($2,000) in sales resulting from a decrease in selling price. The company increased volume by $45,000, but this was more than offset by collection losses of $50,000.

Budgeted sales	$580,000
Plus favorable sales volume variance	45,000
Less unfavorable price variance	(2,000)
Actual sales	$623,000
Less budgeted uncollectible sales	(20,000)
Less unfavorable collection variance	(50,000)
Actual cash from sales	$553,000

4

BUDGETING CASH RECEIPTS AND DISBURSEMENTS

Much of preparing cash budgets is mechanical and straightforward. The difficult part is deciding the dollar amount of sales, purchases, advertising, and other cash inflows and outflows. For example, cash collections in any particular month will often include collections from sales made in preceding months. For this reason, arriving at a specific dollar amount expected to be collected from accounts receivable in a particular month (January, perhaps) requires managers to decide on the dollar amount of sales expected to occur both in that month and in the preceding months (November and December). Managers must decide on what the amount of sales in these months will be ($30,000? $40,000? $50,000?), the pattern in which customers will pay (30 days? 40 days?), and the portion of sales that will not be collected (1%? 3%? 3.5%?).

This chapter introduces the basic mechanics of cash budgeting. The next chapter discusses one way to deal with the uncertainty inherent in all phases of budgeting.

Preparing a Cash Receipts Budget

A company receives cash from only a limited number of sources. Sales of goods or services result in either immediate cash inflows or in receivables that will be collected in the near future. Cash can be obtained from creditors by issuing debt or from investors by issuing stock. In addition, cash can be received as a return on (or of) loans made to others or investments in the stock of other companies. Finally, from time to time a company may sell one of its own long-term assets, such as a building, a patent, or a machine. A company has few other sources of cash.

The most common source of cash is the sale of goods and services in the normal course of operations. Usually, sales are on credit and cash is received during the 30 to 60 days following the sale. If, for example, sales in January are $50,000 and credit terms are net/30 (the customer must pay in 30 days), cash will be received in January, February, and (from late-paying customers) March. It is likely that some portion of the $50,000 will not be collected at all. If the company expects to collect 40% of its cash in the month of sale, 45% in the following month, and 12% in the third month (with uncollectibles of 3%), cash inflows from January sales would be budgeted as follows:

January sales		$50,000
Collected in the month of sale	(40%)	20,000
Collected in the following month	(45%)	22,500
Collected in the third month	(12%)	6,000

Because only 97% of sales are expected to yield cash inflows, only $48,500 is collected, leaving $1,500 (3%) as the estimated uncollectible sales for January.

Cash collected in January depends not only on January sales, but also on the sales and collection pattern for November and December. If sales in November and December are $30,000 and $40,000, respectively, and customers pay in the same pattern as expected for January sales, collections from these two months will be:

Month		November	December
Sales		$30,000	$40,000
Collected:			
In the month of sale	(40%)	12,000	16,000
In the following month	(45%)	13,500	18,000
In the third month	(12%)	3,600	4,800
Total from each month's sales		$29,100	$38,800

Collections in January from November, December, and January sales are budgeted as follows. (December sales and collections from December sales are in boldface so you can see the pattern.)

Month		November	December	January	February	March
Sales		$30,000	**$40,000**	$50,000		
Collected:						
In the month of sale	(40%)	12,000	**16,000**	20,000		
In the following month	(45%)		13,500	**18,000**	22,500	
In the third month	(12%)			3,600	**4,800**	6,000
Total collected in January				$41,600		

Exhibit 4-1 shows a budget of cash collections from accounts receivable for the first quarter, assuming the sales and collection pattern previously discussed and sales for February and March of $40,000 and $30,000, respectively. Exhibit 4-2 shows how a complete cash receipts budget might appear if the company also budgets $5,000 in rents each month, the sale of obsolete equipment for $6,000 in February, and the receipt of a $12,000 dividend from an affiliated company in March.

EXHIBIT 4-1 ACCOUNTS RECEIVABLE COLLECTIONS BUDGET FOR FIRST QUARTER

Month		January	February	March
Sales		$50,000	$40,000	$30,000
Collected:				
In the month of sale	(40%)	20,000	16,000	12,000
In the following month	(45%)	18,000	22,500	18,000
In the third month	(12%)	3,600	4,800	6,000
Total collected each month		$41,600	$43,300	$36,000

EXHIBIT 4-2 CASH COLLECTIONS BUDGET FOR FIRST QUARTER

Month	January	February	March	Total
Cash from accounts receivable	$41,600	$43,300	$36,000	$120,900
Cash from rents	5,000	5,000	5,000	15,000
Sale of obsolete equipment		6,000		6,000
Dividend from affiliate			12,000	12,000
Total cash receipts	$46,600	$54,300	$53,000	$153,900

Preparing a Cash Disbursements Budget

There is a finite number of sources of cash inflow, but an infinite number of causes for cash outflow. Cash is paid for labor, materials, and overhead items (energy, supervision, property taxes, insurance, and other items) required to manufacture products. Cash is used to pay dividends to stockholders and to repay interest and principal to creditors. All sales and marketing costs, any customer refunds, and any litigation settlements require cash.

Cash disbursement budgets frequently begin with the budget for payment of accounts payable. Accounts payable result from a company's doing business with its vendors on credit and includes payables for all materials and supplies. As in accounts receivable, there is a lag between the time the payable is created and the time when it is paid. If purchases of materials and supplies for the company exemplified in Exhibits 4-1 and 4-2 (receivables) amounted to 50% of sales, were purchased in the month preceding the sale, purchases are as follows. (Again, December sales, purchases, and cash payments are in boldface to highlight the pattern.)

Month	November	December	January	February
Sales	$30,000	**$40,000**	$50,000	$40,000
Purchases (50% of sales of next mo.)	20,000	25,000	20,000	15,000
Cash paid for purchases (in next mo.)	15,000	**20,000**	25,000	20,000

Exhibit 4-3 shows a cash disbursements budget for the first quarter, using the cash payments for purchases we just calculated, and additional outflows for dividends, equipment lease and maintenance, debt repayment, and property taxes. Exhibit 4-4 shows a combined budget for receipts and disbursements for the same quarter. Beginning cash balance for the quarter is $16,000, and ending cash balance is $19,900. Notice that the ending cash balance for each month is the beginning balance for the next month.

EXHIBIT 4-3   CASH PAYMENTS BUDGET FOR FIRST QUARTER

Month	January	February	March	Total
Cash paid for:				
Purchases	$25,000	$20,000	$15,000	$60,000
Dividend to stockholders		30,000		30,000
Wages	5,000	4,000	5,000	14,000
Lease and maintenance	3,000	3,000	3,000	9,000
Retire debt	18,000		18,000	36,000
Property taxes	1,000			1,000
Total cash payments	$52,000	$57,000	$41,000	$150,000

EXHIBIT 4-4   CASH RECEIPTS AND DISBURSEMENTS BUDGET FOR FIRST QUARTER

Month	January	February	March	Total
Beginning cash balance	$16,000	$10,600	$ 7,900	$ 16,000
Plus cash receipts from:				
Accounts receivable	41,600	$43,300	$36,000	120,900
Rents	5,000	5,000	5,000	15,000
Sale of obsolete equipment		6,000		6,000
Dividend from affiliate			12,000	12,000
Total cash receipts	$46,600	$54,300	$53,000	$153,900
Less disbursements for:				
Purchases	$25,000	$20,000	$15,000	$60,000
Dividend to stockholders		30,000		30,000
Wages	5,000	4,000	5,000	14,000
Lease and maintenance	3,000	3,000	3,000	9,000
Retire debt	18,000		18,000	36,000
Property taxes	1,000			1,000
Total cash disbursements	$52,000	$57,000	$41,000	$150,000
Net cash increase (decrease)	(5,400)	(2,700)	12,000	3,900
Ending cash balance	$10,600	$7,900	$19,900	$ 19,900

5

USING PROBABILITIES TO BUDGET CASH RECEIPTS AND DISBURSEMENTS

In Chapter 4, we assume that the company "expects" $50,000 in sales in January and puts that amount in its budget. Frequently, that is not the case. A company might "expect" several different amounts for January sales, depending on circumstances. The economy might stall or grow. Competition might increase, or the company might develop a new technology, besting its competition. The winter might be too cold, or too warm for some products (such as skis or down jackets). Other products might be linked to housing starts (such as roofing or lumber) or to the automobile market (steel).

In cases such as these, a company might estimate a range of possible January sales, perhaps $40,000 to $60,000. Managers might feel much more confident estimating high, low, and most-likely sales levels. They might predict sales for January as most likely $50,000, but with $40,000 as a pessimistic, worst-case estimate, and $60,000 as an optimistic, best-case estimate. This allows the company to develop three budgets: high, most likely, and low.

Best case $60,000
Most likely   50,000
Worst case   40,000

A sales forecast also includes an estimate of how customers will pay. In our example in Chapter 4, managers believe that customers will pay 40% in the month of sale, 45% in the next month, and 12% in the third month. Here again, managers might feel they can best describe their expectations about the receivables cash collection pattern by giving worst-case, best-case, and most-likely estimates. Exhibit 5-1 shows three estimates managers might make for sales and collection patterns for the first quarter.

EXHIBIT 5-1 ESTIMATES OF SALES AND COLLECTION PATTERNS FOR THE FIRST QUARTER

January sales estimates:

Best-case estimate	$60,000
Most likely estimate	50,000
Worst-case estimate	40,000

February sales estimates:

Best-case estimate	$55,000
Most likely estimate	40,000
Worst-case estimate	35,000

March sales estimates:

Best-case estimate	$45,000
Most likely estimate	30,000
Worst-case estimate	20,000

Sales collection patterns possible for all months:

	Best Case	Most likely	Worst Case
In the month of sale	50%	40%	25%
In the following month	40%	45%	50%
In the third month	9%	12%	20%
Uncollectible	1%	3%	5%
	100%	100%	100%

When these estimates are made and used in budgets, nine different possible cash flow patterns are possible for January sales: each sales projection (best, most likely, worst) is combined with three collection pattern possibilities (best, most likely, worst). Exhibit 5-2 shows the nine cash flow patterns that may arise from January sales. For example, depending on the collection pattern, January sales of $50,000 can result in any of three different amounts of cash from January sales collected in January: $12,500, $20,000, or $25,000.

EXHIBIT 5-2 NINE POSSIBLE CASH FLOWS FROM JANUARY SALES

Collections from January Sales

Sales: 50,000

	Worst Case	Amount	Most Likely	Amount	Best Case	Amount
In month of the sale	0.25	12,500	0.40	20,000	0.50	25,000
In the following month	0.50	25,000	0.45	22,500	0.40	20,000
In the third month	0.20	10,000	0.12	6,000	0.09	4,500
Estimated uncollectible	0.05	2,500	0.03	1,500	0.01	500

Collections from January Sales

Sales: 60,000

	Worst Case	Amount	Most Likely	Amount	Best Case	Amount
In month of the sale	0.25	15,000	0.40	24,000	0.50	30,000
In the following month	0.50	30,000	0.45	27,000	0.40	24,000
In the third month	0.20	12,000	0.12	7,200	0.09	5,400
Estimated uncollectible	0.05	3,000	0.03	1,800	0.01	600

Collections from January Sales

Sales: 40,000

	Worst Case	Amount	Most Likely	Amount	Best Case	Amount
In month of the sale	0.25	10,000	0.40	16,000	0.50	20,000
In the following month	0.50	20,000	0.45	18,000	0.40	16,000
In the third month	0.20	8,000	0.12	4,800	0.09	3,600
Estimated uncollectible	0.05	2,000	0.03	1,200	0.01	400

EXHIBIT 5-3 NINE POSSIBLE CASH FLOWS FROM FEBRUARY SALES

Collections from February Sales

Sales: 40,000

	Worst Case	Amount	Most Likely	Amount	Best Case	Amount
In month of the sale	0.25	10,000	0.40	16,000	0.50	20,000
In the following month	0.50	20,000	0.45	18,000	0.40	16,000
In the third month	0.20	8,000	0.12	4,800	0.09	3,600
Estimated uncollectible	0.05	2,000	0.03	1,200	0.01	400

Collections from February Sales

Sales: 55,000

	Worst Case	Amount	Most Likely	Amount	Best Case	Amount
IIn month of the sale	0.25	13,750	0.40	22,000	0.50	27,500
In the following month	0.50	27,500	0.45	24,750	0.40	22,000
In the third month	0.20	11,000	0.12	6,600	0.09	4,950
Estimated uncollectible	0.05	2,750	0.03	1,650	0.01	550

Collections from February Sales

Sales: 35,000

	Worst Case	Amount	Most Likely	Amount	Best Case	Amount
In month of the sale	0.25	8,750	0.40	14,000	0.50	17,500
In the following month	0.50	17,500	0.45	15,750	0.40	14,000
In the third month	0.20	7,000	0.12	4,200	0.09	3,150
Estimated uncollectible	0.05	1,750	0.03	1,050	0.01	350

EXHIBIT 5-4 NINE POSSIBLE CASH FLOWS FROM MARCH SALES

Collections from March Sales

Sales: 30,000	Worst Case	Amount	Most Likely	Amount	Best Case	Amount
In month of the sale	0.25	7,500	0.40	12,000	0.50	15,000
In the following month	0.50	15,000	0.45	13,500	0.40	12,000
In the third month	0.20	6,000	0.12	3,600	0.09	2,700
Estimated uncollectible	0.05	1,500	0.03	900	0.01	300

Collections from March Sales

Sales: 45,000	Worst Case	Amount	Most Likely	Amount	Best Case	Amount
In month of the sale	0.25	11,250	0.40	18,000	0.50	22,500
In the following month	0.50	22,500	0.45	20,250	0.40	18,000
In the third month	0.20	9,000	0.12	5,400	0.09	4,050
Estimated uncollectible	0.05	2,250	0.03	1,350	0.01	450

Collections from March Sales

Sales: 20,000	Worst Case	Amount	Most Likely	Amount	Best Case	Amount
n month of the sale	0.25	5,000	0.40	8,000	0.50	10,000
In the following month	0.50	10,000	0.45	9,000	0.40	8,000
In the third month	0.20	4,000	0.12	2,400	0.09	1,800
Estimated uncollectible	0.05	1,000	0.03	600	0.01	200

Exhibits 5-3 and 5-4 show the same multiple estimates for February and March. Using these multiple estimates, worst-case sales combined with the worst-case collection pattern results in a worst-case budget of cash collections by accounts receivable for the first quarter, as shown in Exhibit 5-5. Exhibit 5-6 shows first quarter cash collections, using the best-case sales and cash collection pattern. In both exhibits, our budget

process begins at the first of the year; cash flows from November and December sales are presumed as "actual" and continue as in our original budget in Exhibit 4-1.

EXHIBIT 5-5 ACCOUNTS RECEIVABLE COLLECTIONS BUDGET FOR FIRST QUARTER WITH WORST-CASE SALES AND WORST-CASE COLLECTION PATTERN

Month		January	February	March
Sales		$40,000	$35,000	$20,000
Collected:				
In the month of sale	(25%)	10,000	8,750	5,000
In the following month	(50%)	18,000	20,000	17,500
In the third month	(20%)	3,600	4,800	8,000
Total collected each month		$31,600	$32,750	$30,500

Note: November and December sales are collected as in Exhibit 4-1.

EXHIBIT 5-6 ACCOUNTS RECEIVABLE COLLECTIONS BUDGET FOR FIRST QUARTER WITH BEST-CASE SALES AND BEST-CASE COLLECTION PATTERN

Month		January	February	March
Sales		$60,000	$55,000	$45,000
Collected:				
In the month of sale	(50%)	30,000	27,500	22,500
In the following month	(40%)	18,000	24,000	22,000
In the third month	(9%)	3,600	4,800	5,400
Total collected each month		$41,600	$45,300	$49,900

Note: November and December sales are collected as in Exhibit 4-1.

Exhibits 4-1, 5-5, and 5-6 result in the following three budgets of monthly cash flow:

Month	January	February	March
Best-case sales and collections (5-6)	$41,600	$45,300	$49,900
Most-likely sales and collections (4-1)	$41,600	$43,300	$36,000
Worst-case sales and collections (5-5)	$31,600	$32,750	$30,500

The greatest change occurs in March, when the budget period contains all estimated results (no actual cash flow amounts from November or December). The difference between best- and worst-case scenarios is $49,900 − $30,500 = $19,400. Cash flows in months following March (not budgeted here) will, like those in March, be based entirely on budgeted amounts and should show variations of similar magnitude between best and worst cases.

But what about all the other possible combinations of sales and collection pattern assumptions? What about best-case sales and the most-likely collection pattern? Or best-case sales and the worst-case collection pattern? There are nine combinations in all. How likely to occur are the three cases shown in our exhibits? The rest of the chapter addresses this question.

Cash Flows and Probabilities

If we question sales managers and others, we might find that collection patterns are much more likely to improve than to deteriorate. Perhaps managers will tell us that they believe there is a 60% chance that collections will occur in the most-likely pattern. If the collection pattern does change, it is three times more likely to improve than to get worse. Put into percentage probabilities that explain (or add up to) 100 percent, those estimates become:

Best-case collection pattern has a 30% probability of occurrence.

Most-likely collection pattern has a 60% probability of occurrence.

Worst-case collection pattern has a 10% probability of occurrence.

When sales are budgeted at three levels, managers should also be able estimate a probability of occurrence for each level. Top managers may plan differently if middle managers are 90% certain that sales will be $50,000 than if they are only 50% certain. If managers can attach a probability of occurrence to the three levels, January sales can be stated as follows:

Best-case $60,000, with a 25% probability of occurrence
Most-likely   50,000, with a 50% probability of occurrence
Worst-case   40,000, with a 25% probability of occurrence

How likely are the best-case sales and the best-case collection pattern to occur together (as shown in Exhibit 5-6)? If these are independent events, probability theory tells us that the likelihood of the two events occurring together is the product of the two likelihoods (or probabilities) that either will occur alone:

.25(for best-case sales) $\times$ .30 (for best-case collection pattern) = .075

The occurrence of best-case/best-case is expected to occur only 7.5 times in 100. What about most-likely/most-likely and worst case/worst case? How likely are they to occur?

.50 (for most-likely sales) $\times$ .60 (for most-likely collection pattern) = .30

.25 (for worst-case sales) $\times$ .10 (for worst-case collection pattern) = .025

Neither worst-case/worst-case nor best-case/best-case is expected to occur frequently. Even most-likely/most-likely is expected to occur less than one-third of the time. According to our managers' best judgment, neither of these three estimates of cash flows is very likely to occur.

The Expected Values of Cash Flows

Using the three possible sales levels for January and the probability of each occurring, we can calculate a weighted average, or expected value of sales for January. Calculating an expected value works like this: If the likelihood of the three amounts of January sales occurring is as presented earlier, and next year occurs 100 times, we expect the 100 times to yield sales as follows:

Sales of $60,000 will occur 25 times.
Sales of $50,000 will occur 50 times.
Sales of $40,000 will occur 25 times.

The average sales for the 100 recurring years is $50,000, calculated as follows:

$60,000 × 25 times	=	$1,500,000
50,000 × 50 times	=	2,500,000
40,000 × 25 times	=	1,000,000
Total for 100 repeats of the year	=	$5,000,000
Divided by 100 occurrences	=	$ 50,000

Truly, $50,000 is the *weighted average* of the sales for January, because it was calculated by weighing each possible sales figure by its probability of occurrence (25, 50, or 25 times in 100). Another name for this weighted average is *expected value*, the term we use from this point on.

What is the expected value of cash collections for January sales? We know from earlier calculations that several different amounts might be collected, depending on (1) January sales and (2) the collection pattern. If the expected value of sales in January is $50,000, then the amount of January sales budgeted to be collected in January, and the occurrence of each in 100 Januarys is as follows (see $50,000 of sales in Exhibit 5-2).

Best-case pattern, collecting $25,000, will occur 30 times. ($50,000 × .50)
Most-likely pattern, collecting $20,000, will occur 60 times. ($50,000 × .40)
Worst-case pattern, collecting $12,500, will occur 10 times. ($50,000 × .25)

Thus, the expected value of cash collected in January from $50,000 in January sales is $20,750.

$25,000 × 30 times	=	$ 750,000
20,000 × 60 times	=	1,200,000
12,500 × 10 times	=	125,000
Total for 100 repeats	=	$2,075,000
Divided by 100	=	$ 20,750

Exhibit 5-7 shows the calculation of the expected values of cash collections from January sales. The calculation of the dollar amounts used is shown in Exhibit 5-2 for sales of $50,000. (The most likely sales level and the expected value are both $50,000.) Perhaps an easier approach to determining the expected values of cash flow each month is to calculate the expected value of the percentage of cash that will be collected in the month of sale and in the following two months. Exhibit 5-8 shows the calculation of those expected values. Exhibit 5-9 determines the expected value of sales in February and March. Exhibit 5-10 uses the expected values from Exhibits 5-8 and 5-9 to construct a budget of cash flows for the first quarter.

EXHIBIT 5-7 EXPECTED VALUES OF CASH COLLECTIONS FROM JANUARY SALES

Cash from sales in January collected in February:
$20,000 × .30 = $ 6,000
22,500 × .60 = 13,500
25,000 × .10 = 2,500
Expected value $22,000

Cash from sales in January collected in March:
$ 4,500 × .30 = $ 1,350
6,000 × .60 = 3,600
10,000 × .10 = 1,000
Expected value $ 5,950

Uncollectible sales from January:
$ 500 × .30 = $ 150
1,500 × .60 = 900
2,500 × .10 = 250
Expected value $ 1,300

Summary of expected values of cash flows from January sales:
Cash from sales in January collected in January (from text)	$20,750
Cash from sales in January collected in February	22,000
Cash from sales in January collected in March	5,950
Uncollectible sales from January	1,300
Expected value of January sales (from text)	$50,000

EXHIBIT 5-8 EXPECTED VALUE OF CASH COLLECTION PATTERN

	Probability of occurence		Percentage collected		
Expected value of percentage of cash collected in the month of sale:					
Best case	.30	×	.50	=	.150
Most likely	.60	×	.40	=	.240
Worst case	.10	×	.25	=	.025
Expected value					.415
Expected value of percentage of cash collected in the second month:					
Best case	.30	×	.40	=	.12
Most likely	.60	×	.45	=	.27
Worst case	.10	×	.50	=	.05
Expected value					.44
Expected value of percentage of cash collected in the third month:					
Best case	.30	×	.09	=	.027
Most likely	.60	×	.12	=	.072
Worst case	.10	×	.20	=	.020
Expected value					.119
Expected value of percentage of uncollected sales:					
Best case	.30	×	.01	=	.003
Most likely	.60	×	.03	=	.018
Worst case	.10	×	.05	=	.005
Expected value					.026

EXHIBIT 5-9 EXPECTED VALUE OF SALES IN FEBRUARY AND MARCH

Expected value of February sales:
Best case $55,000 × .25 = $13,750
Most likely   40,000 × .50 = 20,000
Worst case   35,000 × .25 = 8,750
Expected value $42,500

Expected value of March sales:
Best case $30,000 × .25 = $ 7,500
Most likely   45,000 × .50 = 22,500
Worst case   20,000 × .25 = 5,000
Expected value $35,000

EXHIBIT 5-10 **BUDGET OF FIRST QUARTER CASH
COLLECTIONS FROM ACCOUNTS
RECEIVABLE, USING EXPECTED VALUES
FOR SALES AND COLLECTION PATTERN**

Month		January	February	March
Sales		$50,000	$42,500	$35,000
Collected:				
In the month of sale	(41.5%)	20,750	17,637.5	14,525
In the following month	(44.0%)	18,000	22,000	18,700
In the third month	(11.9%)	3,600	4,800	5,950
Total collected each month		$42,350	$44,437.5	$39,175

Note: November and December sales are collected as in Exhibit 4-1.

The same technique can be used with other estimates of cash inflows (from investments or equipment disposals, for example) and cash outflows. The resulting cash flow estimates will be more likely to occur than any other single value.

6

AVOIDING PITFALLS IN GRANTING CREDIT:
Cash Flow Management

Often, a company uses credit as a sales tool. U.S. business practice has a long tradition of extending credit to purchasers of goods and services. The credit period extends from the time the goods are shipped until the buyer is required to make payment for them. In essence, the buyer is lending the seller an amount equal to the purchase price of the goods sold. This form of funding is a significant source of financing for most companies. Therefore, the cash manager must know how to effectively manage the factors that will reduce credit abuses and the amount of time receivables remain uncollected.

The availability of credit can help a company expand its market share if potential buyers perceive little difference between the company's product and those of its competitors. In addition, the availability of credit can increase the size of the total market. The automobile and housing markets would be much smaller if these items could be purchased only for cash.

What Is Credit?

Credit transactions result in an assumption of risk by the seller that payment will be delayed or not received. The credit period is from the date of the invoice to the date that payment is required. The standard credit period is usually 30 days and expressed on the invoice as *net 30* or *n/30*. Many times, the credit arrangement calls for a *cash discount* for the buyer if he or she pays within a stipulated period of time, called the *discount period*. For example, a company might sell merchandise on terms of 2/10, n/30. This means the buyer can deduct 2% of the invoice price if it is paid within 10 days; otherwise, the gross amount of the invoice is due at the end of 30 days. Most companies take advantage of cash discounts, because the cost of not paying within the discount period is extremely high. For example, a 2% discount foregone for 20 days each month results in an annual interest rate of 36.5% (365 days/20 × 2%). Even if the buyer must borrow, it makes sense to take advantage of the discount. Borrowing from most sources is less expensive than failing to pay during the discount period.

A company's management must carefully consider its policy regarding credit terms because of its effect on sales, profits, and uncollectible accounts. If a company has a strict credit policy, it will experience lower sales and profits, but less cash is tied up in accounts receivable. In addition, this will result in lower bad-debt losses, but, possibly, also disgruntled customers. The more lenient a company's credit terms, the more attractive are the products and services it offers to customers. However, if a company's credit policy is too loose, sales will be higher, but so will bad-debt losses and the amount of cash tied up in customer accounts.

Who Gets Credit?

A company establishes credit standards in order to reject customers who will be slow to pay or whose delinquency will result in a bad-debt loss. Credit standards should measure *credit quality*, or the probability that a particular customer will pay on a timely basis. There are several sophisticated methods, including statistical techniques, that can be used in deciding who gets credit; however, the final decision will still require the judgment of a skilled and experienced credit manager.

The credit manager will consider a number of factors in making the final decision as to who gets credit. The basic qualitative principles in such a case are often referred to as the "four C's of credit granting." (Some analysts refer to the "five C's" and treat collateral as a separate item.) The first principle relates to the *willingness* to pay, and the other three deal with the *ability* to pay.

1. *Character* relates to the reputation the customer has developed regarding his or her willingness to pay obligations as they become due. The company is interested in such traits as the customer's integrity and honesty and how they relate to the customer's intention to pay for purchases by the designated due date.

2. *Capacity* refers to the ability of the customer to pay existing obligations as they become due, as opposed to the willingness to pay. Capacity relates to the financial and managerial capabilities of the customer company to create profits.

3. *Capital* measures the financial resources and capitalization of the customer company.

4. *Conditions* refers to the economic and political environment in which the customer operates. This principle is concerned with how changes in the customer's economic and political environment might affect its ability to pay.

These principles provide the credit manager with a framework for evaluating creditworthiness.

Sources of Information Relating to the Four C's

Credit managers realize that in order to make a decision regarding the granting of credit, they must gather information: however, *more* information does not mean a *better* decision. The value of the information must be weighed against the cost in time and money associated with obtaining that information. The following sources of information assist the credit manager in evaluating each of the four C's of credit.

Character—Personal interviews are conducted, and the customer's credit application is reviewed. The customer's references, such as banks, suppliers, and insurance companies, should be called and the customer's payment record examined.

A customer's payment record is also available from external sources. Credit reporting agencies such as Dun & Bradstreet, Inc. and TRW furnish credit reports on individuals and companies. They provide credit reports and ratings on thousands of companies throughout the world. Both agencies can transmit credit reports in seconds to subscribers through a computer-based telecommunications network.

Local credit bureaus also provide credit information on individuals and companies. These local bureaus are normally affiliated with the Associated Credit Bureaus of America, which facilitates the exchange of credit information among member credit bureaus.

Capacity—Credit managers obtain evidence about a customer's ability to pay on schedule from an examination of its income statement and statement of cash flows. They make inquiries regarding the customer's quality of management, its product markets, trends in profits and sales, and bill-paying history. They also check background information on the customer company's officers.

Capital—Capital has to do with the financial resources (including collateral) of the customer. While the statement of cash flows is one aspect of capacity, the major emphasis in examining a company's capital is the company's wealth and the focus is on its balance sheet. The customer's working capital position and form of capitalization are investigated. Using trend analysis, key ratios (such as the current ratio, debt-to-equity ratio, and times-interest-earned ratio) are also examined and compared with industry norms.

Conditions—A customer has little or no control over the factors that affect its economic and political environment.

Changes in product demand, management, competitor's strategies, or in the national or international environment—all may impact the company's ability to pay its debts. Information on such conditions is obtained from sources other than those used for the assessment of character, capacity, and capital and include industry trade association publications and the business press.

As previously stated, the four C's present a general framework for credit investigation; however, they are still difficult to translate into a manageable course of action. Difficulties arise in how the credit manager measures each of these factors, as well as how much weight is given to each one in the decision-making process. In addition, the weighting of the four principles will vary from one credit analyst to another and from customer to customer. Based on experience, the credit analyst uses judgment to make his or her decision. Although the credit analyst uses quantitative analysis to assist in the credit-granting decision, the process cannot be reduced to a mechanical one.

Credit Scoring Systems

Even though experience and judgment play major roles in the credit-granting process, companies still maintain credit scoring systems based on quantitative measures (such as ratios) and qualitative assessments (such as "good," "fair," or "poor"). The criteria used to make the qualitative assessments are so important that the Equal Credit Opportunity Act requires that com-

panies maintain well-defined policies on these subjective types of assessments. This means that if credit decisions are made without the use of an empirically verified, mechanical scoring model, the company must keep written policy statements to avoid the possibility of discriminating among customers.

These credit scoring systems or models, used to weight the characteristics relevant to a customer's willingness and ability to pay, result in a numerical score. The numerical score is used to determine whether or not credit is granted. In general, the higher the score, the more creditworthy the customer. One such model used by many companies is called multiple discriminant analysis.

Multiple discriminant analysis (MDA) is a statistical technique that mathematically classifies a population (in this case, customers) into certain categories based on a set of characteristics. With MDA, a company uses historical data from its total customer base to determine the particular set of credit variables that best distinguish between good and bad credit risks. MDA relates the data to the characteristics associated with prompt payment, late payment, or no payment, and assigns a "usefulness weight" to each measure that helps discriminate between good and bad credit risks. MDA also creates credit score levels and provides information on how these are related to payment behavior.

Assume that a company used MDA and identified the appropriate weights and score levels, as shown in Exhibit 6-1, after analyzing data from its corporate credit customer base.

EXHIBIT 6-1   MULTIPLE DISCRIMINANT ANALYSIS

Weights

Measures	Usefulness Weight
Debt-to-Equity Ratio	5.3
Times Interest Earned	1.5
Years in Business	.9
Current Ratio	3.4
Number of Employees	.6
Inventory Turnover	2.1

Scoring Levels

Credit Score	Credit Quality
Less than 20	Poor—deny credit
20–45	Fair—further investigation required
Greater than 45	Good—grant credit

Now assume a corporate applicant has the following measures:

	Measures ×	Weight ×	Weighted Value
Debt-to-Equity Ratio	.6	5.3	3.18
Times Interest Earned	3.0	1.5	4.50
Years in Business	4.0	.9	3.60
Current Ratio	2.1	3.4	7.14
Number of Employees	60.0	.6	36.00
Inventory Turnover	50.0	2.1	10.50
			64.92

Since 64.92 exceeds the value of 45 (See Exhibit 6–1), credit should be granted to the customer.

We should note, however, that while credit scoring is a valuable tool, it should not be used blindly. A scoring system should be used to assist in the decision to grant credit, but it should not be used as a substitute for judgment.

Overall Credit Policy

A company's credit policy must adapt to changes in a company's economic environment. For example, when the economy is growing, a company might wish to extend additional credit or make its credit terms more favorable in order to increase its sales. On the other hand, when the economy is contracting, many customers have trouble paying on time or paying at all. In this case, the company might tighten its credit policy.

Credit policy is related also to the types of products or services the company markets, the costs and selling prices of those products, and the overall strategy and goals of the company. In addition, a company's competitors, its liquidity, solvency, inventory levels, and cash position, all influence credit policy.

The company must extract as much payment as possible before the customer consumes the product's value. Once full value has been received, customers are much more reluctant to pay. As an old Russian proverb says, "No one pays for a dead mule."

The type of business in which a company engages also affects credit policy. For example, a business that supplies accounting or legal services normally bills either in advance (seeking a retainer) or when the accounting or legal work is performed. A company that sells refrigerators or automobiles usually sells on credit, using the installment method because of the high selling price of the items and because of the long-lived nature of these items. The sale of produce is normally transacted on a cash basis because of the problem of perishability. Management must constantly be aware of these linkages when setting or changing credit policy.

7

CASH COLLECTION AND DELAYED PAYMENT TECHNIQUES

Cash for investment can be increased, or borrowing needs decreased, by minimizing the time required to collect cash from customers. Similarly, delaying payments to suppliers and creditors results in holding cash for a longer time, because payment is made only when necessary.

We begin with an overview of how customer remittances to a seller (and, conversely, payments by a buyer), are processed by the banking system. We then provide general guidelines for accelerating cash collections and delaying cash payments.

Check-Clearing Operations

When a bank receives checks for deposit from its customers, several steps must be taken before the checks can be sent to their final destination for clearing. First, all checks are coded with their dollar amounts and totals of checks are reconciled to the amount of the deposit. Second, the checks are computer-sorted and totaled by destination (Federal Reserve Bank, local or automated clearinghouse, or correspondent bank). Finally, the computer runs are totaled and reconciled to the total deposits received each day. The checks are then sent to their destinations.

Federal Reserve Bank

The Federal Reserve operates regional processing centers across the United States. Each processing center is linked by air, wire, and computer and serves a certain geographic area. Normally, banks using the Federal Reserve system must deposit checks for collection with the processing centers in their areas. The vast majority of checks processed by a Federal Reserve center are those presented from drawees within its area. If the checks must be collected from a bank in another Federal Reserve area, air or ground transport is usually used to transport the checks to the area from which they were drawn. The Federal Reserve bank then presents the checks to the drawee banks for payment. Checks presented to the Federal Reserve normally clear in one to three days.

The Federal Reserve Wire System is another way for companies to transfer large amounts of cash. These transfers become immediately available funds to the receiving company as soon as the wire transaction is executed. The amounts also immediately reduce the account of the sending company. Federal Reserve Wire System transfers are expensive, and companies should assess the benefits and associated costs to determine the optimum transfer amount.

Local Clearinghouses

In many instances, local banks form clearinghouse associations. A clearinghouse association generally meets each day to exchange checks. Before the daily meetings, each individual bank sorts and processes the checks it has received. At the meeting the checks are physically exchanged and the Federal Reserve (where each bank has an account) is notified of the net settlement of each bank for the exchanged checks.

Automated Clearinghouses

The automated clearinghouse (ACH) network is an improvement over the manual check-clearing process. ACHs simply provide an electronic means of sending check data from an account at one bank to a checking or savings account at another bank or financial institution. An ACH is an example of an electronic funds transfer (EFT) network. Instead of financial institutions manually exchanging checks to settle accounts, computers do the work. All entries for each individual bank are electronically delivered to that bank for immediate processing, and checks do not have to be exchanged to facilitate processing and payment.

Sending and receiving banks are normally linked directly to the ACH national computer center. If a bank is not directly linked to the center, it must depend on physical transportation of the computer media to and from the ACH center. Funds are available for use by the receiving bank one day after an ACH transaction is started in either instance.

Correspondent Banks

A bank that specializes in check clearing is called a *correspondent bank*. Such banks normally have the most modern and up-to-date check-processing equipment, are usually located in larger cities, and have access to air transportation. They are normally part of an extensive direct-send (discussed next) correspondent bank network. These features allow correspondent banks to move larger numbers of checks and offer later deposit deadlines than do local clearinghouses. If a bank sends a check for deposit to a correspondent bank located in the city of the drawee, it will usually clear in one day.

Smaller banks (called *respondents*) typically use correspondent banks to avoid using the Federal Reserve system, thus reducing check-clearing time. Settlement occurs by accounting entries made on the books of the smaller banks, kept by the correspondent banks, and often results in the smaller banks receiving same-day credit.

Direct Sends

If a bank desires to have immediate availability of funds, it can transport the checks it receives, usually by air, to the bank of the drawee and deposit it directly in the drawee's bank. This is a *direct send*. To determine whether a direct send is cost-justified, a bank must compare the cost of additional processing and transportation against the benefit of having the funds available for investment sooner than would be the case if the checks were processed through the Federal Reserve System.

Another form of direct send involves using a correspondent bank. In this case, a correspondent bank accepts deposits in the form of a cash letter. A *cash letter* is a deposit ticket that lists checks drawn on one or more banks in another city. The correspondent bank immediately credits the account of the sending bank and presents the checks to the Federal Reserve Bank, the paying bank, or a local clearinghouse.

Wire Services

Banks also move funds by using wire systems, another form of EFT network. These wire systems provide a medium for information exchanges through recurring fund transfers. Recurring transactions are those of a frequent and predictable nature. Transactions are settled through individual or correspondent banks' balances. At the conclusion of daily trading of funds transfers, each bank's net credit or debit (plus or minus) position is determined. Net minus positions are eliminated by wire transfers from one bank to another. Wire transfers can be very useful, because they allow a company to receive same-day use of cash.

In addition, many companies make nonrecurring transfers. Unlike recurring wire transfers, these individual wire transfers are not of a standard amount and are made at various times. Such transfers are normally settled immediately.

Which Method Does Your Bank Use?

It is important for a company to be aware of the policies and procedures used by its bank(s) regarding the processing and movement of funds. Knowledge of check-clearing practices is important in setting the company's cash collection and payment strategies.

To determine which method to use to clear checks, a bank must consider several factors:

1. The type of check-sorting equipment a bank has will determine its ability to use the Federal Reserve system or a correspondent bank, because each has its own special sorting and processing requirements.

2. The location of the bank will affect its ability to process direct sends or to use the Federal Reserve system. If a bank is not close to a Federal Reserve bank or depository, or does not have easy access to air transportation, then a local clearinghouse may have to be used.

3. The cost of check clearing through the Federal Reserve or correspondent banks (and the resulting availability of funds) must be compared with that of clearing checks through a local clearinghouse.

4. The volume of checks cleared affects the clearing mechanism used by a bank. Generally, the volume of checks cleared must be large enough to be cost-effective.

Methods to Accelerate Cash Collections

The primary function of the cash manager in the collection process is to accelerate the collection of cash receipts. The cash manager must transform credit sales into cash as rapidly as possible so that these funds can be used to satisfy payments of the company's debts. Among the methods used to accelerate collection of cash receipts are the following:

1. Use of EFT, ACH, and wire transfers to speed collections

2. Billing as soon as possible

3. Creativity in setting credit terms

4. Use of lockboxes

5. Monitoring the handling of checks

6. Periodic auditing of the system of cash processing

7. Knowing bank deadlines

8. Use of preauthorized checks and debits

9. Use of depository transfer checks

Use of EFT, ACH, and Wire Transfers to Speed Collections

The use of EFT, ACH, and wire transfers allows funds to be available faster because they are automatically transferred and credited to a company's account from its customer's account on the same day. Collection problems are also reduced through the use of EFT. Moreover, charges for returned checks and check-clearing float are decreased.

Billing as Soon as Possible

Accelerating invoice data is a critical starting point in the cash manager's focus on accelerating cash receipts. The company must ensure that invoices are mailed promptly to reduce the delay in receiving customer payments. Many companies know which customers centralize their accounts payable function. To expedite payments to accounts receivable, companies can bill those customers directly at their centralized locations.

Other cash-acceleration strategies associated with the billing function include billing when the order is processed, rather than when it is shipped, and using specially coded return envelopes. Coded envelopes are sent directly to the company's bank.

Creativity in Setting Credit Terms

Cash discounts, as discussed in Chapter 6, encourage payment of an amount due prior to the agreed-upon due date. Although discounts are often an expensive way of accelerating cash receipts, many companies use them.

In addition, the company should charge interest on past due accounts receivable balances. The company should also consider the costs and benefits of allowing its customers to pay bills by credit card. Accepting credit cards reduces collection problems, and vendors often find that companies that use credit cards are less price-sensitive and buy more than those that pay cash. The disadvantage of accepting credit cards is the processing fee the company must pay the bank for the use of the card.

Use of Lockboxes

Processing customer receipts can be accelerated by using a lockbox system. Lockboxes are discussed in greater detail in Chapter 10. The primary advantage of a lockbox is that the cash is collected and made available for use more quickly, because the recordkeeping associated with accounts receivable is done after the cash is deposited, rather than before.

Monitoring the Handling of Checks

A company can lose valuable time and money in handling customer remittances. The cash manager must constantly monitor check preparation and the deposit process. The time required must be reduced so that the daily deposit can be made before the bank's deadline, in order to obtain the optimum use of the funds received each day.

Periodic Auditing of the System of Cash Processing

Even if the cash manager feels that the handling and processing of deposits is under control, administrative and clerical staff may become more involved in the bookkeeping aspects of the collection process than in making the funds available for use. Periodic auditing of the cash-processing system may indicate areas where improvement can be made in the handling and processing of deposits.

Knowing Bank Deadlines

Even though a company's bank may be open until 6:00 P.M. during the week, this does not mean that a check deposited late in the day will receive same-day credit. The bank might use a 2:00 or 3:00 P.M. deadline as its cutoff. Receipts deposited after this time lose one additional day of availability.

Use of Preauthorized Checks and Debits

Collections can be accelerated by using preauthorized checks and debits. Preauthorized checks and debits allow the selling company to write a check on or charge customer accounts routinely. The company can obtain funds sooner and reduce clerical costs because of the reduction in invoicing and mailing costs. Preauthorized checks have, for the most part, been replaced by automated, preauthorized debits.

Use of Depository Transfer Checks

Depository transfer checks are checks requiring no signature that are used for moving funds between a company's bank accounts. These checks can be manually prepared or automated and allow a company to concentrate its funds in a central cash pool for more effective cash management.

Methods to Delay Payments

Disbursing cash efficiently is critical to effective cash management. The cash manager's primary objectives are to have the correct amount of cash available at the company's bank when it is needed and to time the company's payments so that cash balances earn the maximum additional funds.

There are a number of ways a company can conserve cash through its payment program:

1. Mailing payments on Friday
2. Centralization of accounts payable
3. Slowing the bill-paying function
4. Paying through draft
5. Remote disbursement
6. Zero balance accounts
7. Paying by charge card

Mailing Payments on Friday

Mailing payments on Friday or late in the day increases float (discussed in Chapter 10) and allows the company to maintain a higher cash bank balance than shown on its books.

Centralization of Accounts Payable

Centralized disbursement payments on accounts payable reduces the cash tied up in different accounts because all accounts payable payments are made from one location. In addition, centralization allows the company to exercise greater control over disbursements, lowers administrative costs, and assures that all discounts are taken and bills are paid before their due dates. Centralization also maximizes disbursement float by ensuring that payment is made at the most appropriate and profitable time.

Slowing the Bill-Paying Function

To slow the bill-paying function, a company must schedule its payments. That is, the company must prioritize its creditors to determine whom to pay when, rather than automatically paying invoices as they arrive.

Paying Through Draft

Payment can be delayed by the use of drafts. Drafts are drawn on a company, not on a bank. When the company pays with a draft, the vendor remits it to the company's bank. The bank acts as collection agent and asks the company for permission to pay the draft. If the company accepts the draft, it deposits funds equal to the amount of the draft into its account. Drafts are often used when a company purchases items requiring inspection or examination prior to payment.

Remote Disbursement

Although it is discouraged by the Federal Reserve, remote disbursement, discussed in Chapter 10, is used by some companies. Remote disbursement involves mailing checks drawn on banks located in remote areas of the United States. This practice forces checks to be processed through numerous processing points, thus increasing float.

Zero Balance Accounts

Zero balance accounts, also called *controlled disbursement* accounts, are special checking accounts that contain no cash balance. Checks for purchases are written by the company. When these checks reach the company's bank, the bank's computer system funds the account from a master account. That is, deductions from the zero balance account are automatically offset by transfers from the master account, allowing the company to earn interest on funds in the master account until the funds are needed to cover checks. Zero balance accounts are also discussed in Chapter 10.

Paying by Charge Card

When making payments on accounts payable, simply say, "Charge it!" By using the credit card's credit feature as a line of credit, the cash manager has an effective tool to slow the disbursing of cash. The company has use of the funds from the date of the charge, as well as use of the merchandise, until the date of payment to the credit card company.

8

AN EFFECTIVENESS MEASURE FOR MANAGEMENT'S INVESTMENT OF IDLE CASH

When managers perform a task, they must evaluate their effectiveness at performing the task against some standard if they are to become good at it. The technique most used by managers to evaluate the effectiveness of their activities is some sort of feedback loop. Managers act, evaluate the results of their action, then act again, modifying this action according to the information obtained from the result of the previous action.

Companies often have surplus cash balances that could be invested to generate additional income. When a company has surplus or idle cash, the problem for managers is to invest the maximum amount of this cash for the longest possible time, and at the best rate of return in keeping with the company's policies regarding risk. Exhibit 8-1 shows how a simple feedback loop works in solving the problem of investing idle cash balances.

This chapter explains one way to measure a manager's success in investing idle cash balances. Because the rate of return managers want varies with a company's policies on risk, the technique does not attempt to evaluate management's effectiveness in optimizing the return on its idle cash investments. Rather, it measures the proportion of idle cash invested versus the maximum amount of idle cash available to invest, and gives managers a benchmark against which to measure improvement.

EXHIBIT 8-1 THE FEEDBACK LOOP USED BY MANAGERS

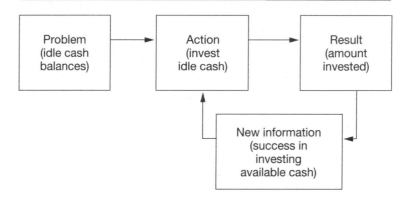

Available Cash Balance

Let us assume that Exhibit 8-2 shows budgeted cash inflows and outflows in thousands for a company for one year, by months. From these cash flows, we calculate a budgeted available balance of idle cash that can be invested each month. (Flows could just as likely be given weekly. The calculations would be the same and the results more precise.) For January (month 1 in the exhibit) the calculation of available cash surplus is (000 omitted):

Available cash at the beginning of the month	$1,726
Plus cash inflow during the month	7,534
Total before outflows	9,260
Minus outflows	6,965
Available surplus during January	$2,295

EXHIBIT 8-2   BUDGETED CASH INFLOWS AND OUTFLOWS (000 OMITTED)

(1) Month (Point in Time)	(2) Cash Inflow	(3) Cash Outflow
0		
1	$7,534	$6,965
2	8,021	8,174
3	9,523	9,480
4	9,560	9,712
5	9,040	7,766
6	8,690	8,628
7	7,995	8,379
8	7,230	7,536
9	6,850	6,881
10	6,250	6,495
11	6,800	7,230
12	7,425	7,595

The available balance for each month is shown in Exhibit 8-3. We have calculated the budgeted available cash, but it is difficult for managers to use this information to determine blocks of cash that can be invested for longer than one month.

EXHIBIT 8-3 BUDGETED BALANCES OF CASH AVAILABLE EACH MONTH (000 OMITTED)

(1) Month (Point in Time)	(2) Cash Inflow	(3) Cash Outflow	(4) Available Balance (4+2−3)
0	(Beginning of the Year)		$1,726
1	$7,534	$6,965	2,295
2	8,021	8,174	2,142
3	9,523	9,480	2,185
4	9,560	9,712	2,033
5	9,040	7,766	3,307
6	8,690	8,628	3,369
7	7,995	8,379	2,985
8	7,230	7,536	2,679
9	6,850	6,881	2,648
10	6,250	6,495	2,403
11	6,800	7,230	1,973
12	7,425	7,595	1,803

EXHIBIT 8-4 GRAPH OF BUDGETED CASH INFLOWS (000 OMITTED)

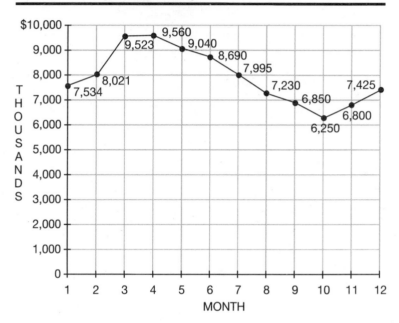

To better illustrate how cash inflows and outflows relate, these flows are graphed in Exhibits 8-4 and 8-5. Next, the graphs are combined, one on top of the other, in Exhibit 8-6. The space between the lines shows the difference (positive or negative) between inflows and outflows each month, but it is still difficult to determine how blocks of cash can most be most profitably invested.

EXHIBIT 8-5 GRAPH OF BUDGETED CASH OUTFLOWS (000 OMITTED)

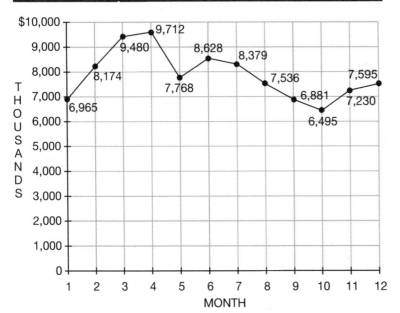

EXHIBIT 8-6 COMBINED GRAPH OF BUDGETED CASH INFLOWS AND OUTFLOWS (000 OMITTED)

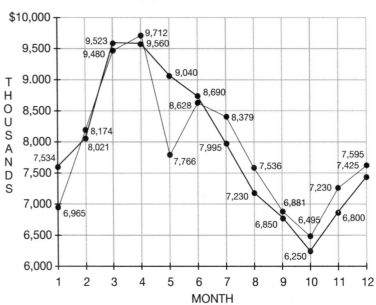

EXHIBIT 8-7 GRAPH OF AVAILABLE CASH BALANCE MONTH BY MONTH (000 OMITTED)

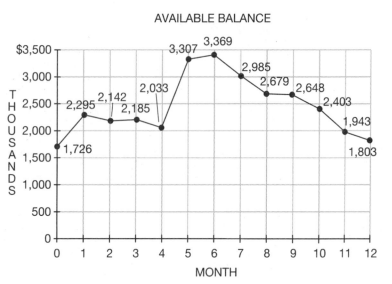

AVAILABLE BALANCE

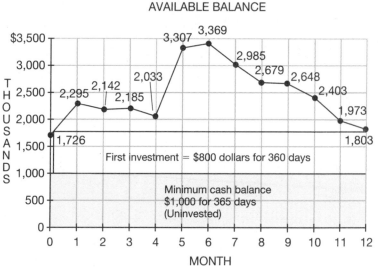

AVAILABLE BALANCE

Exhibit 8-7 is a graph of the available cash balance, taken from amounts calculated in Exhibit 8-3. Now we can clearly see from the area under the graph how much idle cash is available for investment, and for how long. If management wishes to maintain cash on hand of $1,000,000, managers will at-tempt to invest all the area above $1,000,000 and below the curve in Exhibit 8-7. Perhaps managers decide to invest one block of $800,000 from January 5 through the rest of the year. This investment and the minimum cash balance are shown in Exhibit 8-8.

Dollar Days as a Unit of Measurement

The unit of measure used to examine cash available and invested is a "dollar day," one dollar day being one dollar invested (or not invested) for one day. One dollar held for one week is seven dollar days. Ten dollars invested for ten days is 100 dollar days. One thousand (000 omitted) dollars minimum cash available is one million dollars × 365 = three hundred sixty-five million dollar days. Eight hundred thousand dollars invested for 360 days is $800,000 × 360 = 288,000,000 dollar days.

Exhibit 8-9 shows one series of investments management might make. The total dollar days of investment that result from this plan are calculated in Exhibit 8-10.

EXHIBIT 8-9   GRAPH OF AVAILABLE CASH BALANCE AND MANAGEMENT'S INVESTMENT PLAN (000 OMITTED)

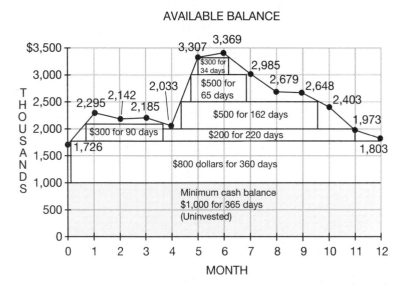

**EXHIBIT 8-10 TOTAL DOLLAR DAYS OF INVESTMENT
USING THE PLAN IN EXHIBIT 8-9
(000 OMITTED)**

$800	×	360 days =	288,000 dollar days
300	×	90 days =	27,000 dollar days
200	×	220 days =	44,000 dollar days
500	×	162 days =	81,000 dollar days
500	×	65 days =	32,500 dollar days
300	×	34 days =	10,200 dollar days
Total			482,700 dollar days

Maximum Dollar Days Available

Exhibit 8-11 shows the calculation of the average cash available each month. The cash balance at the beginning and end of each month is added together and divided by 2. Exhibit 8-12 multiplies the average available cash balance for each month by the length of the month in days to determine the number of dollar days in each month.

EXHIBIT 8-11   AVERAGE AVAILABLE CASH EACH MONTH (000 OMITTED)

(1) Month (Point in Time)	(2) Available Balance	(3) During Month	(4) Sum for Beginning and End of Month	(5) Average (4)/(2)
0	$1,726	(Beginning of Year)		
1	2,295	0–1	$4,021	$2,010.5
2	2,142	1–2	4,437	2,218.5
3	2,185	2–3	4,327	2,163.5
4	2,033	3–4	4,218	2,109.0
5	3,307	4–5	5,340	2,670.0
6	3,369	5–6	6,676	3,338.0
7	2,985	6–7	6,354	3,177.0
8	2,679	7–8	5,664	2,832.0
9	2,648	8–9	5,327	2,663.5
10	2,403	9–10	5,051	2,525.5
11	1,973	10–11	4,376	2,188.0
12	1,803	11–12	3,776	1,888.0

EXHIBIT 8-12   MAXIMUM POTENTIAL INVESTMENT IN DOLLAR DAYS (000 OMITTED)

(1) Month (Point in Time)	(2) Available Balance	(3) During Month	(4) Sum for Beginning and End of Month	(5) Average (4)/(2)	(6) Length of Month	(7) Dollar Days (5)× (6)	(8) Cumulative Dollar Days
0	$1,726	(Beginning of Year)					
1	2,295	0–1	$4,021	$2,010.5	31	62,310	62,310
2	2,142	1–2	4,437	2,218.5	28	62,132	124,442
3	2,185	2–3	4,327	2,163.5	31	67,084	191,526
4	2,033	3–4	4,218	2,109.0	30	63,270	254,796
5	3,307	4–5	5,340	2,670.0	31	82,770	337,566
6	3,369	5–6	6,676	3,338.0	30	100,140	437,706
7	2,985	6–7	6,354	3,177.0	31	98,487	536,193
8	2,679	7–8	5,664	2,832.0	31	87,792	623,985
9	2,648	8–9	5,327	2,663.5	30	79,920	703,905
10	2,403	9–10	5,051	2,525.5	31	78,306	782,211
11	1,973	10–11	4,376	2,188.0	30	65,640	847,851
12	1,803	11–12	3,776	1,888.0	31	58,528	906,379
						906,379	

Minus $1,000 uninvested cash balance (1,000× 365)   365,000

Total Available   541,379

Column 7 of Exhibit 8-12 shows the dollar days in each month; column 8 shows the cumulative dollar days during and at the end of the year. The total of dollar days for the year is 906,379,000. The total of dollar days of investible cash above the desired $1,000,000 available balance is $906,379,000 − $365,000,000 = $541,379,000.

How Well Did Management Do?

The effectiveness of management's investment schedule is calculated as:

$$\text{Invested percentage} = \frac{\text{Dollar Days of Investment}}{\text{Dollar Days Available}}$$

This measure can be used prospectively to evaluate a planned investment schedule of budgeted cash flows, or respectively to evaluate management's actual investment of actual available cash balances. Exhibit 8-11 shows dollar days accumulating during the year, allowing managers to assess the ongoing investment activity at any time during the year.

If management uses the investment schedule shown in Exhibits 8-9 and 8-10, cash will be invested for 482,700,000 dollar days. If cash flows are exactly as proposed in Exhibit 8-2, managers will have 541,379,000 maximum dollar days available (as calculated in the preceding section). Management's effectiveness in investing idle cash is 89.16%, calculated as follows:

$$\text{Invested Percentage} = \frac{482,700,000 \text{ Dollar Days of Investment}}{541,379,000 \text{ Dollar Days Available}}$$

$$\text{Invested Percentage} = 89.16\%$$

Could the managers have done better? We do not know, but at least now they have a benchmark against which to measure their performance. We do know that managers in very stable, predictable entities (such as governmental units) are often able to invest 100% of available idle cash, and sometimes, using float or the delay in checks processed by the banking system, to invest more than 100 percent.

Now, *that's* a benchmark!

9

HEDGES, OPTIONS, AND DERIVATIVES

Hedges, options, and derivative financial instruments are frequently useful, sometimes dangerous, cash management tools. Although these tools are intended to reduce risks associated with an uncertain future, they may instead create risks that scare even the most sophisticated Wall Street bankers. It is interesting that with financial derivatives, the bigger the risk and the harder it is to measure and manage, the more likely it is that the risk will not be disclosed in a company's financial statements. This chapter begins by explaining hedges and how they are used, then explains options, and, finally, discusses some of the riskiest financial derivatives.

We hope you are not easily frightened.

Hedges

When a company has business activities outside the United States, earnings may become less predictable because of changes in the value of the U.S. dollar. For example, assume the United States Wool Company (USW) buys wool cloth from a Scottish company for £10,000 when the exchange rate is £1 = US$2. The transaction, denominated in British £, will require £10,000 to be paid when the account comes due. The purchase is recorded on the books of USW as an increase in Inventory and Accounts Payable of $20,000 (£10,000 × 2 = US$20,000).

The wool is purchased when the exchange rate is £1 = US$2, but because the debt is in British pounds and is to be paid in the future, the exchange rate may go up or down and thus require a payment of more or less cash than $20,000.

If USW pays the liability when the exchange rate is £1 = US$2.2, the company will pay cash of US$22,000 because now the liability of £10,000 × 2.2 = $22,000. Because the exchange rate change is unfavorable, the $2,000 additional cost of the wool is an Exchange Loss in USW's income statement.

Conversely, if USW pays the liability when the exchange rate is £1 = US$1.7, USW will pay cash of only US$17,000 because £10,000 × 1.7 = $17,000. Because the exchange rate change is favorable, the $3,000 savings is an Exchange Gain in USW's income statement.

Forward Exchange Contract

When a company has a foreign currency transaction, the risk of exchange rate losses can be eliminated if the company uses a forward exchange contract. A *forward exchange contract* is an agreement to buy or sell foreign currency at some specified date at a specified rate. The current rate is called the *spot rate*, and the future rate specified in the forward contract is called the *forward rate*. Forward exchange contracts are used for speculation and for three common types of hedges.

1. The hedge of a recorded but unsettled foreign currency transaction

2. The hedge of an identifiable foreign currency commitment

3. The hedge of a net investment or monetary position

In all hedges, the initial hedge contract is a promise to purchase or sell currency and has no immediate effect on cash flows. We illustrate how hedges work with an example of a hedge of a recorded but unsettled foreign currency transaction.

Again, assume USW buys wool from a supplier in Scotland and agrees to pay £10,000. The risk of an unexpected fluctuation in the exchange rate can be controlled by entering into a forward exchange contract. When the wool is purchased, USW contracts with a foreign currency dealer to purchase the £10,000 owed to the Scottish supplier. The dates of the foreign currency purchase and the forward exchange rate are specified in the forward exchange contract.

The exchange rate at the time of the inventory purchase (the spot rate) is £1 = US$2. A forward exchange rate is usually different from the spot rate for at least two reasons:

♦ Interest rates in the international money market may be different for the two currencies, making future values different.

♦ Economic or political uncertainties may affect the strength of one or both currencies.

Assume the forward exchange rate is £1 = US$2.1. USW records the wool purchased and its liability to pay at $20,000, as we saw earlier. When USW enters into the forward exchange contract, it buys (on credit) the right to receive £10,000 for a premium of $1,000 over the $20,000 liability at the spot rate. The $1,000 premium is calculated from the forward exchange rate as follows:

Foreign Currency Receivable (in £)	$20,000
Premium on Forward Exchange Contract	1,000
Liability to Foreign Currency Dealer	$21,000

(£10,000 × 2.1 = $21,000)

The liability to the foreign currency dealer is a fixed amount. The receivable of £10,000 is recorded in U.S. dollars at the spot rate ($20,000). The premium is expensed over the life of the contract.

When the $21,000 payment is made to the foreign currency dealer, the last of the premium is expensed, and the £10,000 in foreign currency is received and paid to the Scottish supplier.

In this example, USW "fixes" its liability at $21,000. USW avoids the possibility of incurring an exchange rate loss if the rate rises higher than £1 = $2.1, perhaps to $2.2 or $2.3. But because USW is obligated to purchase the currency regardless of the exchange rate, it forfeits the possibility of an exchange gain if the rate drops to less than £1 = $2, perhaps to $1.8 or $1.7. USW gives up the possibility of a gain to avoid the possibility of a loss.

Options

Another way USW might control its risk is to purchase an option rather than a forward exchange contract. With an option USW purchases, not the foreign currency, but the *right* to purchase foreign currency at a specific rate on the date the foreign currency liability is due. For example, assume USW buys an option to purchase £10,000 at a rate of £1 = $2.1 and that this option costs USW $1,000.

If the exchange rate rises above £1 = $2.1, USW has the right to purchase £10,000 for $21,000 (£10,000 × $2.1). The greatest total cost that USW can incur, including the cost of the option, is:

Foreign currency	$21,000
Cost of option	1,000
Total cost	$22,000

However, if the exchange rate goes down (to $1.8 or $1.7, perhaps), USW will not exercise its option and will purchase its foreign currency in the market. Thus, with an option, USW can limit its potential loss from a change in the foreign currency exchange rate but still have a chance to realize a gain if rates go down.

Put and Call Options

An option is a right to buy or sell an asset (such as a foreign currency) at a specified price within a certain period. The price set for the asset is called the exercise, striking, or strike price. The period during which the option can be exercised is called the maturity of the option.

Options are classified according to the underlying assets that are to be bought or sold. If an option confers the right to purchase stock, it is a stock option. A currency call option confers the right to buy a foreign currency. The underlying assets for commodity, index, and interest rate options are commodities, stock indices, and Treasury debt, respectively.

Call Options—A call option is the right to buy an asset (such as foreign currency) at a specified price within a certain period or at a certain time. If the right to buy an asset can be exercised only at the maturity of the call option, it is called a European call option. If the right to buy the asset can be exercised prior to maturity, it is called an American call option. Examples of underlying assets that pay cash distributions are stocks that pay cash dividends and bonds that pay coupon interest. Foreign currencies and commodities are examples of underlying assets that do not pay cash distributions.

If the price at which an asset can be bought in the market (for example $3) is greater the price set by the option (perhaps $2), the value of a call option is equal to the difference between these two prices ($1 in this case). The option has value because an investor could purchase at the exercise price of the option ($2) and immediately sell the asset at its market price ($3).

Because most asset values tend to increase over time, and because increasing the time until an event occurs increases uncertainty about the future values of the assets involved, increasing the time to maturity of a call option increases its value. The longer the time to maturity of a call option, the more likely that the value of the asset to be purchased will be above the option price.

Suppose, for example, you own an option to buy British pounds tomorrow at today's exchange rate. This option will have little value because the likelihood of a significant unfavorable change (so that you would want to exercise the option) in the exchange rate within 24 hours is small. But suppose the option were to purchase British pounds at today's exchange rate one year from today—that option has greater value because the likelihood of significant unfavorable change over a year is much greater.

Put Options—A put option is the right to sell an asset at a set price within a certain period or at a certain time. Like a call option, a put option may be either American or European, depending on whether it can be exercised prior to maturity. The value of a put option behaves in a manner opposite to that of a call option. If the market value of the asset that can be sold using the option is greater than the option exercise price, the option is worthless.

If the price at which the asset can be sold using the put option (for example, $4) is greater than the market value of the asset (perhaps $2), the value of the put option is equal to the difference between these two prices (in this case, $2). The option has value because the asset can be purchased at its market value ($2) and immediately sold at the option's exercise price ($4).

Although increasing the time to maturity of a call option increases its value, increasing the time to maturity of a put option reduces its value, since most asset values are expected to increase over time.

Derivative Financial Instruments

Derivative financial instruments are financial assets whose value is derived from the value of another financial asset. An option is a derivative financial instrument because it is valued based on the value of the underlying asset. For example, the value of an option to purchase or sell British pounds depends on the value of the British pound.

Financial instruments may be classified according to the use to which the instruments are put, either investing and financing, or operating and hedging. This classification is based on the intent of the option holder to hold the option either long term or short term. If the option holder intends to hold the option long term, the option is classified as an investing and financing option. If the holder intends to hold the option for only a short term, it is classified as an operating and hedging option.

Financial instruments may also be classified by the kinds of markets in which they are bought, sold, or originated. There are four kinds of markets for financial instruments:

1. Exchange market
2. Dealer market
3. Brokered market
4. Principal-to-principal market

Financial instruments are valued by several methods. If quoted market prices are available, financial instruments should be valued at market price. If market prices are not available, financial instruments should be valued at an estimated price based on the quoted market prices of other financial instruments with similar characteristics. If there are no other financial instruments with similar characteristics, valuation may be based on either the present value of future cash flows, or theoretical option pricing models.

A derivative instrument may be standardized and traded in secondary markets, or custom-tailored as a contract between two parties. For this reason, determining the value of derivatives is sometimes difficult and accounting for derivatives is almost always done off the balance sheet. Consequently, derivative financial instruments pose a significant potential for off-balance-sheet assets and liabilities.

Off-Balance-Sheet Risk

Financial Accounting Standard (FAS) No. 107 defines off-balance-sheet risk as the risk of accounting loss where (1) the loss may exceed the amount recognized as an asset, or (2) the ultimate liability that results may exceed the amount recognized as a liability in the balance sheet.

The risk of accounting loss from a financial instrument includes:

1. The possibility that a loss may occur from the failure of another party to perform according to the terms of a contract (*credit risk*),

2. The possibility that future changes in market prices may make a financial instrument less valuable or more onerous (*market risk*), and

3. The risk of theft or physical loss.

Derivative financial instruments hold the greatest potential for off-balance-sheet risk and, consequently, the greatest risk for companies and their investors. Derivative financial instruments include a wide variety of financial assets and liabilities mostly used in banking, such as forward, futures, and option contracts, swaps, swaptions, and hybrid securities including convertible bonds and other debt contracts with equity or income participation. Full definitions and descriptions of all these derivatives are beyond the scope of this book, but we can describe the type of hybrid derivative security that creates the most unmeasurable risks.

Assume, for instance, that you operate a company in the United States that contracts with grocery chains to supply commodities (produce and coffee) from Brazil. You want to be protected from fluctuations in the Brazilian currency. You are also concerned about fluctuations in the prices of the commodities. If the prices of the commodities go up and exchange rates change unfavorably after you have contracted with grocery stores, you will suffer. To protect your business from exchange rate changes, you can purchase an option to buy Brazilian currency at harvest time. You can also purchase options on various Brazilian commodities. You want options rather than forward contracts so that you can benefit if the exchange rate or commodity prices change favorably.

So far, the options you have purchased are easy to value because they are available on organized markets. But suppose you negotiate an option that protects you only when the prices of *both* Brazilian currency *and* commodities change unfavorably. If the price of only currency or only commodities goes down, you have no rights under the option; if both go down, you are protected from the fall in one or both of these prices. This option is custom-tailored for your business and is very hard to value with any certainty.

In addition to being hard to value, derivatives are risky because they are a zero-sum game. Unlike most business activities, a zero-sum game means that, when someone benefits from an option, someone else loses by the same amount. When *Fortune* magazine discussed derivatives in a lead article on March 7, 1994, it put the open mouth of an alligator on the cover with a banner saying, "The risk that won't go away."

Recently, the nominal value of derivatives in the world was estimated to be in the tens of trillions of dollars and to be growing at a rate of 40% per year. National and international banking authorities are concerned about banks whose economic liabilities, whether on or off balance sheet, are usually guaranteed in whole or in part by various governments or their agents. The rapid, unregulated growth of the derivatives market has led to speculation about whether major defaults on derivatives could lead to a chain reaction that might threaten the solvency of the international banking system.

Exhibit 9-1 lists the financial instruments identified by the Financial Accounting Standards Board as having off-balance-sheet (OBS) risk. Credit risk is identified as CR, market risk as MR.

EXHIBIT 9-1 FINANCIAL INSTRUMENTS THAT HAVE OFF-BALANCE-SHEET RISK

	Type of OBS Risk	
OBS Risk to the Issuer Only	CR	MR
Put option on stock (premium paid up front		
Put option on interest rate contracts (premium paid up front)	x	x
Call option on stock, foreign currency, or interest rate contracts (premium paid up front)		x
Loan commitments:		
Fixed rate	x	x
Variable rate	x	
Interest rate caps		x
Interest rate floors		x
Financial guarantees	x	
Note issuance facilities at floating rates	x	
Letters of credit (also standby letters of credit) at floating rates	x	
OBS Risk to Both Issuer and Holder		
Interest rate swaps—accrual basis		x
Interest rate swaps—market to market		x
Currency swaps		
Financial futures contracts—hedges (marked to market and gain or loss deferred—FAS Statement 52 or 80 accounting)		x
Financial futures contracts—nonhedges (marked to market—FAS Statement 52 or 80 accounting)		x
Forward contracts—hedges (marked to market and gain or loss deferred)		x
Forward contracts—nonhedges (marked to market and gain or loss recognized)		x
Forward contracts—not marked to market		x

10

UNDERSTANDING FLOAT AND LOCKBOX SYSTEMS

Critical cash management functions include the acceleration, collection, and concentration of remittances from customers and clients. Opportunities for increased investments or decreased borrowing needs are created by minimizing the time to collect, process, and concentrate cash from customers. In addition, delaying payments to creditors for as long as possible enables the company to use the funds for an extended period.

A critical factor influencing the cash management function is the creation of various types of float. *Float* can be defined simply as the difference between the cash balance in the accounting records and the cash balance as shown by the company's bank. Float affects a company's cash management by slowing the collection of checks deposited at the bank or delaying the clearing of checks mailed to creditors. There are two basic types of float, collection float and disbursement float. These types of float overlap, in that one company's collection float is another company's disbursement float, and vice versa. Exhibit 10-1 is a schematic of float from the perspective of both the sending (buyer) and receiving (seller) parties.

Cash managers attempt to reduce collection float because of the negative effect it has on his or her company and to increase disbursement float because of its positive effect. Most companies attempt to measure float analytically to accomplish these goals. These negative and positive effects are explained in the next sections of this chapter.

EXHIBIT 10-1   FLOAT SCHEMATIC

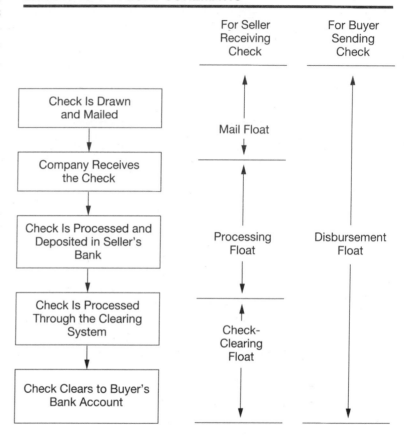

Collection Float

Collection float results from delays in processing checks. Customer checks that have been received but not yet cleared by the bank cost the company time. Because of the time value of money, collection float represents lost revenue to the company. The company forgoes the opportunity to invest the funds or reduce its debts. The cash manager's responsibility is to find strategies that will reduce collection float.

Exhibit 10-1 shows that collection float consists of three components: mail float, processing float, and check-clearing float. *Mail float* is measured as the time from when a check is mailed by a customer until it is received by the company. *Processing float* is the time from when a check is received by the company until it is deposited into the company's bank account. Processing float normally includes the time it takes for the check to move through the company's accounting system, plus the time required for the payment to be recorded as having been received. *Check-clearing float* is measured from the time the check is deposited in the company's bank until the check clears back to the drawee (buyer's) bank. Therefore,

$$\text{Collection Float} = \frac{\text{Mail Float} + \text{Processing Float} +}{\text{Check-Clearing Float}}$$

If a company has 5 days of mail float, 2 days of processing float, and 3 days of check-clearing float, its collection float is 10 days. The company's cash manager would look for ways to reduce each of these float periods to decrease collection float. Specifically, he or she would examine the possible causes of delay in depositing cash receipts from customers. The manager must answer questions such as:

1. What is the length of the period between the time a check is received by the company and the time it is deposited?

2. In what manner are cash receipts transmitted to the company?

3. Where are the cash receipts received, and how are cash receipts transferred to the company's bank account?

4. What policies does the bank have in place regarding the availability of funds to the company from its deposits of cash receipts?

The reduction of collection float, resulting in the acceleration of cash receipts, is extremely important because the company can profit from this reduction. For example, if a company's deposits average $45,000 a day and collection float can be reduced by two days, the company will have $90,000 in additional funds to use for other purposes. At an interest rate of 8%, the company will realize an annual savings of $7,200 on those funds. Higher rates would yield greater savings; lower rates, lower savings.

Lost float also is an important consideration. If the collection period is extended (instead of reduced), the company loses interest on the money it would have collected had the collection period not increased. For example, if the collection period is extended by two days, the company loses $7,200 in interest.

Lockbox Systems

One way a company can accelerate cash receipts is through the use of a lockbox. A lockbox is not an actual box secured with a padlock. A *lockbox* is a collection system whereby a company rents a post office box or private mail box in a particular city or cities. A bank or other third party is responsible for management of the box. Customers are instructed to mail payments to the lockboxes that are strategically located close to them. This reduces mailing time. The bank or a third party monitors the lockbox and, when checks arrive, deposits them in the company's account. Deposit documents, including a photocopy of each check, are forwarded to the company's office daily, and, in many cases, the company also receives a daily deposit report of lockbox deposit totals via computer terminal.

A lockbox collection system is a very effective way to improve collection of a company's cash receipts. Lockboxes also eliminate the need for the company's staff to process remittances. However, this improvement has additional costs. A lockbox system is cost-effective when a company has many checks of high dollar amounts that justify the increase in processing costs. The dollar value of reduced collection float must exceed the cost of this specialized bank service. As of 1990, fewer than 5% of small businesses in the United States used lockboxes. For medium and large corporations, the percentage using lockboxes was more than 30% and 60%, respectively. Exhibit 10-2 is a flowchart of the lockbox process.

Lockbox systems can reduce mail, processing, and check-clearing float. Mail float is reduced because customers send their checks to the closest lockbox and the company receives its mail sooner. For example, a Los Angeles company may have a lockbox in Chicago. Customers in the Chicago area mail their remittances to the Chicago lockbox, and the company receives its mail sooner than if the remittances were mailed from Chicago to Los Angeles.

Processing float is reduced by the use of a lockbox system because the bank or third party that manages the lockbox concentrates on remittance processing as one of its primary objectives. The bank or third party uses high-speed processing equipment and normally operates around the clock. In addition, the bank generally has a large staff to handle, process, and clear checks within hours of receipt of the customer remittances. This is not always the case when the remittances are sent directly to the company. For example, when remittances are received directly by the company, the priority may be to update the accounts receivable file instead of making funds available as soon as possible. The objectives of the credit manager and the cash manager may not coincide. A lockbox system avoids this potential conflict, because the funds are available sooner and the bank or third party simultaneously provides the

EXHIBIT 10-2   LOCKBOX FLOWCHART

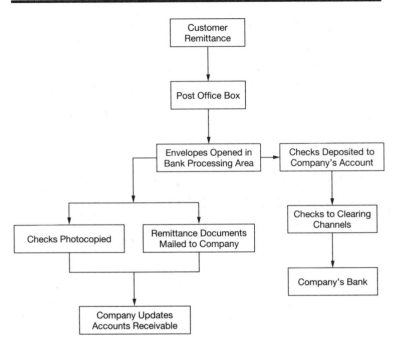

documentation needed to update the accounts receivable files. Moreover, most companies process customer receipts only during normal working hours, while many lockbox systems operate 24 hours a day, seven days a week.

A lockbox system can also reduce check-clearing float because checks sent to a particular lockbox are from customers in the surrounding geographical area. Thus, these checks are likely to be drawn on banks located in the same area. In our example, the company in Los Angeles will more than likely receive checks drawn on Chicago banks in its Chicago lockbox. Therefore, the Los Angeles company will take less time to collect the Chicago checks than it would if the checks were mailed to Los Angeles. Exhibit 10-3 presents the benefits of using a lockbox system.

EXHIBIT 10-3   BENEFITS OF LOCKBOX PROCESSING

♦ Accelerates collections

♦ Increases available funds

♦ Saves employee processing time

♦ Increases cash flow information for better cash management

♦ Increases accounting information with daily forwarding of accounts receivable documents

Disbursement Float

Disbursement float is the flip side of collection float and, as seen in Exhibit 10-1, disbursement float is equal to mail float plus processing float plus check-clearing float. Cash managers attempt to increase disbursement float and use cash until the precise moment when the cash is needed to meet an obligation for outstanding checks. For example, suppose a company makes a $350,000 payment that takes six days to travel from the company's accounts payable department, through the mail, to the seller's accounts receivable department, to the seller's bank, through the banking system, and finally back to the buyer's bank account for clearance. Suppose also that the company has $50,000 in a non-interest-bearing checking account and $400,000 in an interest-bearing account. The company writes a check for $350,000 and mails it to the seller. On the sixth day, the company transfers $300,000 from the interest-bearing account into the non-interest-bearing checking account to cover the $350,000 check. The company has successfully used disbursement float to earn interest on $300,000 for six days. The check to the buyer will clear because the checking account has a balance of $350,000.

Managing disbursement float involves monitoring company bank balances as well as centralizing control of payments.

Recall from the example of collection float that a decentralized collection system (lockbox) was used to speed cash inflows. Conversely, if a payment system is centralized, the company has the ability to slow payments. Thus, the cash manager can evaluate the timing of bills and payments for the entire company and, in the meantime, earn interest on available funds. For example, it is prudent for a cash manager to make a payment to a vendor in Chicago from the company's Los Angeles location rather than from an office in Chicago. In this instance, the cash manager in Los Angeles, who disburses the check to the vendor in Chicago, has several more days of mail float than he would if the check was disbursed from the Chicago branch.

Sometimes cash managers extend disbursement float through remote mailings. A *remote mailing* involves mailing company checks from a location some distance from the payee. A company located in Los Angeles might mail payments from its Boston branch to vendors in Seattle. Assuming the Boston checks are drawn on Boston banks, the checks have to cross the United States twice before the vendor or supplier can use the funds.

Remote disbursement is not looked upon favorably by the Federal Reserve. In fact, in 1979 the Federal Reserve issued a policy statement indicating that banks should not offer any service that delays the presentment of checks. However, the policy statement is not law and companies still engage in this practice.

Float Reports

Another requirement in monitoring disbursement float is to obtain a float report from the company's bank. The float report gives detailed and summary statistics on the average time it takes for the company's checks to clear the banking system. An overall weighted average for all paid checks is computed, which indicates the company's average disbursement float time. The average float time can be monitored from period to period to detect changes in check-clearing times.

Bank Drafts

Another procedure companies use to increase disbursement float is to make payments by draft instead of by check. A *bank draft* is an order drawn by a company on itself. The draft is sent to a vendor as payment. The vendor then presents the draft to the bank on which it was drawn. A draft differs from a check in that after it is presented to the bank by the vendor, the bank presents the draft to the company that created it for formal approval. (Normally, this is done within 24 hours of receiving the draft.) When the company accepts the draft, it deposits funds into its account to cover the amount of the draft. Generally, by using a draft for payment instead of a check, a company delays payment for an additional day and increases disbursement float. Another advantage of using a draft is that it allows the company to maintain a lower average checking account balance than it would if it instead used a check to settle its account.

Zero Balance Accounts

Companies also use zero balance accounts (ZBAs) to extend disbursement float and increase available cash. ZBAs are checking accounts used for the payment of expenditures such as payroll and petty cash. These accounts are intentionally managed to have a zero balance. When a company's checks are presented to its bank each day, they are automatically totaled by the bank's accounting system. Each of the company's ZBAs then receives a deposit for the total amount of the checks, which brings the balance in the account to zero. The deposits to the ZBAs are transferred from another company account in the bank called a "master" or "concentration" account.

There are several advantages to using ZBAs. Float disbursement is increased, because only enough cash is transferred to cover the deficiency in the ZBA and additional balances are not maintained by the company in several different accounts. Moreover, automatic funding is provided from a master or concentration account in the same bank.

11

DEALING WITH THE BANK:
Banking Relationships

Checking accounts, also called transaction accounts, can have a variety of features. These features are different for business accounts than for the accounts of individuals. For example, except for the bank accounts of partnerships and not-for-profit organizations, banks do not pay interest on business checking accounts. When selecting a bank, managers should be very careful to ask about the prices of different kinds of activities, such as overdrafts and payments against uncollected funds. Accounts are often described as "free" when, in truth, they are not.

The fees charged for their different services vary from bank to bank. Some banks, for example, charge a very high fee for overdrafts to discourage such activity; others may consider overdraft charges a revenue source and be much more reasonable. Managers, in addition to pricing the services at several banks before selecting a company's primary bank, should repeat the process from time to time, because there may be changes in both the fees banks charge and the mix of banking services the company needs.

Banking Services

Examples of business banking services offered by First Federal of Anderson (South Carolina) are shown in Exhibit 11-1.

Overdrafts

Some banks will pay a company's overdrafts and then call the company, requesting it to make a deposit to reimburse the bank. Banks charge a fee for each overdraft check, whether or not the bank covers the overdraft. Despite the fee, most banks do not want a company to overdraw its account. Overdrafts covered by the bank constitute a type of interest-free loan to the company and are expensive for the bank to process because they require special handling.

Uncollected Checks

Sometimes a company deposits a check drawn on Bank A into an account in Bank B and begins to use the cash. *Uncollected checks* are Bank A checks that have not yet been returned to Bank A. No funds have been transferred from Bank A to Bank B. Uncollected checks are also interest-free loans to the company, because Bank B provides cash to the company without interest.

EXHIBIT 11-1   TYPICAL BUSINESS BANKING SERVICES

Description	Fee
Monthly Account Maintenance	$xxx Per Month
Debits Posted	$ xxx Per Item
Credits Posted	$ xxx Per Item
Night Deposit Bag Service	$ xxx Per Month
Additional Statements	$ xxx Per Statement
Items in Deposit	
Local	$ xxx Per Item
Foreign	$ xxx Per Item
Stop Payments	$ xxx Per Item
Telephone Notification	$ xxx Per Call (For Customer)
Returned Items	
Charge Back	$ xxx Per Item
Overdraft Charge (NSF)	$ xxx Per Item
Currency and Coin Deposited	$ xxx Per Dollar
Currency Paid Out	$ xxx Per Dollar
Coin Paid Out	$ xxx Per Roll
Wire Transfer with Phone Advice (Domestic)	$ xxx Per Wire
Incoming Wire Transfer with Phone Advice (Domestic)	$ xxx Per Wire
Wire Transfer (Overseas)	Negotiated
Food Coupons Deposited	$ xxx Per $100
Bond Coupon Collection/Redemption per Envelope	
First Federal Customers	$ xxx each
Non-Customers	$ xxx each
Collection Items	$ xxx% of face value

($10.00 minimum, $50.00 maximum per item, plus amount charged by processing bank)

Large Cash Transactions

Banks are required to report certain large cash transactions. Banking regulations require them to report deposits of cash in excess of $10,000 a day. The $10,000 is the total of all cash deposits to a single account, regardless of how many separate branches or deposits are used. Regulations also require banks to report anyone (company or individual) who uses cash to purchase more than $3,000 in cashier's checks, money orders, traveler's checks, or bank-certified and cashier's checks.

Earning Interest

A company can have a savings account, but a savings account does not pay as high interest as a money market deposit account. Regulations limit the number of transfers in or out of the money market account by check each month, but there is no limit on the number of transfers if a manager goes to the bank each time. Requiring managers to go to the bank for each transfer can quickly become costly for a large or even medium-sized company.

Certificates of deposit (CDs) pay higher interest than savings or money market deposit accounts. The interest on CDs is also generally higher than the company's share of interest income from an account analysis (discussed in Chapter 12). CDs can be good investments for temporarily idle funds, but it can be difficult to time the maturity date of CDs to correspond precisely with the company's cash requirements, and banks generally charge a penalty for early withdrawal.

Reconciling a Bank Statement

Each month the bank sends the company a statement for each of its bank accounts. A bank statement shows:

♦ The beginning cash balance,

♦ All deposits and other additions to the account,

♦ All checks and other deductions from the account, and

♦ The account balance at the end of the month.

A bank statement generally includes any checks processed during the month, plus advice slips that show any other charges or credits to the account. Some banks maintain microfilm copies of processed checks rather than returning them to the company. If the company wants a copy of any check, the bank supplies it from the microfilm record.

The ending cash balance on the company's bank statement usually does not agree with the balance in the company's cash account, and the two must be reconciled. There are several reasons that the bank statement balance is different from the cash account, which are discussed in the following paragraphs.

Outstanding Checks

Outstanding checks may cause the bank and book balances to be different. Outstanding checks are checks written by the company and recorded in the cash account, but not yet presented to the bank for payment. Checks are outstanding because of the time it takes a check to travel (usually by mail) from the company to the check's payee, plus the time it takes the payee to process the check, plus the time required for the check to clear the payee's bank and be presented to the company's bank for payment.

Deposits in Transit

Deposits in transit are deposits the company has recorded and taken to the bank, but which the bank has not credited to the company's account as of the date of the statement. Normally, deposits are made after the end of the business day when the bank is closed. Deposits are recorded by the company on the date the deposit is taken to the bank, but by the bank when it opens the next day.

If a deposit is made on the day the statement is prepared, it will appear on the company's books but not on the bank statement. In addition, because the bank statement is mailed to the company, several other deposits may be made (which will not be on the statement) before the statement is received by the company.

Bank Charges

Charges for the banking services listed in Exhibit 11-1 can cause the book and bank statement balances to differ, because often the charges have been incurred but have not been recorded in the company's books. The bank deducts its fee from the company's account when the service is performed and notifies the company of the charge by sending a debit memo. The debit memo is often mailed with the monthly statement.

The company's checking account is debited because a debit reduces the company's bank balance.

Unrecorded Credits

A bank may credit (increase) the company's checking account balance for an item the company does not know about and, hence, does not immediately record on its own books. The bank notifies the company that its account has been increased by sending a credit memo, frequently in the same envelope with the monthly statement. Company managers may not know of the increase until they receive the statement. Only then will the company's cash account be increased.

An example of an unrecorded credit is the collection of a note receivable by the bank. If the company has a note receivable for $20,000 it will be reluctant to surrender the note until

full payment is received. Likewise, because the note is a negotiable instrument, the debtor will be reluctant to pay the $20,000 without receiving the note. This can be a problem if the debtor and creditor are hundreds of miles apart.

The solution is for the creditor to give the note to its bank. The bank then sends the note to a correspondent bank in the same city as the debtor. The debtor is given the note when the $20,000 is paid, and the cash (minus bank fees) is transferred to the creditor company's account. Notice of this credit (deposit) may not be received until the statement is received. At that time, the company can remove the note receivable from its books, record the bank fees as expenses, and increase the cash account for the difference between the two.

Accounting Errors

Errors made by either the bank or the company can cause the book and statement balances to differ. Frequently, errors in posting to these accounts are discovered when the balances are reconciled. Most errors result from the human part of the system (for example, through entering incorrect amounts or posting manually to a wrong account).

Bank Reconciliation Case

Assume the bank statement for DapperWear, Inc. contained the following:

1. The bank balance was $4,252, but the cash balance on DapperWear's books was $2,878.
2. A $500 deposit made on the date of the statement did not appear on the bank statement.

3. Check #2101, returned with the bank statement, was incorrectly recorded as being for $206 instead of $602. The check was a payment for office supplies.

4. After comparing the checks written with those paid by the bank, the company found the following checks still outstanding:

#2098	$ 463
#2117	27
#2120	2,185
	$2,675

5. The statement contained a credit memo showing that the bank had collected a note receivable for the company, adding the proceeds of $400, less a $25 collection fee, to the company's account.

6. A (NSF) check for $400 was returned in the statement. This check was received from a customer and deposited.

7. There was a $350 charge for a check that could not be accounted for. After discussion with the bank, it was discovered that the bank had incorrectly charged the company's account for a check drawn on another company. The bank said it would correct the DapperWear account.

8. Bank service charges for the month were $30.

EXHIBIT 11-2   DAPPERWEAR, INC. BANK RECONCILIATION

Balance per bank	$4,252		Balance per ledger	$2,878	
Add: Deposit in transit	500		Add: Note receivable	400	
Bank error	350				
Subtotal		5,102	Subtotal		3,278
Less: Outstanding checks			Less: Corrections and charges		
#2098	$ 463		NSF check	$ 400	
#2117	27		Collection fee	25	
#2120	2,185	2,675	Service charge	30	
			Error (602–206)	396	851
Adjusted ledger balance		$2,427	Adjusted ledger balance		$2,427

DapperWear's bank reconciliation is shown in Exhibit 11-2. After the reconciliation is completed, DapperWear must adjust its cash account to the actual cash balance of $2,427 by:

1. Recording the collection of the note receivable (and related charge),

2. Changing the NSF check to a receivable (the customer still owes the $400),

3. Correcting the error in recording the check, including correcting the record of office supplies purchased, and

4. Recording the bank service charge expense.

No adjustment is necessary on DapperWear's records for the bank's error. The bank corrects its own records for its mistake.

12

ACCOUNT ANALYSIS AND OTHER BANKING SERVICES

Although regulations do not allow banks to pay interest on business checking accounts, most companies can achieve about the same result by maintaining their accounts on analysis basis. When accounts are on an analysis basis, the bank gives the company an earnings credit for most of the interest earned by the bank on the company's average balance. The bank gives the credit, then charges the costs of servicing the account against it. The bank sends the company an account analysis report each month, which shows the company's credit for interest earnings and the banking charges against it.

Types of Bank Balances

An account analysis contains three types of bank balances:

1. Ledger balances,
2. Collected balances, and
3. Available balances.

Ledger Balances

A ledger balance is the amount of outstanding checks deposited but not yet collected. For example, if a company deposits a $1,000 check received from a customer on the day its statement period ends, the statement will show the check included in the ledger balance even though the check is uncollected at the time. Because ledger balances are uncollected, the bank does not actually have the cash and cannot invest it to earn interest.

Collected Balances

Of the checks drawn on Bank A but deposited in Bank B on day 1, 90% are collected by day 2 and the rest are generally collected by day 3. When a company deposits a $1,000 check, the $1,000 is usually not recorded in the company's account by the bank until after the close of the business day. By the next business day, the bank has (nine times in ten) collected the $1,000.

That collected balance, sometimes called a "good balance," is the cash that the bank has and can actually invest to earn interest.

Available Balances

An available balance is the collected balance in an account, reduced by the amount the bank must maintain as a reserve at the Federal Reserve Bank. Reserves do not earn interest. The available balance is sometimes called the "investable balance," because it is the amount the bank can invest to earn interest. When a company has its account on an analysis basis, it is only the available balance that can be invested to earn income.

Exhibit 12–1 shows the balances defined by Wachovia for its corporate checking customers.

EXHIBIT 12–1   EXPLANATION AND FEE SCHEDULE— WACHOVIA CORPORATE CHECKING

This fee schedule gives you the information you need about charges on your Wachovia Corporate Checking account. It contains some banking terms with which you may not be entirely familiar. The following definitions may help you understand some of these terms better.

Ledger Balance—Your balance shown on your records after all the deposits and withdrawals are processed each day.

Collected Balance—Your ledger balance shown on our records minus any uncollected funds.

Uncollected Funds—Funds in the process of being collected by Wachovia from another financial institution (for example, a check drawn on another out-of-state bank).

Average Ledger Balance—The sum of your daily ledger balances divided by the number of days in the statement cycle.

Wachovia Corporate Checking

Rate Information

No interest is earned. The Financial Management Account Money Market Savings option is available for this account.

Minimum Balance Requirements

An earnings allowance based on the balance in your account is calculated to offset service charges. See "Monthly Service Charge Information" for Business Flex Checking and Corporate Checking.

Fees

The following fees will be assessed against your account:

Monthly maintenance	$ x per month
Debits processed	$ x each
Credits processed	$ x each
Items deposited	$ x each
Currency deposited	$ x/$100
FDIC insurance premium	$ x/$1,000 of ledger balances based on a 30-day month

Other fees noted in our Business Deposit Accounts Explanation and Fee Schedule, when applicable.

Understanding an Account Analysis

A bank account analysis statement usually has three sections. One section determines the company's available balances; another section shows the account activities, the cost of each activity, and the balances that would have produced sufficient earnings to offset the costs. A third section summarizes the account analysis.

The section that determines the company's available balances might appear as follows:

Average ledger balance	$101,000
Adjustments	(1,000)
Adjusted ledger balance	100,000
Minus average float	60,000
Average collected balance	40,000
Minus required reserve	4,400
Average available balance	35,600
Earnings credit on average available balance @ 5%	$1,780

The average float amount is the number of days each check is uncollected (usually just one day) multiplied by the dollar amount of each check. The last line in the account analysis converts the average available balance to an earnings figure. The rate changes each month as rates in the marketplace change.

The second section in the analysis statement shows account activities and charges and is formatted as in the following example. We show only the format here; a complete example is shown in Exhibit 12–2. This part of the statement is useful, because it allows management to analyze the company's balances and the extent to which they were larger or smaller than the amount needed to generate earnings that offset the bank's charges.

ACCOUNT ACTIVITY AND SUMMARY SERVICES

	Number of Items	Price per Item	Activity Charges	Available Balance Required
Account Maintenance				
Debits Paid on Account				
Deposits Made to Account				
Deposited Items:				
Items Deposited				
Returned Unpaid				
FDIC Insurance Assessment				
Total Activity Charges				
Total Available Balance Required to Support Account Activity				
Average Available Balance				
Difference				

Exhibit 12–2 contains a prototype analysis statement produced by NationsBank. The explanation that follows is provided by NationsBank so that customers can read and understand their analysis statements. Each comment explains the like-numbered item on the analysis statement in the exhibit.

EXHIBIT 12–2   BANK ACCOUNT ANALYSIS STATEMENT

Nations Bank

JOHN Q. CUSTOMER, INC.
PO BOX 1234
ANYTOWN, USA

ANALYSIS
STATEMENT

❶	CORPORATE DEMAND DEPOSIT	01 1234567890
	BANK AND COST CENTER NUMBER	099 1234567
	DATE PREPARED	06–08–94
	MONTH ENDING	05–31–94
❷	MONTHLY SETTLEMENT	05-31-94
	SETTLEMENT TYPE	DEBIT
	OFFICER NUMBER	1234
	PAGE	1 OF 1

BALANCE SUMMARY

❸	AVG POSITIVE LEDGER BALANCE	$103,773.99
❹	AVG LEDGER BALANCE	69,008.69
	LESS AVG FLOAT ❺	11,234.89
❻	AVG COLLECTED BALANCE	57,773.80
❼	AVG NEGATIVE COLLECTED BALANCE	34,676.10
❾	AVG POSITIVE COLLECTED BALANCE ❽	92,449.90
	LESS RESERVES	9,253.91
❿	AVAIL BAL FOR EARNINGS CREDIT	83,195.99
	AVAIL BALANCE REQUIRED ⓫	228,539.34
⓬	NET AVAILABLE BALANCE	145,343.35
⓭	REQ RESERVES ON NET AVAIL BALANCE	16,149.26
⓮	DEFICIT COLLECTED BALANCE	$161,492.61

EARNINGS CREDIT SUMMARY

⓯	AVAIL BAL FOR EARNINGS CREDIT	$83,195.99
⓰	EARNINGS ON AVAILABLE BALANCE	221.87
	LESS TOTAL SERVICE CHARGES ⓱	609.48
⓲	DEFICIT	387.61
⓳	PERIOD TO DATE DEFICIT	387.61
⓴	CURRENT PERIOD SERVICE CHARGE	$ 387.61

CURRENT MONTH'S EARNINGS CREDIT RATE = 3.14% ㉑

CURRENT MONTH'S MULTIPLE = $374.97 ㉒

SERVICE ㉓	NUMBER OF UNITS ㉔	UNIT PRICE* ㉕	SERVICE CHARGE ㉖	BALANCE REQUIRED ㉗
BALANCE RELATED SERVICES				
COLL OVERDRAFT INTEREST CHARGES	34,676	9.0000	265.06	99,390.69
FDIC INSURANCE CHARGE	1,000		.16	59.99
CHECKING ACCOUNT SERVICES				
ACCOUNT MAINTENANCE	2	11.0000	22.00	8,249.43
CHECKS PAID	219	.1700	37.23	13,960.29
CREDITS-DEPOSITS	265	.4000	106.00	39,747.27
COIN PER ROLL	400	.0800	32.00	11,999.17
DEPOSITED ITEMS-OTHER	1	.1100	.11	41.24
ACCOUNT RECONCILIATION				
DEPOSIT MAINTENANCE	1	50.0000	50.00	18,748.71
DEPOSIT ITEM	101	.0700	7.07	2,651.06
WIRE TRANSFER				
DOMESTIC WIRE-INCOMING	3	7.0000	21.00	7,874.46
WIRE ADVICE-MAIL	3	.5000	1.50	562.46
BALANCE REPORTING				
NBW-PER DETAIL ITEM	149	.1500	22.35	8,380.67
NBW-IN DATA EXCHG	3	15.0000	45.00	16,873.84
㉘ TOTAL SERVICE CHARGES			609.48	228,539.34

Price/rate information is for illustrative purposes only.

Basic Account Information

1. **Account Number.** Indicates your checking account product name and account number or your analysis Group Summary Number.

2. **Analysis Account Information.** Shows the calendar month being analyzed, the settlement frequency and corresponding scheduled settlement date, and the settlement type.

Balance Summary Information

3. **Average Positive Ledger Balance.** The positive ledger balances for each day of the calendar month are totaled and divided by the actual number of days in the month.

4. **Average Ledger Balance.** Displays the average of all positive and negative or overdrawn ledger balances during the calendar month.

5. **Average Float.** Shows the average daily dollar amount of items in the process of collection during the calendar month.

6. **Average Collected Balance.** Denotes the Average Ledger Balance less Average Float.

7. **Average Negative Collected Balance.** The negative or overdrawn collected balances for each day of the calendar month are totaled and divided by the actual number of days in the month. This figure is used to calculate the Collected Overdraft Interest Charge.

8. **Average Positive Collected Balance.** The positive collected balances for each day of the calendar month are totaled and divided by the actual number of days in the month. This figure, less Reserves, is equal to the Available Balance for Earnings Credit.

9. **Reserves.** Indicates the portion of your balances that are maintained with the Federal Reserve. Reserves are calculated using the Average Positive Ledger Balance less Average Float, multiplied by the current reserve rate.

10. **Available Balance for Earnings Credit.** Denotes the Average Positive Collected Balance less Reserves. This figure is used to calculate the monthly Earnings on Available Balance.

11. **Available Balance Required.** This figure is calculated by multiplying the Total Service Charges by the Current Month's Multiple to show the balances required to support total service charges. (*Note:* The Current Month's Multiple on the statement example has been rounded for illustrative purposes.)

    Available balances required to support each service charge are listed in the service section "Balance Required" column.

12. **Net Available Balance.** Shows the Available Balance for Earnings Credit less the Available Balance Required. A positive figure represents excess balances; a negative figure indicates additional balances required to compensate for service charges.

13. **Required Reserves on Net Available Balance.** Denotes reserves that would have been required on the additional balances needed to fully compensate for services charges.

    Deficit Collected Balance × Current Reserve Rate

14. **Deficit Collected Balance.** Indicates the additional balances that would have been required to fully compensate for account activity during the current month

when the Net Available Balance is negative. This amount includes the reserve requirement for those additional balances.

Net Available Balance/(1 − Reserve Rate)

Earnings Credit Summary Information

15. **Available Balance for Earnings Credit.** This Balance was calculated in the Balance Summary column and repeated here for Earnings Credit Summary information.

16. **Earnings on Available Balance.** Denotes the current month's earnings credit based on the Available Balance for Earnings Credit.

$$\frac{\text{Available Balance for Earnings Credit} \times \text{Earnings Credit Rate} \times \text{\# of Days in Month}}{365 \text{ Days}}$$

17. **Total Service Charges.** Displays the total of all charges for services rendered during the calendar month. This figure and the Earnings on Available Balance are netted to determine the excess allowance or deficit.

18. **Excess Allowance or Deficit.**
    - Excess Allowance occurs when the Earnings on Available Balance exceed the Total Service Charges.
    - Deficit occurs when the Total Service Charges exceed the Earnings on Available Balance.

19. **Period to Date Excess Allowance or Deficit.** Shows excess position or cumulative amount due for the current settlement period.

20. **Current Period Service Charge.** Indicates the amount due, if any, for the current settlement period.
    - When it is not a settlement month, this amount will be $0.00.
    - If an account in a group is debited for service charges, the account to be charged will be provided.
    - If the group or single account is invoiced for service charges, the invoice number will be provided.

Services

21. **Current Month's Earnings Credit Rate.** This rate is applied to the Available Balance for Earnings Credit to calculate the value of that balance during the current month.

22. **Current Month's Multiple.** This is the amount of available balance required to support $1.00 of service charges.

    $1/(\text{Earnings Credit Rate} \times \text{\# of Days in Month}/365)$

    (*Note*: This amount is rounded for statement illustration.)

23. **Service.** Lists the services used during the current analysis month. Services are grouped according to their product family.

24. **Number of Units.** Shows the total number of units used for each service.

25. **Unit Price.** Displays the per unit charge for the service.

26. **Service Charge.** Shows the total charge to the customer for each service provided.

    Number of Units × Unit Price

27. **Balance Required.** Provides the amount of Available Balance Required to offset the calculated charge for the service. The Current Month's Multiple is used to calculate the Balance Required.

   Current Month's Multiple (before rounding) $\times$ Service Charge

28. **Total Service Charges.** Denotes total of all charges for services rendered during the current calendar month.

Most banks have an account maintenance charge that covers such items as printing, postage, paper, and staff expense.

The rest of the items in the activity analysis refer to specific activities for which the bank charges. Debits paid are largely checks written on the account.

A company may transfer cash out of the account in one month so that two months averaged together show a balance close to zero. This works best if the bank allows negative available balances without significant penalty. If the bank charges a penalty on negative balances that is higher than the rate at which the company borrows or invests, the penalty makes negative balances unattractive.

Deferred Funds

Loan Applications

Amounts of checks that have been deposited but that the bank will not permit to be withdrawn are *deferred funds*. Funds may be deferred for as long as a few days up to 30 days. Most banks defer funds only on new accounts. Banks defer funds because thieves often take advantage of the time it takes to process a bad check through the system. The processing delay allows such thieves to make withdrawals or to write checks before the bad check is returned.

Regulations require that banks not defer funds for more than 2 days for local items, or 5 days for nonlocal items. However, regulations recognize the danger with new accounts and do not restrict the deferral of funds into new accounts for the first 30 days.

Compensating Balances

Compensating balances are not deferred funds. A bank customer may be required to leave money in the bank so the bank can earn income on those funds and use that income to offset expenses incurred in operating the depositor's account.

A first-time loan application to a financial institution that does not know you or your business should be much more detailed than one to a lender to whom you are already known. In such a case, you should prepare a business plan to support your loan application. The business plan can be prepared to conform to a specific bank's requirements or it may be prepared in sufficient detail to meet all bank requirements.

Loan application packages vary from bank to bank, but some requirements are common to essentially all packages. Most loan application packages contain the components shown in Exhibit 12–3. Exhibit 12–4 shows the general loan-to-value ratios used to set the upper limits on loans.

EXHIBIT 12–3   COMPONENTS OF A BUSINESS LOAN APPLICATION

- INTRODUCTORY STATEMENT OR COVER LETTER including the amount, purpose, and repayment schedule for the financing needed.
- SUMMARY OF APPLICATION, containing essentially the Executive Summary from the business plan, plus the security or collateral to be provided.
- PERSONAL INFORMATION, including resumes, personal financial statements, credit references, and tax returns for all officers, directors, and major stockholders or owners.
- COMPANY INFORMATION, consisting primarily of the company's business plan.
- BUDGETS OF PROFITS, CASH FLOWS, AND BALANCE SHEETS, as described in the business plan.

EXHIBIT 12–4   GENERAL LOAN-TO-VALUE RATIOS

Asset	Loan to Value Guide
Real estate	
Developed	75%–80%
Undeveloped	50%–80%
Equipment	
New	70%–90%
Used	50%
Inventory (of real property)	35%–50%
Accounts receivable	70%–75%

Many banks require a business plan as part of a company's loan application. The business plan shows that company management has studied both the activity to be supported by the loan and the impact it will have on cash flows, operating results, and financial position.

A business plan can help company management choose the most appropriate type and source of financing, because it offers a format for analyzing different forms of debt, different repayment schedules (a note versus a mortgage, for instance), and different proportions of stockholder and creditor capital.

The Contents of a Business Plan

Although there is no one format for a business plan, all business plans have some common elements:

1. Business description
2. Products and services
3. Sales and marketing plan
4. Operating plan
5. Financial information (past, present, and projected)

Each section can be expanded to highlight the company's strengths and to address questions that might be raised.

Exhibit 12–5 contains a detailed business plan format, based largely on a client loan package used by the Small Business Development Center at Clemson University.

Exhibit 12–6 shows two of the loan application forms used by First Federal of Anderson (South Carolina) to collect and organize a small company's balance sheet and income (operating) statement information. Most banks use forms that look much like these.

EXHIBIT 12-5   A DETAILED BUSINESS PLAN FORMAT

EXECUTIVE SUMMARY

A. Company name, address, and phone number

B. Name(s), address(es), and phone number(s) of key personnel

C. Brief description of the business

D. Brief overview of the market

E. Brief overview of the company's strategic plan

F. Brief description of the experience of the key people

G. Brief statement of financial needs (purpose of the loan)

DETAILED BUSINESS PLAN

A. Background. Brief history of the business and current situation

B. Description of the business
   1. What makes your business unique?
   2. How does it create value for others?
   3. Describe the key success factors, such as price, quality, durability, dependability, and technical features.

C. Market Analysis
   1. Who are the potential buyers?
   2. Why will they buy from you?
   3. How large is the market?
   4. What are the potential annual sales?
   5. What is the nature of the buying cycle?

      (Is the product a durable good that lasts for years or a product that is repurchased on a regular basis? Or is the product likely to be purchased only at seasonal periods during the year?)

   6. What is the target market?
      a. What are the product features that influence the consumer's buying decision?
      b. What research supports your conclusion?
      c. Does the consumer have a preference as to where he or she purchases products?

   7. Financial analysis

      What will be the cost of each unit of product or service?

      What volume do you need to sell at what price to break even?

      Why and how did you set prices?

   8. Market influences: How might each of the following affect the sale or profitability of your product?

Economic Factors

   Inflation/recession

   High/low unemployment

Social Factors

   Age of customers

   Location demographics

   Income levels

   Size of household

   Societal attitudes

D. Competitor Analysis

   Existing Competitors

      List major known competitors. Why do you believe the potential customers in your target market buy from them now?

   Potential competitors

      Who are they? When and why might they enter the market, and what would be their impact in your target market segment?

   List the strengths and weaknesses of each competitor.

E. Strategic Plan
   1. How will you market your products to the target market you have identified? (Describe your specific marketing strategy for key factors such as pricing, product promotion and advertising, customer service.)
   2. How will your products compare with those presently in the market on a competitor-by-competitor basis?

F. Organization and Management
   1. How is your business organized? (corporation, subchapter S corporation, partnership, sole proprietorship)
   2. Who are your key people, and what are their backgrounds?

G. Financial Plans
   1. How much cash do you need?
   2. What sources (loans, owner investment, etc.) can be used to finance proposed activities?
   3. How will debt be repaid? (Include a cash budget.)
   4. Provide current and prior year financial statements.
   5. Do you have collateral? Include a list of market values for assets (including any assets to be purchased).
   6. How will proposed activities affect your financial statements? Prepare projected income statements and balance sheets.

EXHIBIT 12–6   LOAN APPLICATION FORMS

Fiscal Year Ends _____

OFFICE _____

		( )			( )			( )			( )			( )	
1	NAME:						ADDRESS:								
2	BUSINESS:			IND. _____ CORP. _____ PART. _____ PROP. _____											
3	Date of Statement, Opinion	( )			( )			( )			( )			( )	
4	SPREAD: In Thousands Omit 000)		MM	M		MM	M		MM	M		MM	M		MM	M
5	Cash on Hand and in Banks															
6	Accounts Receivable (Net) (Trade)															
7	Notes Receivable (Net) (Trade)															
8	Inventory															
9																
10																
11	TOTAL CURRENT ASSETS															
12	Real Estate and Buildings															
13	Leasehold Improvements															
14	Machinery, Equipment, Fixtures															
15	Less: Depreciation (RED)															
16																
17	Due from Officers, Empl., or Affiliates															
18	Other Non-Current Receivables															
19	Investments															
20	Prepaid Expenses (Deferred Charges)															
21																
22																
23	TOTAL FIXED AND OTHER ASSETS															
24	TOTAL ASSETS															
25	Notes Payable to Banks															
26	Notes Payable—Other															

(continued)

27	Current Maturities—Deferred Debt																
28	Accounts Payable (Trade)																
29	Due to Officers, Empl., or Affiliates																
30	Income Taxes																
31	Accrued Items—Other																
32																	
33																	
34	TOTAL CURRENT LIABILITIES																
35	Mortgage Debt																
36	Other Term Debt																
37																	
38																	
39	TOTAL FIXED AND OTHER DEBT																
40	TOTAL DEBT																
41	Preferred Stock																
42	Common Stock																
43	Retained Earnings (Deficit)																
44																	
45	NET WORTH (Book Value)																
46	TOTAL LIABILITIES AND NET WORTH																
47	Tangible Net Worth																
48	Working Capital (11–34)																
49	Net Sales (or Total Income)																
50	Net Profit (Loss) BTX _____ ATX ____																
51	Depreciation Charged for Period																
52	Cash Dividends or Withdrawals																
53	Cash Flow (50 + 51 − 52)																
54	Contingent Liabilities																
55	Current Ratio (11 ÷ 34)																
56	Worth to Debt (47 ÷ 40)																
57	Liquid (Quick) Ratio ((5 + 6 + 7) ÷ 34)																

58	Sales to Receivables (Days) (49 ÷ (6 + 7))															
59	Sales to Inventory (Days) (49 ÷ 8)															
60	Profit to Net Worth (%) (50 ÷ 47)															
61	Profit to Net Sales (%) (50 ÷ 49)															

Fiscal Year Ends _____

_____
OFFICE

OPERATING STATEMENT

			MM	M	%		MM	M	%		MM	M	%		MM	M	%
1	NAME:					ADDRESS:											
2	BUSINESS:				IND. _____ CORP. _____ PART. _____ PROP. _____												
3	Date of Statement, Opinion	( )				( )				( )				( )			
4	SPREAD: In Thousands Omit 000)		MM	M	%		MM	M	%		MM	M	%		MM	M	%
5	GROSS SALES																
6	Less: Net Returns and Allowances																
7	NET SALES																
8	Material Used																
9	Labor																
10	Manufacturing Expenses																
11																	
12	COST OF GOODS SOLD																
13	GROSS PROFIT																
14	Selling Expenses																
15	General & Adm. Expenses																
16	Officers Salaries																
17																	
18	TOTAL OPERATING EXPENSES																
19	OPERATING PROFIT																
20	Other Income																
21																	

(continued)

22	Other Expense																			
23																				
24	Extraordinary Items																			
25	TOTAL OTHER ITEMS																			
26	PROFIT BEFORE TAX																			
27	INCOME TAXES																			
28	MINORITY INTEREST																			
29																				
30	NET PROFIT AFTER TAX																			
31																				
32																				
33																				
34																				
35																				
36																				
37	RECONCILIATION OF RETAINED EARN.			X			X			X			X							
38	Retained Earnings—Beginning			X			X			X			X							
39	Add: Net Profit			X			X			X			X							
40				X			X			X			X							
41				X			X			X			X							
42	Less: Net Loss			X			X			X			X							
43	Dividends			X			X			X			X							
44	Withdrawals			X			X			X			X							
45				X			X			X			X							
46	Retained Earnings—Ending			X			X			X			X							
47																				
48																				
49																				
50																				
51																				
52																				

53																	
54																	
55																	
56																	
57																	
58																	
59																	
60																	
61																	
62																	

Trust Services

If your company is publicly held, a bank's trust department can provide a number of services in issuing and maintaining stock, and in maintaining shareholder relations. A trust department can serve as registrar and transfer agent for stock and can manage dividend distribution and reinvestment programs.

A trust department helps with pension plans, profit-sharing plans, 401(k) salary deferral plans, employee stock ownership plans (ESOPs), and HR10 plans. A 401(k) plan allows employees to invest untaxed dollars in a retirement plan in which earnings are not subject to taxes until the funds are withdrawn.

An HR10 or Keogh plan is used by self-employed individuals and their employees who work more than 1,000 hours a year. An ESOP is a trust that invests company contributions in the company's own stock, giving employees ownership in the company.

A trust department can also be the trustee, registrar, and paying agent for bond issues. Here, the trust department makes interest payments and records changes in ownership of the bonds.

13

FRAUD AND EMBEZZLEMENT: EFFECTS OF INTERNAL CONTROL ON CASH MANAGEMENT

Most people think fraud and embezzlement are the same thing, and for all practical purposes they are. Still, technically, embezzlement refers to a theft whereby a person steals something that is already in his or her custody. A lawyer may embezzle money from the trust fund of a client, or an employee may embezzle from the petty cash fund, for example. Embezzlement is one type of fraud; white-collar crime is another. White-collar crime refers to a theft committed by nonviolent, nonphysical means, usually involving a violation of trust. A business owner may misrepresent the financial condition of the company to avoid repaying a loan or to gain a business advantage. Fraud generally includes embezzlement, white-collar crime, and a whole range of other thefts based on deceptions such as false promises, misrepresentations, lies, and concealment.

This chapter discusses the prevalence of fraud, the type of environment necessary for fraud to occur, and the red flags or warning signs that indicate the possible presence of fraud.

Up, Up, and Away: America's Fastest-Growing Business

Each year the international accounting firm of KPMG Peat Marwick conducts a survey of fraud in companies in the United States. The findings of the KPMG survey are quite interesting, and most are included here. The exhibits in this chapter are largely reproductions of visual aids prepared by the national director of KPMG Peat Marwick's Forensic and Investigative Services.

The KPMG 1994 Fraud Survey found that 77% of the companies surveyed suffered fraud in the preceding year. Seventy-six percent believed that fraud was a major problem for business in general, 54% believed that it was a major problem in their own organizations, and 67% (up from 52% in the previous year) believed that fraud would increase in the future. These responses are shown in Exhibits 13-1, 13-2, and 13-3.

Poor internal controls were seen as the single most influential factor in allowing frauds to occur, being present in 59% of the cases. The factors contributing to an environment where fraud can occur are shown in Exhibit 13-4. Collusion by employees and management override of controls were each a factor in approximately one-third of the frauds.

EXHIBIT 13-1   THE EXTENT OF BUSINESS FRAUD

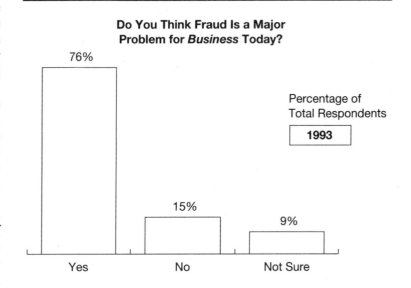

Do You Think Fraud Is a Major Problem for *Business* Today?

Percentage of Total Respondents

1993

76% Yes
15% No
9% Not Sure

EXHIBIT 13-2   MANAGER'S PERCEPTION OF FRAUD AS A MAJOR PROBLEM

Do You Think Fraud Is a Major Problem for *Your Organization* Today?

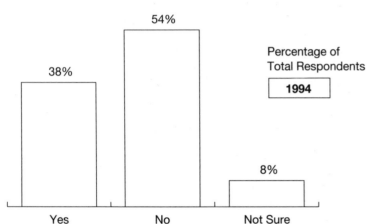

Percentage of Total Respondents
1994

Yes 38%
No 54%
Not Sure 8%

EXHIBIT 13-3   MANAGER'S EXPECTATIONS REGARDING THE GROWTH OF FRAUD

Do You Believe the Incidence of Fraud Will Increase, Decrease, or Stay the Same?

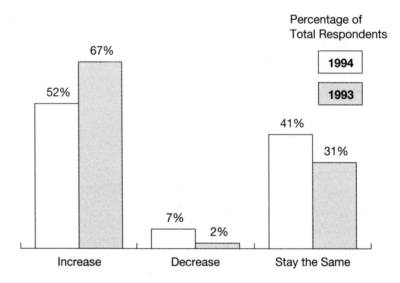

Percentage of Total Respondents
1994
1993

Increase 52% / 67%
Decrease 7% / 2%
Stay the Same 41% / 31%

Oddly, as shown in Exhibit 13-5, internal controls, the leading cause, was also the most frequently occurring single factor leading to the discovery of fraud, being a factor in the discovery of 52% of the frauds in the survey. Internal audit review, considered a part of internal control by many business people, was a factor in the discovery of 47% of the frauds, and notification of managers by an employee or a customer was the third most frequent factor. Discovery of approximately one-third of the frauds was accidental.

EXHIBIT 13-4 CONDITIONS THAT ALLOW FRAUD TO OCCUR

What Allowed the Frauds to Happen?

	1994	1993
• Poor internal controls	59%	56%
• Collusion—employees/third parties	33%	44%
• Management override of controls	36%	40%
• Industry at high risk	34%	38%

Red Flags were ignored in 48% (46%) of instances

EXHIBIT 13-5 DISCOVERY OF FRAUD

How Were the Frauds Discovered?

	1994	1993
• Internal controls	52%	59%
• Notification by employee	51%	10%
• Internal audit review	47%	47%
• Specific management investigation	42%	46%
• Notification by customer	34%	38%
• Accident	28%	32%
• External auditor review	5%	3%

What Did Companies Do?

Once a fraud was detected, the KPMG Peat Marwick survey tells us that most companies (83%) began an investigation and 74% immediately dismissed the perpetrator. Two-thirds of the companies reported the fraud to the police. One-third initiated a civil action to recover lost cash. These responses are shown in Exhibit 13-6.

To reduce or prevent fraud in the future, 79% of the corporate victims indicated that they were establishing a corporate

EXHIBIT 13-6   HOW COMPANIES RESPOND TO FRAUD

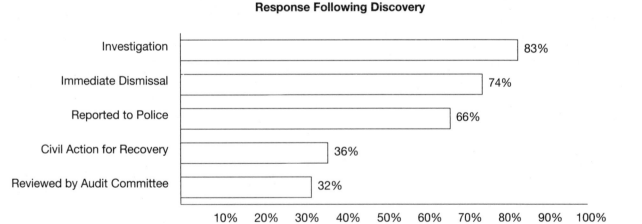

Response Following Discovery

Investigation	83%
Immediate Dismissal	74%
Reported to Police	66%
Civil Action for Recovery	36%
Reviewed by Audit Committee	32%

10% 20% 30% 40% 50% 60% 70% 80% 90% 100%

code of conduct. Corporate codes of conduct are strongly recommended by the National Commission on Fraudulent Financial Reporting as a means of establishing an ethical "tone at the top," and empower employees and managers at all levels of the company to reduce fraud.

Seventy percent of the victims say they will focus on reference checks for new employees. Forty-seven percent intend to review and improve internal controls. These and other steps that victims intended to take are shown in Exhibit 13-7.

EXHIBIT 13-7   STEPS TO REDUCE FRAUD

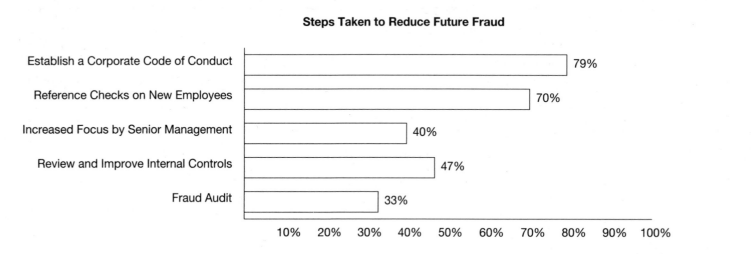

Steps Taken to Reduce Future Fraud

Step	Percentage
Establish a Corporate Code of Conduct	79%
Reference Checks on New Employees	70%
Increased Focus by Senior Management	40%
Review and Improve Internal Controls	47%
Fraud Audit	33%

Red Flags That Signal Fraud

Three conditions must be present for fraud to occur. There must be a need, a rationalization, and an opportunity. The need can be real or imagined. The rationalization can be as creative as people are different. Exhibit 13-8 contains examples of rationalizations cited by KPMG Peat Marwick.

The situational pressure red flags in Exhibit 13-9 are examples of personal and company pressures that can create a perceived need in an employee. These red flags and the remainder of the exhibits in the chapter are from KPMG Peat Marwick materials used in seminars for internal auditors.

Red flags that indicate that an employee may have the opportunity to commit fraud are listed in Exhibits 13-9 and 13-10. These exhibits contain an elaborate compendium of both personal and company red flags. Situational red flags are shown in Exhibit 13-9, and opportunity red flags in Exhibit 13-10.

Managers cannot prevent fraud from occurring. Responsible managers should learn the red flag warning signs and stay on the alert. As soon as a control to prevent fraud is developed, someone starts probing for weaknesses.

EXHIBIT 13-8   HOW EMPLOYEES RATIONALIZE FRAUD

Possible Rationalizations
- "I'm just borrowing the funds."
- "I deserve it—I'm underpaid or underpromoted."
- "I'm not hurting anyone."
- "Others are doing it—either the boss or other employees."

EXHIBIT 13-9   SITUATIONAL PRESSURE RED FLAGS

Personal

A. Financial Pressures

1. High personal debts

2. Severe illnesses in family

3. Inadequate income and/or living beyond means

4. Extensive stock market speculation creating indebtedness

5. Loan shark involvement

6. Excessive gambling

7. Heavy expenses incurred by involvement with other women/men

8. Undue family, peer, company, or community expectations

9. Excessive use of alcohol or drugs causing indebtedness

B. Revenge Motives

1. Perceived inequities (e.g., underpaid, poor job assignment)

2. Resentment of superiors

3. Frustration, usually with job

Company

A. Financial Pressures

1. Unfavorable economic conditions within the industry

2. Heavy investments or losses

3. Lack of sufficient working capital

4. Success of the company dependent on one or two products, customers, or transactions

5. Excess capacity

6. Severe obsolescence

7. Extremely high debt

8. Extremely rapid expansion through new business or product lines

9. Tight credit, high interest rates, and reduced ability to acquire credit

10. Pressure to finance expansion through current earnings rather than through debt or equity

11. Profit squeeze (costs and expenses rising higher and faster than sales and revenues)

12. Difficulty in collecting receivables

13. Unusually heavy competition (including low-priced imports)

14. Existing loan agreements with little flexibility and tough restrictions

15. Progressive deterioration in quality of earnings

16. Significant tax adjustments by the IRS

17. Long-term financial losses

18. Unusually high profits with a cash shortage

19. Urgent need for favorable earnings to support high price of stock, meet earnings forecast, etc.

20. Need to gloss over a temporary bad situation and maintain management position and prestige

21. Significant litigation, especially between stockholders and management

22. Unmarketable collateral

23. Significant reduction in sales backlog, indicating future sales decline

24. Long business cycle

25. Existence of revocable and possibly imperiled licenses necessary for the continuation of business

26. Suspension or delisting from a stock exchange

27. Fear of a merger

EXHIBIT 13-10   OPPORTUNITY RED FLAGS

Personal

A. Personally Developed Opportunities

  1. Very familiar with operations (including cover-up capabilities)

  2. In a position of trust

  3. Close association with cohorts, suppliers, and other key people

B. Firm Environments That Foster and/or Create Opportunities

  1. A firm that does not inform employees about rules and disciplining of fraud perpetrators

  2. A firm in which there is rapid turnover of key employees—quit or fired

  3. A firm in which there are no annual vacations of executives

  4. A firm in which there are no rotations or transfers of key employees

  5. A firm that does not use adequate personnel

  6. A firm in which there is an absence of explicit and uniform personnel policies

  7. A firm that does not maintain accurate personnel records of dishonest acts or disciplinary actions for such things as alcoholism and/or drug abuse

  8. A firm that has no documented code of ethics

  9. A firm that does not require executive disclosures and examinations

  10. A firm that has weak leadership

  11. A firm that has a dishonest management and/or environment

  12. A firm that has a dominant top management (one or two individuals)

  13. A firm that is always operating in a crisis

  14. A firm that pays no attention to details

  15. A firm in which there is too much trust in key employees

  16. A firm in which there are relatively few interpersonal relationships

  17. A firm that does not have viable dissatisfaction and grievance outlets

  18. A firm that lacks personnel evaluations

  19. A firm that does not have operational productivity measurements and evaluations

Company

A. Nature of Firm

  1. A firm that has related-party transactions

  2. A firm that has a very complex business structure

  3. A firm that does not have an effective internal auditing staff

  4. An extremely large and decentralized firm

  5. A highly computerized firm

  6. A firm that has inexperienced people in key positions

B. Relationship with Outside Parties

  1. A firm that uses several different auditing firms

  2. A firm that is reluctant to give auditors needed data

  3. A firm that changes auditors often

  4. A firm that hires an auditor who lacks expertise

  5. A firm that persistently brings unexpected information to the auditor's attention

  6. A firm that changes legal counsel often

  7. A firm that is reluctant to give accounting information to its legal counsel

  8. A firm that has several different legal counsels

  9. A firm that uses several different banks, none of which can see the entire picture

  10. A firm that has continuous problems with various regulatory agencies

C. Accounting Practices

  1. A firm that has large year-end and unusual transactions

  2. A firm in which many adjusting entries are required at the time of the audit

  3. A firm that supplies information to auditors at the last minute

  4. A firm that has a poor internal control system or does not enforce internal control procedures

  5. A firm that has unduly liberal accounting records

  6. A firm that has poor accounting records

  7. A firm that has inadequate staffing in the accounting department

14

INTERNAL CONTROLS TO PREVENT LOSSES AND ERRORS

From the perspective of a thief, cash is a company's most desirable asset. Cash is small and easily concealed. It is generally not recognizable once it has left the premises, and it is easy to convert to other assets. If a thief steals any other asset, marketable securities or industrial diamonds, for example, he or she must first convert these items to cash if they are to be exchanged for sports cars, furs, or other things the thief desires. Management must be very careful to safeguard the company's cash and to protect employees (including themselves) from unnecessary temptation.

Internal control is the primary tool for safeguarding cash. Internal control is any policy, procedure, or management action that directs employees and safeguards the company's assets. There is a great deal of information on internal control available, much of it developed by the American Institute of Certified Public Accountants (AICPA) and the Institute of Internal Auditors (IIA). The IIA standards state that internal controls have five objectives, which concern the following:

1. The reliability and integrity of information,

2. The extent of management's compliance with company policies, plans, and procedures, and government laws and regulations,

3. The safeguarding of assets,

4. The effectiveness and efficiency of operations, and

5. The accomplishment of established objectives and goals.

There are general internal control principles which, if used, are intended to protect all types of assets, and there are an array of procedures specific to controlling and safeguarding cash. Because the theft or misuse of any asset requires an expenditure of cash to replace it, we start by discussing general internal control measures for all assets; measures specific to safeguarding cash are discussed in Chapter 15. In Chapter 16, we discuss the internal control problems unique to small companies.

Types of Control

Internal controls are frequently divided into administrative controls and accounting controls. Administrative controls are all the measures used to guide, limit, or direct employee actions and business operations in areas other than accounting. Accounting controls are concerned with the accuracy of the accounting system. Of the five objectives of control listed, only the first is concerned with the reliability and integrity of accounting information. The rest relate to complying with rules or performing operating activities.

The internal control literature of the AICPA is predominantly involved with accounting controls. The following AICPA guidelines on accounting internal control are widely accepted by accountants and auditors and were written by Congress into the Foreign Corrupt Practices Act.

Accounting controls should assure:

1. That business transactions of all kinds are (a) properly authorized by management and (b) recorded in the accounting records so that company financial statements can be prepared and the accountability of employees and managers maintained.

2. That access to company assets is limited to specifically authorized people so the assets cannot be stolen or misused.

3. That accounting records from time to time are compared or reconciled to the underlying company assets so that any differences due to error or crime can be detected.

All controls, accounting and administrative, can be categorized as one or more of the following types:

- Preventive controls
- Detective controls
- Corrective controls
- Compensating controls
- Directive controls

The first four types of controls focus on negative results. Directive controls focus on positive results.

Preventive Controls

Preventive controls are usually the most cost-effective, because preventing a theft or an error avoids the cost of correction. Hiring honest employees with sufficient education and skills is a control that prevents theft and unsatisfactory performance.

Detective Controls

Detective controls are more expensive, because they assess the effectiveness of preventive controls. A manager who checks the work of a subordinate is acting as a detective control. Reconciling the bank account is another type of detective control. Even when exceptional employees are hired, not all errors can be prevented and detective controls are still necessary.

Corrective Controls

Corrective controls either correct an error when it is detected or spotlight the error until it is corrected. Corrective controls are necessary, because unless corrections are made, detective controls are useless. A manager who checks the work of a sub-ordinate may tag defective items to spotlight them for correction. The tag is a corrective control. Another might be to require a worker to attend an educational program if mistakes are excessive, or to buy a calculator for an employee who adds poorly.

Compensating Controls

Compensating controls compensate for deficiencies in other controls, as detective control may compensate for the failure of a preventive control. The manager seeks to prevent errors by hiring skilled, capable workers but still monitors output to detect any defective work product. The monitoring compensates for any failure of hiring practices to prevent errors.

Directive Controls

Directive controls focus on, and are designed to produce, positive results rather than to prevent, detect, or correct bad outcomes. A management directive that the company hire graduates of the best colleges as accountants is intended to produce good results (as well as to prevent bad results).

Separation of Duties

Separation of duties is a preventive control. Managers presume that if an act requires collusion, it is less likely to occur. If two employees must conspire to conceal an error or commit a crime, the concealment or crime is less likely than if it can be accomplished by one employee acting alone. Under this presumption, certain duties are incompatible and cannot be assigned to the same person. If incompatible duties are assigned to one employee, they make concealment of an error or theft possible by the single employee. If these duties are separated and assigned to two people, however, collusion is necessary to conceal an error or commit a theft.

For example, no one employee should be allowed to receive customer payments and maintain the balances in customer accounts. If both duties are assigned to the same employee, a criminal activity called "lapping" may occur. Suppose Raymond's responsibilities include the incompatible duties of receiving customer payments and maintaining the balances in customer accounts. When a payment of $1,000 is received from Red Company, Raymond steals the money. He does not credit the Red account receivable for the $1,000 payment. The next day, Raymond receives a $1,000 payment from White Ltd. He credits the $1,000 received from White to the Red account. Now the Red account is correct and the White account is short. The next day when a payment is received from Blue Corporation, that payment is used to cover the shortage in the White account. And so on.

No account is ever short more than one day, because Raymond "laps" the payments. Raymond has successfully removed $1,000 from the system. If he is responsible for a large number of accounts, he can, by lapping the payments for many accounts, steal a great deal of money.

Even if Raymond is honest and does not steal, an employee having custody of cash and accounting for customer accounts might be tempted to avoid a reprimand by concealing errors. Concealing errors causes accounts to be misstated, possibly changing reported earnings and other amounts in the financial statements.

Examples of other incompatible functions include ordering and receiving materials, or issuing checks and reconciling the bank balance. In the first instance, the employee can create a bogus order, indicate receipt when no goods are received, and cause a payment to be made to a fictitious supplier (himself). In the second, an employee can issue a check to a fictitious payee (again himself) and conceal the check when it is returned with the bank statement.

Prenumbered Documents

Forms and documents are used to record and communicate important information. For example, a purchase requisition lists items requested, who made the request, and the date the items were requested. Other forms authorize activities: an approved purchase order authorizes the purchase of the items on the requisition. Some documents, such as cents-off coupons and gift certificates, have value in and of themselves. A cents-off coupon on coffee is redeemed at face value from the manufacturer by the grocer.

Exhibit 14-1 shows a prenumbered gift certificate from the Old Time Tavern restaurant. A gift certificate may be accepted by all restaurants in a chain and is equivalent to cash when used in the restaurant. Such gift certificates can be stolen and used to buy food or can be placed in the cash register to make it balance by an employee stealing cash. Using prenumbered certificates requires employees to account for all certificates and allows managers to track a missing certificate.

The forms, coupons, and other documents that management wants to control should be prenumbered. If documents are prenumbered, management can control their use and require employees to account for all documents in their possession.

Old Time Tavern

1233 Green Road
Anderson, SC 29621

Gift certificate good for $10 (ten dollars)

Presented to

Signed _____   No. 128

For example, the owner of a certain restaurant was concerned about low sales and poor cash flow. Sales appeared good, yet recorded sales were significantly below the level achieved by other restaurants in the chain. The procedure followed by waitresses was to write an order on an order pad and submit the order to the kitchen. When the food was given to the waitress, the order was returned so it could be used as the customer's bill. When the customer paid, the waitress took the order/bill and payment to the cash register.

When the owner checked prenumbered order pad pages, she found many pages missing. All missing pages were from the order pads of one waitress. On some of the large orders each evening, the waitress had pocketed both the cash payment and the order. By placing the prenumbered pages in numerical sequence, the owner discovered the theft.

Often, using prenumbered documents is both a preventive and a detective control. If workers know that the manager accounts for all documents, or even that this is possible, theft may be deterred.

Mandatory Vacations

Mandatory vacations, taken all at once, are both a preventive and a detective control, because fraudulent schemes often require constant attention by the criminal. In our illustration of lapping, Raymond must constantly monitor and redirect customer payments to avoid being caught. In many cases, managers and other employees are shocked to learn of fraud committed by a fellow worker.

"Why, Raymond was so devoted!" they might exclaim. "He hasn't missed a day's work in seven years. He never took a vacation or even a sick day. I just can't believe it!"

Raymond never missed work because he could not let anyone else do his job without risking exposure of his crime. Mandatory vacations allow someone new to perform each job. Thus, unusual or fraudulent activities can be uncovered.

Limited Access

Limited access is a preventive control. Companies often require badges or other identification for access to the plant or offices. Access can be limited on a "need to know" or "need to go" basis. A hospital may limit access to computerized patient records and billing information. Access to these records might be accomplished only with proper authentication, a password, perhaps.

Access to information or physical facilities can be limited by:

1. Something you know, such as a password, or data encryption requiring a decrypting "key." Coding computer data before it is transmitted through a public telephone system is becoming more common.

2. Something you have, such as a key or a smart card imprinted with your access code. Your bank electronic teller machine recognizes you only by your card (something you have) and your personal identification number (something you know).

3. Something you are, such as the retina of your eye or your handprint. Interestingly, intelligence agencies have become reluctant to use machine-read handprints or fingerprints to permit access to secure areas, because a determined enemy can steal these items!

4. Somewhere you are, such as determined by dial-back security on a computer modem. After you give your password (something you know) the computer must be able to dial you back at an approved location or access will be denied.

Physical Barriers

Physical safeguards deter thieves and reduce losses. A fence around the warehouse, a lock on the storeroom back door, and a safe in which to keep the change fund at night are examples of physical barriers that are part of a company's internal control system.

15

MAINTAINING CONTROL OVER CASH

Internal control of cash is based on the principles of internal control discussed in the preceding chapter. A manager should separate incompatible duties: the employee who has custody of cash should not be responsible for maintaining the cash records; companies should use numbered checks and receipts and make employees take annual vacations. This chapter discusses four areas that are particularly important in establishing internal control over cash. The second and third relate specifically to cash. The first and last are important for safeguarding all assets.

1. Hire honest people.

2. Deposit cash daily.

3. Make all disbursements by check.

4. Monitor internal controls.

Hire Honest People

Perhaps the single most important thing a company can do to prevent fraud or the mishandling of cash or cash records is to hire honest people and use them wisely. The largest proportion of fraud is committed by company employees, not outsiders. But if controls fail, honest people will not take advantage. Honest people will not conspire to defeat controls or probe for weaknesses. Honest people will not conceal their mistakes from management. A control system is only as good as the employees who implement the controls.

Even after having attempted to hire honest people, managers should make the best possible use of employees. Managers should assign duties commensurate with the training, skills, interests, and abilities of each employee. If managers scrimp to save pennies and assign complex duties, such as purchasing specialty chemicals, to lower-paid, untrained employees, they may find they have increased the incentive for the employees to conceal errors or take short-cuts, perhaps bypassing controls. An employee who is not properly trained in chemical purchasing procedures may, for example, accept help from another employee who also receives incoming shipments.

Receiving shipments is incompatible with initiating purchases because, in combination, these duties allow an employee to steal from the company. For instance, an employee can generate both a purchasing order to a phony company (perhaps a mail drop) and a record that the goods ordered were received, when they were not. This will cause management to write a check to the phony company, which the employee then cashes. When a purchasing employee allows a receiving employee to informally assume purchasing duties, the control established by separating incompatible functions is circumvented.

Bond Employees in Positions of Trust

All people in positions of trust should be bonded. A bond is an insurance policy against loss from employee theft—but a bonding company will pay only when the loss is proven and proven to result from the action of the bonded employee. Providing the required proof can be expensive, or even impossible, if no controls exist. Bonding employees is no substitute for good internal controls.

Fix Responsibility

Fixing responsibility involves linking actions with the individuals who perform them. At all points in the cash-handling process, formally identify the employee who takes each action and have the employee take responsibility for that action. Have employees sign the documents they handle. A salesperson should sign sales slips and the final tally on the change drawer at the end of the day. People who count money and make up deposits should sign the calculator tapes and deposit slips. Anyone making a refund, or approving a refund to be made, should sign the credit memo.

Fixing responsibility causes employees to perform better because they must explain any deviations from the established control procedures. In addition, fixing responsibility has a psychological effect that tends to increase efficiency and effectiveness by focusing the employee's attention on the task and stressing the employee's responsibility for seeing that it is done correctly.

Deposit Cash Daily

Deposit all cash receipts intact daily. This means that none of the receipts are used to pay cash items that come due during the day. All expenditures are made by check, as explained in the discussion that follows. If this practice is followed:

1. Employees cannot "borrow" the company's cash, because it goes (with little delay) straight from the customer to the bank, and

2. The accounting record of daily cash sales corresponds exactly to the company's deposit records.

If cash sales of $13,786.34 are made on Monday and deposited intact, both the bank's records and the company's own cash account will show a deposit of $13,786.34. Cash sales should be recorded when they are made, using a cash register or prenumbered sales receipts. Copies of the register tape, or sales receipts, should be sent to the company cashier (with the cash) and the originals sent to the bookkeeper.

Customer payments received in the mail are usually checks or money orders. An employee who is neither the company cashier nor the bookkeeper should open the mail and list the checks and money orders. This employee should make three copies of the list: one copy to keep, and one copy each for the company cashier and the bookkeeper.

The company cashier is responsible for depositing the cash, and the bookkeeper for maintaining the cash records. The company cashier never has access to the accounting records, and the bookkeeper never has custody of the cash.

The daily deposit slip should be compared with (and should be the same as) total (1) cash receipts on the list of payments received and (2) the register tape or cash sales receipts. Cash deposits must reconcile with amounts received each day. Any difference should be investigated.

The reconciliation forces the cashier to deposit all receipts, so that the bank balance will agree with the bookkeeper's accounting record. Likewise, employees who receive cash must record all cash receipts, or risk having customers question their account balances or the amount rung up on the cash register.

Make All Disbursements by Check

All cash disbursements should be made by check, never from the day's receipts. When all disbursements are made by check, the bank statement amounts correspond to the company's accounting records. If expenditures are made for $300 of office supplies and $900 of computer software, the $300 and $900 amounts will be recorded in the accounting records and will also appear on the company's bank statement.

Because many thefts of cash are payments of fictitious invoices, control over cash disbursements is usually considered more important than control over cash receipts. The following procedures provide guidance in controlling and safeguarding cash disbursements. The first three procedures ensure that the company pays only properly authorized invoices. The last four maintain the separation of cash recordkeeping and custody.

1. All disbursements should be made by check or from the petty cash fund.

2. All checks should be prenumbered.

3. Access to checks should be limited to the employee(s) responsible for writing checks.

4. All disbursements should be authorized by a designated manager and supported by documentation such as invoices, written requests, or purchase orders.

5. Only original documentation should be accepted in support of payments. (Accepting copies may result in duplicate payment.)

6. Supporting documentation should be stamped "PAID" when cash is disbursed (to prevent duplicate payments).

7. The manager responsible for authorizing a payment should not be the person who signs the check.

8. Signed checks should be mailed by employees who do not have access to cash or cash records.

9. The employee who signs the checks should not have access to canceled checks.

10. The employee who signs the checks should not reconcile the bank account.

11. The bank account should be reconciled promptly when statements are received.

Petty Cash Procedures

We have said that companies should deposit cash receipts daily and make all disbursements by check. Many times, however, common sense tells you that such a procedure is not practical. A delivery truck arrives with a package, for which the company must pay $15.61 in delivery charges, or an employee goes to the post office to buy $20 worth of postage stamps. It is not practical or cost-efficient to request that a check be written for such payments. In order to pay by check, someone must obtain approval, write the check (or have it written), and then take the check to the delivery person or the post office. It is much more convenient to have small amounts of cash on hand to pay for small expenditures. This small amount of cash is called a petty cash fund.

A petty cash fund is established by writing a check for a small amount, perhaps $100, to a person called the petty cashier. The cashier cashes the check and keeps the currency in a safe place. The petty cashier is responsible for maintaining the fund and performing all cash activities involving the fund.

Exhibit 15-1 shows a petty cash voucher used by Calvin Floor Coverings. A petty cash voucher (or some other form of support document) is prepared by the cashier each time cash is disbursed from the fund. The voucher shows the date, amount, and reason for the expenditure. Approval for the expenditure is shown by the signature of the cashier, and the voucher is signed by the person receiving the cash.

From time to time the petty cash fund must be replenished. The sum of the remaining cash and the payment vouchers should always equal the total amount initially put into the

EXHIBIT 15-1   PETTY CASH VOUCHER

No. _____102_____   Amount _____$20.00_____

Date _____January 21, 1996_____

Explanation _____Payment to post office for stamps._____

Approved by _____D.M._____   Received _____Bob Dukes_____

fund. The fund in our example was established for $100 and on February 15 contains cash and voucher records as follows:

Cash	$ 18.50
Voucher #101 Supplies	23.75
Voucher #102 Postage	20.00
Voucher #103 Freight	15.00
Voucher #104 Supplies	12.50
Voucher #105 Employee Advance (Loan)	10.25
Total of Petty Cash Fund	$100.00

To replenish the fund, a check to the petty cash cashier is drawn for $81.50, the amount of the five vouchers. The fund is restored to $100.

The expenses recorded on the vouchers have not been entered into the accounting system, only into the petty cash control system. Thus, when the check is written to restore the fund, it is recorded as being for the expenses recorded on the vouchers, and the following expenses are recorded in the accounting records:

Supplies Expense	$36.25
Postage Expense	20.00
Freight Expense	15.00
Employee Advance Receivable	10.25

The vouchers are removed from the petty cash fund so that its balance (cash plus vouchers) remains $100.00. If the cashier makes an error somehow and the total of vouchers plus cash in the fund is not equal to the $100.00 fund balance, the fund is "short" or "over." These shortage and overages are charged to an account called Cash Short or Over. If cash remaining in the fund is only $15.25, the fund is $3.25 short.

Cash	$ 15.25
Voucher #101 Supplies	23.75
Voucher #102 Postage	20.00
Voucher #103 Freight	15.00
Voucher #104 Supplies	12.50
Voucher #105 Employee Advance (Loan)	10.25
Cash Short or Over	3.25
Total of Petty Cash Fund	$100.00

In this case, the petty cash fund is reimbursed $84.75 so that the balance of cash and vouchers is again $100.00, and the $3.25 shortage is entered into the accounting records in the Cash Short or Over account.

Monitor Internal Controls

It is management's responsibility to establish the company's goals and the internal controls necessary to achieve them. Managers should monitor the controls that direct their subordinates. However, independent monitoring is important too. A company's auditors, internal and external, should monitor and periodically evaluate management's controls.

External Auditors

Unless a company is subject to government regulations and government auditors (who may not be certified), such as an insurance company or a bank, its external auditors are Certified Public Accountants (CPAs). CPAs audit the company so that they can give an opinion on the company's financial statements. An audit is usually performed annually, but in a smaller company it may be done only in conjunction with a loan application. As part of its audit, a CPA firm examines a company's internal controls. Exhibit 15-2 is an example of a management letter that might be issued by Deloitte & Touche, an international accounting firm, to a retail company following an annual financial statement audit. (The observations and recommendations are taken from an actual letter.)

Internal Auditors

Internal auditors may audit the same things that external auditors do. They also audit the efficiency, effectiveness, and economy of operations in a special type of audit called an *operational audit*. Internal auditors performing an operational audit seek the answers to several basic questions:

- Has management established goals?

- Has management put controls in place that are adequate to achieve its goals?

- Are management's controls working to achieve its goals?

- Are management's goals achieved?

Exhibit 15-3 shows the components that an internal audit deficiency finding might contain. Exhibit 15-4 contains an internal audit deficiency finding detailing a specific problem in cash control.

EXHIBIT 15-2 A MANAGEMENT LETTER FROM A CERTIFIED PUBLIC ACCOUNTING FIRM ADDRESSING INTERNAL CONTROL WEAKNESSES

Deloitte & Touche LLP

March 4, 1994

ABC Retailer, Inc.

Dear Sirs:

In planning and performing our audit of the financial statements of ABC Retailer, Inc. (the "Company") for the year ended January 31, 1994 (on which we have issued our report dated March 4, 1994), we developed the following recommendations related to the internal control structure (other than "reportable conditions") and another recommendation related to an accounting matter. Our observations and recommendations and management's response are as follows:

INTERNAL CONTROL STRUCTURE

INACTIVE EDP TERMINAL CONTROLS

Observation—The EDP system control feature which automatically signs off inactive terminals has not been activated. As a result, unauthorized access to computer resources may be obtained through unattended terminals that have not been signed off.

Recommendation—We recommend that the automatic terminal sign-off feature be activated and set at a reasonable period of time to prevent unauthorized users from obtaining access through unattended terminals that have not been signed off.

Management Response—We will activate the computers' time-out feature.

ACCOUNTING FOR DAMAGED MERCHANDISE

Observation—Damaged merchandise on hand was included in the stores' year-end physical inventories. As a result, inventory at year end was misstated for quantities of damaged merchandise in the stores. Subsequent to year end, the damaged merchandise was returned to the warehouse and written off.

Recommendation—A reserve for damaged merchandise should be recorded at year end. If possible, such damaged merchandise may be identified at the year-end physical inventories. Otherwise, it may be practical to develop a procedure to fairly estimate the amount of damaged merchandise on hand at year end.

Management Response—We plan to segregate damaged merchandise from the stores' regular inventory and thereby exclude it from physical counts in the future.

BANK ACCOUNT RECONCILIATIONS

Observation—Controls over bank reconciliations were not adequate to bring to management's attention in a timely manner an irregularity whereby a store employee was withholding funds from the store's daily deposits.

Recommendation—Personnel performing the bank account reconciliations for store depository accounts should be instructed to bring certain findings, such as missing deposits, promptly to the attention of management.

Management Response—The person who was deficient in reporting this irregularity resigned. The supervisor of the sales audit department now reviews all bank reconciliations each month as an additional control.

ACCOUNTING MATTER

FREIGHT IN INVENTORY

Observation—Freight costs included in inventory at year end are based on average freight costs for the year rather than on freight costs determined on a FIFO basis, consistent with the Company's inventory accounting policy. Variation in the cost of sourcing inventories resulting from item mix, geographic location of the vendors, etc., could affect freight cost and the resultant determination of freight costs included in inventory. Also, the freight costs which are included in inventory are based on a blended freight cost for both domestic and import goods.

Recommendation—We recommend that an effort be made to determine freight in inventory on a FIFO basis and based on whether the goods, and related freight costs, are domestic or import.

Management Response—We have developed systems to do this, and it will be done prior to the second quarter closing.

****

This report is intended solely for the information and use of the Audit Committee, the Board of Directors, management, and others within the organization.

We will be pleased to discuss these comments with you and, if desired, assist you in implementing any of the suggestions.

Yours truly,

Deloitte & Touche LLP

EXHIBIT 15-3   CONTENT OF AN INTERNAL AUDIT DEFICIENCY FINDING

An internal audit deficiency finding will contain most or all of the following components:

- The STANDARD the operation was supposed to meet.
- The actual CONDITION of the operation (what was actually accomplished—the facts).
- The PROCEDURES/PRACTICES that should have been followed (Were procedures established? followed? complete?).
- The CAUSE of the departure from standard procedure (answers "Why?").
- The EFFECT of the departure from standard (answers "So what?").
- The auditor's CONCLUSION as to what needs to be corrected (alternatives, cost/benefit).
- A RECOMMENDATION as to how the correction might be made (deciding what to do is management's job).

EXHIBIT 15-4   INTERNAL AUDIT DEFICIENCY FINDING ON CASH CONTROL

INTERNAL AUDIT FINDING OF DEFICIENCY

AUDIT PROJECT:_____207_____

AUDIT ENTITY:_____Regional Administrative Office_____

STANDARD(S):

Policy prohibits the petty cashier from expending, borrowing, using, or otherwise employing the petty cash fund for personal benefit. All disbursements should be supported by a properly completed expenditure voucher. The voucher should be signed by the petty cashier and the person receiving the cash.

CONDITION:

The petty cashier had fiduciary responsibility for the $1,000 imprest petty cash fund of the regional administrative office. When examined during a surprise cash count, the fund contained vouchers supporting expenditures of $518.28, cash of $344.30, and a personal check from the petty cashier for $100.00 dated December 22, last year, leaving the fund short by $37.42. The petty cashier said he had borrowed the money and intended to write a check for the amount, but forgot. The petty cash fund has not been audited or replenished in more than two years (the exact date is uncertain).

CORRECT PROCEDURE(S):

The petty cashier is not allowed to take cash from the petty cash fund, even if a check is written to replace the cash taken.

RECOMMENDATION(S):

1. The petty cashier should be given a copy of company policy on the duties of a petty cashier.

2. The petty cash fund should be reduced to an amount that would require replenishment in not more than six months. (We recommend $250.00.)

3. The activities of the petty cashier should be monitored by the office manager. The monitoring should include examining all vouchers when the fund is replenished and periodically conducting surprise cash counts.

For managers to be able to rely on an auditor's work, the auditor must be independent of the entity or activity audited. Independence is easy for external auditors to achieve. These auditors report only to stockholders and the board of directors and are required by their code of ethics to be free of any relationship with the company or its employees that might appear to compromise independence. An external auditor cannot, for example, own stock in or make a loan to the company, cannot accept gifts from company employees or managers, and cannot have a relative who has a financial or managerial relationship with the company.

Internal auditors, however, are employees of the company and cannot be independent in the same way external auditors can. Yet, although internal auditors cannot be independent of the company as a whole, they can be independent of the parts of the company they audit. This is achieved by having the internal audit department report directly to top management or the board of directors. Ideally, only the board of directors has the authority to set the budget for internal auditing or to dismiss the director of the internal audit department. Such safeguards protect internal auditors from pressures possibly exerted by audit clients in senior management and allows them to be independent.

External auditors evaluate a company's internal control system as it relates to the information in annual reports. This is a valuable service, but internal auditors are better attuned to management's concerns about individual procedures and cash controls. In general, the more cash activity a company has, the more it relies on internal auditors to monitor cash controls. Banks, for example, often spend 10 to 50 times as much money on internal auditors as on external auditors.

Regardless of a company's size, managers should monitor the controls affecting their subordinates and employ auditors to monitor the internal controls of the company as a whole.

16

CASH CONTROLS IN SMALL COMPANIES

Many small businesses cannot justify an elaborate system of internal control. Hiring a staff of accountants and clerical personnel is not feasible, so small companies must be creative. To separate incompatible functions, for example, payments mailed to the company can be opened by any employee, who makes a list of the amounts received. Payments received can then be safely given to another employee responsible for posting to customer accounts. At the end of the day, the total receipts deposited in the bank must be the same as the total on the list prepared by the mail opener.

A night clerk working alone in a small market both receives money and records the sales on the cash register. These functions can be separated by having the customer act as the second person in the system. Signs that request, "Please ask for your receipt" attempt to ensure the customer's involvement. Because the customer expects the purchase to be entered in the cash register, and because the customer wants an itemized receipt, the presence of the customer forces the clerk to ring up the sale. When the sale is rung up, a record not accessible to the employee is created inside the cash register and the cash is placed in the drawer. The accounting (the inaccessible record) and the custody of the cash are separated.

When a company owner has only one employee, that employee may perform the bank reconciliation, write and sign checks, and have access to blank checks. Here, a creative safeguard is to involve the spouse of the owner in accounting for cash. The owner can have all bank statements sent to his or her home, where the owner or spouse can open the statement and inspect or shuffle the contents. When the statement is given to the employee, the opened envelope lets the employee know that the cash flows are monitored.

In addition, "Not good for more than $100" can be written on blank checks left with the employee. This limits the amount of the checks and also makes them easy to pick out (separate from those written by the owner) when the bank statement is opened by the owner or spouse. Examination of returned checks can be more easily limited to those written by the employee.

Control in a Small Business: A Case Study

Consider the creative use of internal cash controls in an illustrative case involving the Neighbor Movie Theater (NMT). The owner of the NMT is also its manager. NMT employs three high school students. One student collects ticket money and admits patrons to the theater. That student tears the ticket in half and gives a stub to each person admitted. The ticket sales receipts are kept in a metal box with the unsold tickets. Because NMT is small, no one checks the stubs once they are given to the customer.

The second student sells snacks at the concession counter. Cash from concession sales is kept in the drawer of an inoperable cash register.

The third student has several duties: sweeping the floor, helping the owner/manager in the projection booth, and serving as a backup in case someone does not come to work.

The owner/manager counts all cash at the end of each night and records a single amount in her ledger as "Ticket and Concession Sales." The cash is deposited in a bank night deposit drop.

NMT has potential problems with cash internal control. The biggest problem is a lack of separation of incompatible duties. One person should not receive customer payments for tickets or concession purchases and maintain the record of cash receipts (determined from the unsold tickets, and the cash in the drawer). When both duties are assigned to the same person, errors and thefts are more likely to occur.

Ticket sales: The student selling tickets can steal or defraud NMT in several ways. The main ways are the following:

1. Because ticket stubs are the only record of the number of persons admitted, the ticket seller can admit friends without charging them.

2. Two halves of the same ticket can be given to different customers, allowing the ticket seller to keep the price of one ticket.

3. The ticket seller can admit people, collecting cash and giving no ticket stub at all, keeping all the cash received.

The problem with ticket sales can be solved by using the third employee to collect ticket stubs when patrons are admitted between movies. When patrons are admitted during a movie, while the third employee is working in the projection booth, the stub can be collected by the employee selling at the concession counter.

All tickets should be prenumbered, and the owner/manager should compare the number of tickets torn from the roll with the cash received and, occasionally, with the number of patrons in the theater as counted from the projection booth.

A sign can be placed in the lobby saying "PLEASE RETAIN YOUR TICKET STUB!" so that customers will participate in the internal control system and insist that they be given a ticket stub. A conspiracy that occurs in some small movie houses involves collecting tickets, rather than tearing them, and reselling the same tickets to additional customers. To prevent this practice, the manager should periodically check either the stubs held by the employee or those held by the customers.

Concession sales: The primary problem with concession sales is the broken cash register. The owner/manager should repair or replace the cash register, if possible. In addition, items in the concession area can be inventoried and the cash that should have been received determined from the number of drink cups, popcorn containers, and candy bars consumed during the night.

A warning, however: counting drink cups and reconciling the number used to cash received may result in a determined employee thief collecting and refilling used cups, then keeping the money from those sales. Should customers discover this practice, they will find it disgusting and may not revisit the theater.

Cost-to-Benefit Analysis

A control in a business of any size must provide the company a benefit that is greater than the cost of the control. This is especially true for small businesses. A Bulgarian proverb says, "Don't build a $100 fence for a $10 cow." Yet benefits may be hard to determine, because they are often measures of the effect of events that did not happen. Moreover, no internal control system is 100% effective. So even if a control is created to address a particular risk, perhaps the theft of concession revenue in the NMT case, not all theft may disappear. If managers attempt to achieve 100% reduction in risk, controls can be very expensive. Managers should closely examine the cost-to-benefit ratio when initiating or improving controls.

For an example of the use of a cost-to-benefit ratio, consider the problem of authorizing payments for purchases. When an invoice is received, how much checking should managers do before paying? Typically, a manager wants to see evidence that the items were indeed ordered and received in good condition before an invoice is paid. But a company that has a long-term, established relationship with a vendor might safely pay with only periodic checking of a sample of supporting documents. In fact, one large manufacturer sends blank checks with its purchase orders. The vendor fills out each check and deposits it.

In another case, however, a criminal found that sending fake invoices to small governmental units often resulted in payment for goods never ordered nor shipped. In fact, the criminal found the scheme worked best if the first phony invoice sent was stamped "SECOND NOTICE—PLEASE REMIT." The decision to safeguard assets by confirming that items were ordered and received in good condition before paying must consider both the cost of the control and the benefit received.

The benefit received is, of course, related to the risk controlled. Often, the loss that can be expected from a specific risk is uncertain. Failure to inspect incoming raw materials might produce a risk of loss ranging from $0 to $100,000 per month. In this case, how much should a small company spend on inspections? One way to decide is to gather subjective assessments of the likelihood of various losses occurring and calculate the weighted average or expected value of the loss. Exhibit 16-1 presents the calculation of the expected value of the hypothetical risk of not inspecting raw materials received from vendors. A poll of managers yielded an estimated probability of occurrence for each loss.

Exhibit 16-1 shows that $28,000 is the expected value of monthly losses resulting from failure to inspect incoming raw material shipments. Managers would probably decide to inspect incoming shipments if inspection can be done for less than $28,000 per month, perhaps for $6,000. If inspection is expected to cost, say $55,000, managers would probably decide to forego inspecting and accept the loss. If the cost of inspection is expected to cost $26,000 or another amount close to the expected value of the loss resulting from not inspecting, managers may wish to attempt better estimates of the benefit of inspection. Because the expected value is completely an estimate, it may be difficult to know what to do.

EXHIBIT 16-1   THE EXPECTED VALUE OF COST OF NOT INSPECTING RAW MATERIALS SHIPMENTS RECEIVED FROM VENDORS

Amount of Loss (1)	Probability of Occurrence (2)	Loss Weighted by Its Probability (1 × 2)
—0—	.05	—0—
$ 5,000	.40	$ 2,000
30,000	.30	9,000
60,000	.20	12,000
100,000	.05	5,000
Expected Value	1.00	$28,000

Benefits of Control

Small businesses can be more sensitive to large losses than large companies. In addition, smaller numbers of employees make some controls more expensive or inconvenient to put in place. Therefore, small companies must be particularly attuned to all the costs and all the benefits of a control system. Exhibit 16-2 lists a few of the benefits a company receives from internal controls.

For an employee to commit fraud, three conditions must be present. The employee must have (1) a (real or imagined) need for money, (2) an opportunity to commit the fraud, and (3) a rationalization that committing the crime is appropriate, everything considered.

Restrictive controls attempt to remove the temptation and thus protect both the employee and the company. When money is stolen from a petty cash drawer from which all employees make change unsupervised, everyone is a suspect and uncomfortable. But if the petty cash is controlled by having a petty cashier designated to perform all petty cash activities, theft is deterred because the temptation is removed and only the cashier is a suspect if improprieties occur. Subjecting employees to unnecessary suspicion and investigation is bad for morale. Properly designed internal controls prevent such situations.

EXHIBIT 16-2   BENEFITS OF CONTROL

The benefits of a good internal control system include:

Removing temptation

Protecting both the employee and the company

Helping the person controlled to establish goals

Motivating employees through auto-control

Documenting the discharge of the fiduciary duty

Creating a control-conscious climate in the company

Preventing the rationalization and opportunity required for fraud

When employees participate in designing controls, the process can lead to auto-control. With auto-control, employees not only participate in setting their own operating goals and budgets, a much-praised management approach, they also participate in designing the controls that will monitor their progress.

Controls assist managers in documenting the discharge of their fiduciary duty of company owner. If internal controls are not in place, operating objectives may not be met, and financial statements and other reports from management cannot be relied on as correct.

Perhaps the greatest benefit resulting from a good internal control system is that it may create a control-conscious environment within the company. Controls that are lacking or poorly structured breed employee contempt for controls in general and aid in the rationalization of fraud.

Certain kinds of problems are associated with internal control. Those most commonly encountered are listed in Exhibit 16-3. Internal control problems occur in companies of all sizes, but can increase control costs significantly in a small company. For example, overemphasis on controls and over-controlling not only cause contempt for controls, an indirect cost, but also cost money directly in wasted time and resources. When controls are overemphasized, the control activity may become an end in itself. A salesperson who must complete overdetailed forms on every prospective customer may come to enjoy data collection more than selling.

Obsolete controls, left in place after the need disappears, are also costly and annoying to workers. Many companies continue manual controls long after a process has been computerized. For instance, a company may continue to require workers to complete, distribute, and file paper copies of requisitions even after the requisition process is computerized and all records stored electronically.

People naturally resist and resent controls. It appears to be an aspect of being human. Some proportion of fraud perpetrators do not fit the need/opportunity/rationalization profile cited earlier, but seem motivated almost completely by a desire to "beat" the controls. To reduce resentment and resistance, controls should be as inoffensive as possible and excessive, redundant, or obsolete controls should be discontinued.

EXHIBIT 16-3   PROBLEMS OF CONTROL

Overemphasis of controls

Too many controls

Control obsolescence

Control resistance and resentment

Management overrides

Employee collusion

Substitution of form for substance

Conflicts of interest

Management overrides of control and employee collusion to circumvent controls are two control violations that are difficult to detect if they occur. So are controls whereby employees substitute form for substance. If, for example, a purchasing agent is required to obtain bids from three suppliers so as to get the best price, the intent of the control is defeated if the purchasing agent allows a "favored" supplier to designate who will be solicited for the other two bids. Likewise, a requirement that all purchases above $50,000 be approved individually is defeated if the purchasing department manager signs such approval requests blindly.

Nepotism by a production head, investment by a purchasing agent in a particular supplier, and other such situations can create a conflict of interest and cause controls to be violated. For example, custody and accounting for cash are not separated if the functions are performed by a father and daughter.

PROFITS ARE AN OPINION, BUT CASH IS A FACT: FINANCIAL STATEMENTS AND CASH FLOW

Successful operating management requires different skills in different industries, but good cash management is the same in every industry. Understanding and managing cash flows is vitally important. Cash is the lifeblood of a new or growing company. It is a rejuvenation tonic that gives life to tired businesses, a fertilizer that grows profits from sales fields thought barren. Chrysler diverted cash of $700 million from its program to redesign the Dodge Ram pickup truck and instead used it to revamp its Windsor, Canada, plant and begin production of the minivan. This seed money produced a product so innovative that Chrysler has "virtually owned" the minivan market, according to *Fortune* magazine.[1] It was the cash from this venture that kept Chrysler in business during the hard times that followed its introduction.

Conversely, a shortage of cash is one of the leading causes of failure in small or new businesses, even profitable ones. New restaurants are notorious for failing to generate enough cash to stay open, even while creating paper profits. But while many companies fail because of cash shortages, cash shortages do not always mean operating losses and business failure. The cash position of a company is, in fact, strongly related to factors other than earnings and, in certain circumstances, a negative cash flow may be a sign of a successful operation.

A company's growth rate and the type of market in which it operates sometimes dictate whether the company will generate cash or consume it. Companies in slow growth markets tend to generate cash. Studies have shown that

[1] For an interesting discussion of the development of Chrysler's minivan, see Alex Taylor III, "Iacocca's Minivan," *Fortune*, 30 May 1994, 56–66.

slow sales growth tends to generate positive cash flows. In contrast, companies in rapidly growing markets tend to consume cash. Rapid sales growth requires cash and produces negative cash flows.

Rapid sales growth often requires large amounts of cash for increased investment in inventories, receivables, and production capacity. Even when growth in sales is caused by inflation rather than growth in market share or market size, the cash flow created from rising selling prices is usually more than consumed by rising costs. As you can see, cash flow often appears to vary inversely with selling prices and rate of market growth.

The biggest cash inflows occur in companies that have a large market share in a slow or no-growth market. In this situation, neither the market nor the company's market share is growing significantly. These companies are called "cash cows."

Companies often try to develop a cash-cow segment or subsidiary. If a company is successful, the cash generated by the cow can be used to finance new ventures in which the company does not have an established market share and expects to consume cash through rapid growth. Despite the strong early growth of the minivan, Chrysler's stable position in this market later prompted *Fortune* magazine to call the minivan "Chrysler's cash cow."[2]

---

[2]The cover of the May 30, 1994, *Fortune* magazine trumpets: "The inside story of Chrysler's cash cow/How Iacocca created the Minivan while GM and Ford dropped the ball."

The Income Statement and Cash Flows

The income statement reports the results of operating activities. These results come from the inflows and outflows of revenues and expenses. Revenues and expenses are not cash flows, and net income is not cash. Revenues are increases in owners' wealth from doing business and are the sources of the company's assets. Expenses are outflows of owners' wealth from doing business and use up assets (cash, trucks, inventories, etc.) in the earning process. Annual income or loss is the change in owners' wealth from doing business and is computed by subtracting the expenses incurred during the year from the revenues earned during the year.

If revenues exceed expenses, the company earned income. If expenses exceed revenues, the company has operated at a loss. However, creating income or loss is often not directly related to increasing or decreasing cash, because of the use of accrual accounting. *Accrual accounting* records the accounts receivable from making sales on credit and requires the recording of liabilities for unpaid expenses and purchases in determining the correct amounts of revenues, expenses, and profit. Accrual accounting recognizes revenue in the period it is *earned*, regardless of when the cash is received, and recognizes expenses when they are *incurred*, regardless of when cash is paid.

Cash Flow Versus Profit

Actually, the cash flow and the profit of a company for a period are measures of the same business activity. It is very unusual for the cash flows of a company to equal its profit (or loss) for a period. This is because the vast majority of companies do business on *credit*. They sell products or services on credit, with amounts uncollected at the end of the accounting period called "accounts receivable." In addition, companies normally buy the goods they sell on credit and incur some operating expenses on account, and therefore have a liability at the end of the year. These amounts owed to others are called "accounts payable."

So you see that cash received during a certain period does not measure revenues earned during that period. The amount of cash received includes amounts from the prior period's sales and does not include amounts owed to the company that will be received in the next period.

Likewise, cash paid does not equal expenses, because it includes payments of amounts owed from the prior period and does not include amounts owed at the end of the current period. These liabilities will be paid in the next period.

In determining whether a company has earned a profit, a distinction is made between the purposes of cash receipts and disbursements. The sources of cash are operations, investment by owners, and borrowings. A company does not count as revenue cash received from creditors and owners. That is, cash received from borrowing and owners' investments are not included as revenues on the income statement.

Disbursements may include payments to suppliers and to employees for salaries, and payments for income taxes, maintenance, insurance, and other operating costs. These payments are certainly expenses. However, dividend payments to stockholders and payments for the purchase of property, plant, and equipment are not expenses. Dividend payments to stockholders are issued in return for their investment in the company, and payments for property, plant, and equipment are for assets that will be used over an extended period of time. It does not make sense to treat the cost of office equipment as an expense in just one year.

The statement of cash flows does not tell whether a company has earned a profit, and the income statement does not tell whether cash has increased or decreased during the year. Nor does the income statement provide any information as to the sources and uses of cash for the period. Adjustments must be made to the amounts in the income statement, and other items not appearing in the statement must be included to determine the cash flows for the period. Chapter 18 discusses the statement of cash flows and these adjustments.

Quality of Earnings

Despite the fact that earnings and cash flows are not the same thing, investors believe that the company's reported net income should not be very different from its cash flows. To have value, all income must generate a cash inflow either before or after the income is earned. For this reason, investors seem to believe that, over time, cash flows show the company's "true" net income. The quality of a company's earnings affects the market value of its stock. The extent to which earnings are matched by cash flows determine the "quality" of a company's earnings. The lower investors perceive the quality of a company's earnings to be, the lower value they place on the company's stock.

Investors believe earnings are of low quality if (1) they generate cash flows that cannot be sustained or (2) they result from accounting or "paper" gains that are not accompanied by an increase in cash. Investors believe earnings that generate cash inflows that can be sustained to be of high quality.

Changing the Timing of Revenues and Expenses One way reported profits are increased without a corresponding increase in cash inflow is by changing the timing of sales or expense recognition. A company may offer liberal credit terms to entice customers to buy who would ordinarily wait until next year. This increase in sales cannot be sustained. A company that promotes its product by allowing "No payment for six months" may motivate customers to buy in one year at the expense of the next.

In addition, managers may accelerate expenses (perhaps repaint this year, rather than next) to move the expense to a current year if earnings are low, and improve prospects for next year. Conversely, managers can delay some expenses to improve the current year's earnings. Travel, maintenance, and advertising are discretionary expenses that may be delayed if managers wish to reduce expenses. Delaying these expenses improves current earnings, and accelerating them improves earnings next year, but changing the timing of revenues and expenses produces changes (normally increases) in earnings that cannot be sustained.

Accounting Methods That Do Not Affect Cash Flows When a company chooses to use an accounting method because it makes earnings greater, investors view the earnings as lower quality than earnings that do not use such "sleight-of-hand" techniques. Different depreciation methods, for example, can increase or decrease earnings but do not affect cash flows. Studies show that a company that chooses to use a depreciation method to increase earnings is seen by investors as having lower-quality earnings than a company that does not.[3] It seems that stockholders (as a group) somehow "see" the com-

pany's real, cash-based earnings, regardless of the accounting method used.

Accounting Methods That Do Affect Cash Flows Some accounting choices do affect cash flows, because often the Internal Revenue Service requires the same accounting method to be used for both financial reporting and tax reporting. The choice of an inventory accounting method is one example: if a company chooses to use the last in–first out (LIFO) inventory method for tax purposes, it must also use the LIFO method for financial accounting purposes. Because cash paid for taxes is in part determined by the inventory method chosen, the choice affects both reported earnings and cash flows and may have a substantial effect on how investors judge the quality of a company's earnings.

[3]See F.L. Ayres, "Perceptions of Earnings Quality: What Managers Need to Know," *Management Accounting* (March 1994), 27–29.

Approximating Cash Generated by Operations

Depreciation and amortization are operating expenses that do not require cash outflows each year. Cash was consumed when the asset being depreciated or amortized was acquired, but in later years the asset's annual depreciation or amortization expense is simply an expensing of the asset's historical cost in each period benefited by the asset. A machine purchased for $10,000 will be paid for when purchased (by a loan or cash) but the $10,000 will be expensed in the years the machine is used. If the machine is expected to last five years, $2,000 may be expensed each year. There is no cash flow associated with depreciation expense.

Because depreciation and amortization reduce earnings without consuming cash, they can be added back to net income to approximate cash from operations. The consolidated

---

[4]When a company owns more than 50% of the outstanding stock of another company, the investor company, referred to as the *parent*, has a controlling interest in the investee, called *subsidiary*. Because the parent owns the majority of the outstanding stock of the subsidiary, the companies are, for all practical purposes, combined, and their financial statements are consolidated and shown as if the two companies were one entity. The combining process is called consolidation and the resulting financial statements are called consolidated financial statements.

income statement of Ametek is shown in Exhibit 17-1.[4] Ametek has net income of $44,357,000 and depreciation expense of $29,360,000. If we assume that all Ametek's revenues and expenses resulted in cash flows except for the depreciation expense, we can approximate Ametek's cash flow from operations as follows:

Net income	$44,357,000
Plus depreciation not using cash	29,360,000
Estimated cash flow from operations	$73,717,000

Ametek's Statement of Cash Flows, seen in Exhibit 17-2, shows cash flows from operations of $78,586,000. In calculating cash from operations in the Statement of Cash Flows, Ametek adjusted earnings, not only by the amount of depreciation expense for the year, but also for amortization (not shown on the face of the income statement) and changes in working capital accounts. Adding back depreciation and amortization is not always accurate but is often used to arrive at a rough approximation of cash generated by operations.

Exhibit 17-3 presents the income statements and statements of cash flows for 10 Fortune 500 companies. By review-

**EXHIBIT 17-1   CONSOLIDATED STATEMENT
OF INCOME —AMETEK, INC.**

(Dollars in thousands, except per share amounts)

Years ended December 31,

	1992	1991	1990
Net sales	$769,550	$715,099	$660,745
Expenses:			
Cost of sales, excluding depreciation	583,357	546,479	498,749
Selling, general and administrative	77,690	74,038	69,563
Depreciation	29,360	28,277	24,063
	690,407	648,794	592,375
Operating income	79,143	66,305	68,370
Other income (expenses):			
Interest expense	(19,721)	(22,079)	(20,818)
Other, net (Note 10)	7,297	8,152	9,103
Income before income taxes	66,719	52,378	56,655
Provision for income taxes (Note 7)	22,362	14,392	19,317
Net income	$ 44,357	$ 37,986	$ 37,338
Average common shares outstanding	44,095,057	43,887,631	44,105,020
Earnings per share	$ 1.01	$ .87	$ .85

See accompanying notes.

ing the statements of each company, you can see that cash flow from operations can be approximated by taking net income and adding back depreciation and amortization.

Exhibit 17-4 is a reconciliation of net income, after adjusting for depreciation and amortization, to cash flow from operations. As you can see, the relative range or difference between the two is between 0% and 4.9% for the 10 companies. For example, when net income is adjusted for depreciation and amortization for the Atmos Energy Corporation, the amount is within 3.7% of cash flows from operations for the company. Although these differences appear to be small, it is important to realize that only in limited cases will adjusting net income for depreciation and amortization approximate cash flows from operations. As you will see in Chapter 18, in general, this technique will not give satisfactory results. However, it is discussed here because it is often used.

EXHIBIT 17-2 CONSOLIDATED STATEMENT OF CASH FLOWS—AMETEK INC.

| | Years ended December 31, | | |
	1992	1991	1990
Cash provided by (used for):			
Operating activities:			
Net income	$ 44,357	$37,986	$37,338
Adjustments to reconcile net income to net cash provided by operating activities:			
Depreciation and amortization	37,263	36,455	33,542
Deferred income taxes and credits	1,814	2,850	751
Changes in operating working capital:			
Decrease (increase) in receivables	2,940	(11,754)	2,686
Decrease (increase) in inventories and other current assets	2,969	10,310	11,043
(Decrease) increase in payables, accruals and income taxes	(5,228)	11,374	(264)
Other	(5,529)	(4,034)	1,700
Total operating activities	78,586	83,187	86,796
Investing activities:			
Additions to property, plant and equipment	(23,990)	(18,808)	(35,683)
Purchase of businesses and investments	(16,992)	(25,526)	(42,475)
Decrease (increase) in marketable securities	15,965	(40,118)	7,456
Proceeds from sale of businesses and investments	12,806	9,778	39,181
Other	781	(2,984)	(2,769)
Total investing activities	(11,430)	(77,658)	(34,290)
Financing activities:			
Cash dividends paid	(29,991)	(28,990)	(28,221)
Additional long-term borrowings	3,755	—	1,720
Repayment of long-term debt	(20,041)	(23,785)	(16,064)
Net change in short-term borrowings	—	(5,608)	(2,366)
Purchase of treasury stock	—	—	(5,669)
Proceeds from issuance of common stock	3,388	831	546
Total financing activities	(42,889)	(57,552)	(50,054)
Increase (decrease) in cash and cash equivalents	24,267	(52,023)	2,452
Cash and cash equivalents:			
Beginning of year	34,871	86,894	84,442
End of year	$ 59,138	$34,871	$86,894

See accompanying notes.

Profits are an opinion, but cash is a fact

EXHIBIT 17-3   APPROXIMATING CASH FLOW FROM OPERATIONS

CONSOLIDATED STATEMENTS OF EARNINGS — J.B. Hunt Transport Services, Inc. and Subsidiaries

(Dollars in thousands, except per share amounts)   **Years ended December 31,**

	1993	1992	1991
Operating revenues	$1,020,921	$911,982	$733,288
Operating expenses:			
Salaries, wages and employee benefits (note 5)	371,849	347,972	293,390
Purchased transportation and spotting	187,726	111,579	51,180
Fuel and fuel taxes	126,966	129,999	119,600
Depreciation	83,210	86,825	69,111
Operating supplies and expenses	73,511	67,215	59,006
Insurance and claims	40,424	43,473	34,210
Operating taxes and licenses	28,905	25,728	21,829
General and administrative expenses	19,032	18,613	15,223
Communication and utilities	10,672	11,488	10,314
Total operating expenses	942,295	842,892	673,863
Operating income	78,626	69,090	59,425
Interest expense	13,800	10,908	10,732
Earnings before income taxes and cumulative effect of changes in accounting methods	64,826	58,182	48,693
Income taxes (note 4)	26,605	21,249	19,234
Earnings before cumulative effect of changes in accounting methods	38,221	36,933	29,459
Cumulative effect on prior years of changes in accounting methods:			
Revenue recognition, net of $1,017 in income taxes (note 1(d))	—	—	(1,558)
Tires in service, net of $1,049 in income taxes (note 1(b))	—	1,825	—
Net earnings (notes 1(b) and 1(d))	$ 38,221	$ 38,758	$ 27,901
Earnings per share:			
Earnings before cumulative effect of changes in accounting methods	$ 1.00	$ 1.03	$ .85
Cumulative effect of changes in accounting methods:			
Revenue recognition (note 1(d))	—	—	(.05)
Tires in service (note 1(b))	—	.05	—
Net earnings (notes 1(b) and 1(d))	$ 1.00	$ 1.08	$ .80
Proforma amounts assuming the new accounting methods are applied retroactively (notes 1(b) and 1(d)) (unaudited):			
Net earnings	$ 38,221	$ 36,933	$ 28,338
Earnings per share	$ 1.00	$ 1.03	$ .82

See accompanying notes to consolidated financial statements.

EXHIBIT 17-3   APPROXIMATING CASH FLOW FROM OPERATIONS (*continued*)

CONSOLIDATED STATEMENTS OF CASH FLOWS —
J.B. Hunt Transport Services, Inc. and Subsidiaries

(Dollars in thousands)

	Years ended December 31,		
	1993	1992	1991
Cash flows from operating activities:			
Net earnings	$ 38,221	$ 38,758	$ 27,901
Adjustments to reconcile net earnings to net cash provided by operating activities:			
Cumulative effect of accounting changes	—	(1,825)	1,558
Depreciation, net of gain on disposition of equipment	83,210	86,825	69,111
Provision for noncurrent deferred income taxes	17,396	16,637	9,925
Tax benefit of stock options exercised	890	723	479
Changes in assets and liabilities:			
Decrease (increase) in deferred tax asset	5,271	(9,864)	—
Increase in accounts receivable	(31,375)	(14,631)	(17,450)
Decrease (increase) in prepaid expenses	1,092	(4,161)	(11,601)
Increase in trade accounts payable	5,583	15,742	2,874
Increase (decrease) in claims accruals	(2,114)	8,374	10,325
Increase in other current liabilities	3,253	1,620	1,269
Net cash provided by operating activities	121,427	138,198	94,391
Cash flows from investing activities:			
Additions to property and equipment	(285,687)	(289,409)	(151,781)
Proceeds from sale of equipment	88,651	40,110	38,774
Increase in other assets	(6,306)	(2,299)	(2,880)
Net cash used in investing activities	(203,342)	(251,598)	(115,887)
Cash flows from financing activities:			
Proceeds from sale of common stock	—	55,563	—
Proceeds from long-term debt	99,691	182,270	72,617
Repayments of long-term debt	(12,446)	(122,946)	(53,284)
Proceeds from sale of treasury stock	3,878	4,849	2,780
Dividends paid	(7,651)	(7,028)	(6,473)
Net cash provided by financing activities	83,472	112,708	15,640
Net increase (decrease) in cash	1,557	(692)	(5,856)
Cash—beginning of year	1,833	2,525	8,381
Cash—end of year	$ 3,390	$ 1,833	$ 2,525
Supplemental disclosure of cash flow information:			
Cash paid during the year for:			
Interest:	$ 12,014	$ 10,395	$ 9,715
Income taxes	$ 3,743	$ 11,056	$ 13,862

See accompanying notes to consolidated financial statements.

CONSOLIDATED STATEMENT OF INCOME —
United Missouri Bancshares, Inc. (in thousands except per share data)

Year Ended December 31

Interest Income	1993	1992	1991
Loans	$142,713	$119,288	$143,514
Securities available for sale	116,044	—	—
Investment securities:			
Taxable interest	$ —	$102,051	$114,424
Tax-exempt interest	11,656	12,496	17,173
Dividends	—	407	402
Total investment securities income	$ 11,656	$114,954	$131,999
Federal funds and resell agreements	9,888	14,720	17,567
Trading securities and other	2,914	4,405	5,119
Total interest income	$283,215	$253,367	$298,199
Interest Expense			
Deposits	$ 99,127	$103,023	$142,137
Federal funds and repurchase agreements	16,155	16,180	23,300
Short-term debt	29	1,036	2,225
Long-term debt	4,407	3,547	4,015
Total interest expense	$119,718	$123,786	$171,677
Net interest income	$163,497	$129,581	$126,522
Provision for loan losses	3,332	2,981	6,044
Net interest income after provision	$160,165	$126,600	$120,478
Noninterest Income			
Trust fees	$ 32,048	$ 27,334	$ 24,785
Securities processing	13,341	13,715	10,473
Trading and investment banking	13,629	12,503	12,162
Service charges on deposit accounts	30,168	24,067	21,294
Other service charges and fees	14,101	9,748	7,105
Bankcard fees	22,440	18,263	19,356
Net security gains	1,607	5,305	116
Other	4,727	2,527	3,400
Total noninterest income	$132,061	$113,462	$ 98,691
Noninterest Expense			
Salaries and employee benefits	$106,329	$ 87,857	$ 80,760
Occupancy, net	14,809	12,180	10,916
Equipment	20,319	15,756	14,192
Supplies and services	17,448	14,492	13,545
Bankcard processing	18,660	15,991	15,805
Marketing and business development	13,563	10,567	8,449
FDIC and regulatory fees	10,955	8,568	7,236
Amortization of intangibles of purchased banks	5,241	2,196	1,939
Other	23,653	17,340	12,932
Total noninterest expense	$230,977	$184,947	$165,774
Income before income taxes	$ 61,249	$ 55,115	$ 53,395
Income tax provision	20,130	15,748	13,910
Net income	$ 41,119	$ 39,367	$ 39,485
Per Share Data			
Net income	$ 2.57	$ 2.85	$ 2.86
Dividends	$ 0.80	$ 0.80	$ 0.73
Average shares outstanding	16,017,547	13,800,197	13,786,984

See Notes to Financial Statements.

Profits are an opinion, but cash is a fact   **169**

EXHIBIT 17-3   APPROXIMATING CASH FLOW FROM OPERATIONS (*continued*)

FINANCIAL STATEMENTS CONSOLIDATED STATEMENT OF CASH FLOWS
(in thousands)

	Years Ended December 31		
Operating Activities	**1993**	**1992**	**1991**
Net income	$ 41,119	$ 39,367	$ 39,485
Adjustments to reconcile net income to net cash provided by operating activities:			
Provision for loan losses	3,332	2,981	6,044
Depreciation and amortization	19,222	13,966	12,453
Deferred income taxes and investment tax credits	(225)	2,781	832
Net (increase) decrease in trading securities	(34,731)	55,390	(19,166)
Gains on sales of:			
Investment securities	(17)	(5,845)	(622)
Securities available for sale	(1,598)	—	—
Losses on sales of:			
Investment securities	—	540	506
Securities available for sale	8	—	—
Amortization of securities premium, net of discount accretion	36,853	28,958	10,271
(Increase) decrease in interest receivable	(6,334)	3,456	5,912
Increase (decrease) in interest payable	311	(6,228)	(5,402)
Other, net	2,581	(6,534)	(10,128)
Net cash provided by operating activities	$ 60,521	$ 128,832	$ 40,185
Investing Activities			
Proceeds from sales of:			
Investment securities	$ 697	$1,114,719	$ 23,056
Securities available for sale	225,587	—	—
Proceeds from maturities of:			
Investment securities	131,723	1,604,693	1,431,341
Securities available for sale	654,769	—	—
Purchases of:			
Investment securities	(158,018)	(3,244,086)	(1,538,105)
Securities available for sale	(1,025,388)	—	—
Net (increase) decrease in loans	(146,800)	(125,756)	213,560
Net (increase) decrease in federal funds sold and resell agreements	113,147	177,257	(166,202)
Purchases of bank premises and equipment	(12,804)	(19,342)	(16,617)
Proceeds from sales of bank premises and equipment	811	646	7
Purchases of financial organizations, net of cash received	57,211	(8,572)	(378)
Net cash used in investing activities	$ (159,065)	$ (500,441)	$ (53,338)
Financing Activities			
Net increase in demand and savings deposits	$ 400,373	$ 513,271	$ 260,856
Net decrease in time deposits	(131,946)	(133,796)	(161,830)
Net increase (decrease) in federal funds purchased and repurchase agreements	(115,439)	(87,121)	239,780
Net increase (decrease) in short-term debt	(689)	(48,964)	11,813
Proceeds from issuance of long-term debt	25,000	—	—
Repayments of long-term debt	(7,801)	(8,695)	(5,123)
Cash dividends	(13,064)	(11,042)	(10,062)
Purchases of treasury stock	(4,859)	(1,722)	(120)
Proceeds from issuance of treasury stock	508	393	259
Net cash provided by financing activities	$ 152,083	$ 222,324	$ 335,573
Increase (decrease) in cash and due from banks	$ 53,539	$ (149,285)	$ 322,420
Cash and due from banks at beginning of year	612,829	762,114	439,694
Cash and due from banks at end of year	$ 666,368	$ 612,829	$ 762,114
Supplemental disclosures:			
Income taxes paid	$ 20,833	$ 13,259	$ 13,252
Total interest paid	119,407	130,014	177,079

Note: Certain noncash transactions regarding the adoption of SFAS No. 115 and common stock issued for acquisitions are disclosed in the accompanying financial statements and notes to financial statements.

STATEMENT OF INCOME — Union Electric Company
(Thousands of Dollars Except Shares and Per Share Amounts)

	Year 1992	Year 1991	Year 1990
Operating Revenues (*):			
Electric	$1,929,468	$2,006,258	$1,939,171
Gas	84,159	86,877	80,310
Other	1,494	3,805	3,536
Total operating revenues	2,015,121	2,096,940	2,023,017
Operating Expenses:			
Operations			
Fuel and purchased power	407,067	411,739	402,453
Other	381,690	374,997	367,365
	788,757	786,736	769,818
Maintenance	187,267	170,454	176,369
Depreciation and nuclear decommissioning	214,029	204,152	200,475
Amortization of phase-in plans deferred costs	32,291	32,459	32,461
Income taxes	179,691	222,700	192,206
Other taxes (*)	201,069	197,626	194,148
Total operating expenses	1,603,104	1,614,127	1,565,477
Operating Income	412,017	482,813	457,540
Other Income and Deductions:			
Gain on sales of electric property	34,810	—	—
Income taxes related to gain on sales of electric property	(16,711)	—	—
Allowance for equity funds used during construction	3,115	2,156	2,188
Miscellaneous, net	(71)	(2,611)	10,118
Total other income and deductions, net	21,143	(455)	12,306

Income Before Interest Charges	433,160	482,358	469,846
Interest Charges:			
Interest	135,319	167,209	187,584
Allowance for borrowed funds used during construction	(4,907)	(6,363)	(11,957)
Net interest charges	130,412	160,846	175,627
Net Income	302,748	321,512	294,219
Preferred Stock Dividends	14,058	14,059	14,693
Earnings on Common Stock	$ 288,690	$ 307,453	$ 279,526

(*) Includes license and franchise taxes of $92,993,000, $96,802,000, and $94,200,000 for the years 1992, 1991, and 1990, respectively.

Earnings per Share of Common Stock (based on average shares outstanding)	$2.83	$3.01	$2.74
Dividends per Share of Common Stock	$2.26	$2.18	$2.10
Average Number of Common Shares Outstanding	102,123,834	102,123,834	102,123,834

See Notes to Financial Statements.

EXHIBIT 17-3   APPROXIMATING CASH FLOW FROM OPERATIONS (*continued*)

STATEMENT OF CASH FLOWS — Union Electric Company (Thousands of Dollars)

	Year 1992	Year 1991	Year 1990
Cash Flows From Operating:			
Net income	$ 302,748	$ 321,512	$ 294,219
Adjustments to reconcile net income to net cash provided by operating activities:			
Depreciation and amortization	237,659	227,684	225,760
Amortization of nuclear fuel	47,816	71,964	58,518
Gain on sales of electric property	(34,810)	—	—
Allowance for funds used during construction	(8,022)	(8,519)	(14,145)
Deferred taxes on income, net	44,950	50,633	42,213
Deferred investment tax credits, net	(7,414)	(7,007)	(7,017)
Changes in assets and liabilities:			
Receivables, net	22,408	(3,663)	15,181
Materials and supplies	(9,938)	(15,182)	14,485
Accounts and wages payable	12,207	6,346	(3,740)
Taxes accrued	(10,958)	7,336	(8,430)
Interest and dividends accrued or declared	(4,242)	5,593	(3,512)
Other, net	(1,393)	5,486	(2,384)
Net cash provided by operating activities	591,011	662,183	611,148
Cash Flows From Investing:			
Construction expenditures	(259,652)	(237,159)	(212,932)
Acquisition of electric property	(62,430)	—	—
Sale of water property	8,500	—	—
Sales of electric property	68,702	—	—
Allowance for funds used during construction	8,022	8,519	14,145
Nuclear fuel expenditures	(63,779)	(25,344)	(43,332)
Net cash used in investing activities	(300,637)	(253,984)	(242,119)

	Year 1992	Year 1991	Year 1990
Cash Flows From Financing:			
Dividends on preferred and common stock	(244,858)	(236,690)	(228,917)
Environmental bond redemption fund—			
1991 Series	42,585	(42,585)	—
1992 Series	(47,500)	—	—
Redemptions—			
Nuclear fuel lease	(50,693)	(60,178)	(68,884)
Short-term debt	(34,500)	(34,000)	—
Long-term debt	(520,076)	(292,396)	(222,539)
Preferred stock	(26)	(212)	(8,087)
Issuances—			
Nuclear fuel lease	40,534	16,669	49,943
Short-term debt	—	—	49,500
Long-term debt	521,500	242,585	60,000
Net cash used in financing activities	(293,034)	(406,807)	(368,984)
Net Change in Cash and Cash Equivalents	(2,660)	1,392	45
Cash and Cash Equivalents at beginning of year	4,917	3,525	3,480
Cash and Cash Equivalents at end of year	$ 2,257	$ 4,917	$ 3,525

Cash and cash equivalents include cash on hand and temporary investments purchased with a maturity of three months or less.

See Notes to Financial Statements.

CONSOLIDATED STATEMENTS OF INCOME — PHH Corporation and Subsidiaries

(Thousands of dollars except per share data)

Years ended April 30.	1993	1992	1991
Revenues:			
Vehicle management services	$1,069,484	$ 992,514	$1,023,857
Relocation and real estate services	829,336	849,871	923,536
Mortgage banking services	122,111	89,099	70,232
	2,020,931	1,931,484	2,017,625
Operating expenses:			
Direct costs of operating leases	707,542	600,109	599,797
Costs, including interest, of carrying and reselling homes	734,640	757,534	812,340
Direct costs of mortgage banking services	47,288	30,738	18,149
Interest	150,894	185,750	243,637
Selling, general and administrative	284,238	271,972	264,477
	1,924,602	1,846,103	1,938,400
Operating income	96,329	85,381	79,225
Other expense, net	(2,091)	(2,264)	(1,466)
Income before income taxes	94,238	83,117	77,759
Income taxes	37,821	33,138	30,680
Net income	$ 56,417	$ 49,979	$ 47,079
Net income per share	$ 3.25	$ 2.92	$ 2.78

See Notes to Consolidated Financial Statements.

EXHIBIT 17-3   APPROXIMATING CASH FLOW FROM OPERATIONS (*continued*)

CONSOLIDATED STATEMENTS OF CASH FLOWS —
PHH Corporation and Subsidiaries

(Thousands of dollars)

Years ended April 30.	1993	1992	1991
Operating Activities:			
Net income	$ 56,417	$ 49,979	$ 47,079
Adjustments to reconcile income to cash provided by operating activities:			
Depreciation and amortization	738,062	620,298	616,333
Deferred income taxes	(13,721)	(8,686)	(14,146)
Changes in:			
Accounts receivable	29,452	104,437	(86,820)
Carrying costs on homes under management	10,510	14,779	10,200
Mortgages held for resale	(28,505)	(258,563)	52,288
Income taxes and interest recoverable	—	—	26,798
Accounts payable and accrued expenses	12,033	5,058	33,543
Advances from clients	(9,329)	(59,986)	(29,890)
Deferred revenue	3,592	4,666	5,327
All other operating activity	(21,969)	(7,179)	(24,984)
Cash provided by operating activities	776,542	464,803	635,728
Investing Activities:			
Investment in leases and leased vehicles	(1,699,971)	(1,744,771)	(2,037,722)
Repayment of investment in leases and leased vehicles	553,822	578,687	758,529
Proceeds from sales and transfers of vehicle management-related assets	90,697	450,163	739,956
Value of homes acquired	(4,102,013)	(3,992,271)	(3,783,740)
Value of homes sold	4,068,422	4,061,685	3,863,949
Proceeds from sale of relocation and real estate-related assets	39,318	59,399	105,354
Additions to property and equipment, net of dispositions	(20,825)	(23,992)	(25,960)
Acquisitions accounted for as purchases	—	(35,381)	—
Proceeds from sale of discontinued operations	—	—	1,033
All other investing activities	3,006	5,501	15,038
Cash used in investing activities	(1,067,544)	(640,980)	(363,563)
Financing Activities:			
Net change in borrowings with terms of less than 90 days	81,453	(227,412)	(207,907)
Proceeds from issuance of other borrowings	1,123,795	927,824	285,165
Principal payment on other borrowings	(947,905)	(515,775)	(302,804)
Stock option plan transactions	9,833	(362)	(35)
Payment of dividends	(20,436)	(20,272)	(20,258)
Cash provided by (used in) financing activities	246,740	164,003	(245,839)
Effect of exchange rate changes on cash	43,601	13,088	(27,334)
(Decrease) increase in cash	(661)	914	(1,008)
Cash at beginning of period	1,183	269	1,277
Cash at end of period	$ 522	$ 1,183	$ 269

See Notes to Consolidated Financial Statements.

CONSOLIDATED STATEMENTS OF INCOME — Texas Industries, Inc. and Subsidiaries

Year Ended May 31,

In thousands except per share	1993	1992	1991
NET SALES	$614,292	$601,129	$619,827
COSTS AND EXPENSES (INCOME)			
Cost of products sold	545,200	542,355	547,806
Selling, administrative and general	43,116	46,622	55,269
Interest	32,596	31,149	30,127
Other income	(6,639)	(24,010)	(9,701)
Sale of United Cement Company	—	—	(43,049)
	614,273	596,116	580,452
INCOME BEFORE THE FOLLOWING ITEMS	19	5,013	39,375
Provision for income taxes (benefit)	(646)	1,737	13,611
	665	3,276	25,764
Minority interest in Chaparral	393	(1,356)	(3,678)
NET INCOME	$ 1,058	$ 1,920	$ 22,086
Average common shares	11,085	11,056	11,030
Net income per common share	$ .11	$ .19	$ 1.97
Cash dividends	$ .20	$ .20	$ .20

See notes to consolidated financial statements.

EXHIBIT 17-3   APPROXIMATING CASH FLOW FROM OPERATIONS (*continued*)

CONSOLIDATED STATEMENTS OF CASH FLOWS —
Texas Industries, Inc. and Subsidiaries

Year Ended May 31,

In thousands	1993	1992	1991
OPERATING ACTIVITIES			
Net income	$ 1,058	$ 1,920	$ 22,086
Gain on disposal of assets	(264)	(13,805)	(44,141)
Non-cash items			
Depreciation, depletion and amortization	49,799	47,495	44,979
Deferred taxes	(4,284)	432	7,689
Undistributed minority interest	(1,528)	206	2,552
Other—net	819	880	4,704
Changes in operating assets and liabilities			
Notes and accounts receivable	(2,125)	(3,645)	8,120
Inventories and prepaid expenses	2,431	(12,719)	(3,403)
Accounts payable and accrued liabilities	2,470	4,575	(5,094)
Real estate and investments	985	878	(14)
Net cash provided by continuing operations	49,361	26,217	37,478
Net cash used by discontinued operations	—	—	(3,224)
Net cash provided by operations	49,361	26,217	34,254
INVESTING ACTIVITIES			
Capital expenditures	(17,212)	(21,621)	(98,386)
Proceeds from disposition of assets	497	21,794	98,496
Purchase of temporary investments	(4,660)	(6,528)	—
Proceeds from temporary investments	4,816	—	—
Final payment for Chaparral acquisition	—	—	(49,968)
Cash surrender value—insurance	5,554	(1,840)	(1,440)
Commissioning costs and other—net	(375)	(8,412)	(2,948)
Net cash used by investing	(11,380)	(16,607)	(54,246)
FINANCING ACTIVITIES			
Proceeds of long-term borrowing	600	20,337	58,226
Proceeds of short-term borrowing	—	—	10,000
Debt retirements	(22,290)	(35,351)	(63,888)
Dividends paid	(2,228)	(2,213)	(2,152)
Other—net	(1,439)	(1,451)	(1,326)
Net cash (used) provided by financing	(25,357)	(18,678)	860
Increase (decrease) in cash	12,624	(9,068)	(19,132)
Cash at beginning of year	14,132	23,200	42,332
Cash at end of year	26,756	14,132	23,200
Temporary investments	6,333	6,528	—
Cash and temporary investments at end of year	$ 33,089	$ 20,660	$ 23,200

See notes to consolidated financial statements.

CONSOLIDATED STATEMENTS OF INCOME — Atmos Energy Corporation

YEAR ENDED SEPTEMBER 30,

	1992	1991	1990
	(In thousands, except per share data)		
Operating revenues	$340,117	$336,047	$351,951
Purchased gas cost	221,546	225,412	239,489
Gross profit	118,571	110,635	112,462
Operating expenses			
Operation	62,118	59,648	57,521
Maintenance	3,254	3,878	4,336
Depreciation and amortization	13,566	12,602	13,472
Taxes, other than income	14,463	13,426	13,570
Income taxes	4,871	3,003	4,247
Total operating expenses	98,272	92,557	93,146
Operating income	20,299	18,078	19,316
Other income (expense)			
Interest income	265	406	404
Other	66	(432)	232
Total other income (expense)	331	(26)	636
Income before interest charges	20,630	18,052	19,952
Interest charges	10,599	10,134	10,993
Net income	$ 10,031	$ 7,918	$ 8,959
Net income per share	$ 1.46	$ 1.20	$ 1.47
Cash dividends per share	$ 1.24	$ 1.20	$ 1.16
Average shares outstanding	6,863	6,596	6,098

See accompanying notes to consolidated financial statements.

EXHIBIT 17-3   APPROXIMATING CASH FLOW FROM OPERATIONS (*continued*)

CONSOLIDATED STATEMENTS OF CASH FLOWS — Atmos Energy Corporation

YEAR ENDED SEPTEMBER 30,

	1992	1991	1990
(In thousands)			
Cash Flows From Operating Activities			
Net income	$10,031	$ 7,918	$ 8,959
Adjustments to reconcile net income to net cash provided by operating activities			
Depreciation and amortization			
Charged to depreciation and amortization	13,566	12,602	13,472
Charged to other accounts	3,934	3,648	2,116
Deferred income taxes	314	(557)	1,650
Other	254	152	182
	28,099	23,763	26,379
Change in assets and liabilities			
(Increase) decrease in accounts receivable	(988)	1,125	(903)
(Increase) decrease in inventories	121	(342)	(833)
(Increase) decrease in gas stored underground	(14)	784	604
Decrease in other current assets	148	423	458
(Increase) decrease in deferred charges and other assets	595	(1,247)	(1,862)
Increase (decrease) in accounts payable	154	(271)	(1,898)
Increase (decrease) in taxes payable	934	(869)	839
Increase (decrease) in customers' deposits	278	49	(1,356)
Increase (decrease) in other current liabilities	229	(8,176)	7,328
(Decrease) in deferred credits and other liabilities	(967)	(2,487)	(228)
Net cash provided by operating activities	28,589	12,752	28,528

	1992	1991	1990
Cash Flows From Investing Activities			
Capital expenditures	(33,293)	(30,223)	(25,345)
Sales and retirements of property, plant and equipment	2,095	3,142	13,336
Net cash used in investing activities	(31,198)	(27,081)	(12,009)
Cash Flows From Financing Activities			
Net increase (decrease) in notes payable to banks	12,300	(6,000)	(13,100)
Proceeds from issuance of long-term debt	10,000	20,000	30,000
Dividends paid	(8,516)	(7,919)	(7,075)
Repayment of long-term debt	(15,308)	(6,750)	(21,745)
Issuance of common stock	4,210	10,557	140
Net cash provided (used) by financing activities	2,686	9,888	(11,780)
Net increase (decrease) in cash and cash equivalents	77	(4,441)	4,739
Cash and cash equivalents at beginning of year	2,378	6,819	2,080
Cash and cash equivalents at end of year	$ 2,455	$ 2,378	$ 6,819

See accompanying notes to consolidated financial statements.

CONSOLIDATED STATEMENTS OF EARNINGS — Willamette Industries

Years ended December 31, 1993, 1992 and 1991 (dollar amounts, except per share amounts in thousands)

	1993	1992	1991
Net sales	$2,622,237	2,372,396	2,004,501
Cost of sales	2,191,448	2,007,703	1,715,197
Gross profit	430,789	364,693	289,304
Selling and administrative expenses	174,413	167,094	145,329
Operating earnings	256,376	197,599	143,975
Other income (expense), net	(3,918)	(1,725)	(7,103)
	252,458	195,874	136,872
Interest expense, net	63,290	66,422	63,263
Earnings before taxes and accounting changes	189,168	129,452	73,609
Provision for income taxes (notes 1 and 3)	78,500	47,900	27,800
Earnings before accounting changes	110,668	81,552	45,809
Accounting changes (notes 3 and 5)	26,364	—	—
Net earnings	$ 137,032	81,552	45,809
Per Share Information			
Earnings before accounting changes	$ 2.02	1.52	0.90
Accounting changes	0.48	—	—
Net earnings	$ 2.50	1.52	0.90
Weighted average number of shares outstanding	54,810	53,788	50,962

Per share earnings are based upon the weighted average number of shares outstanding and have been adjusted for all stock splits.

EXHIBIT 17-3   APPROXIMATING CASH FLOW FROM OPERATIONS (*continued*)

CONSOLIDATED STATEMENTS OF STOCKHOLDERS' EQUITY — Willamette Industries

Years ended December 31, 1993, 1992 and 1991 (dollar amounts, except per share amounts, in thousands)

	1993	1992	1991
Common Stock:			
Balance at beginning of year	$ 27,385	12,741	12,712
2-for-1 stock split	—	13,683	—
Shares issued for options exercised	64	86	29
Shares issued in stock offering	—	875	—
Balance at end of year	$ 27,449	27,385	12,741
Capital Surplus:			
Balance at beginning of year	$284,487	165,115	163,217
2-for-1 stock split	—	(13,683)	—
Shares issued for options exercised	4,159	6,875	1,898
Shares issued in stock offering	—	126,180	—
Balance at end of year	$288,646	284,487	165,115
Retained Earnings:			
Balance at beginning of year	$852,956	816,604	811,510
Net earnings	137,032	81,552	45,809
Less cash dividends on common stock ($ .88, $ .84, $ .80 per share in 1993, 1992 and 1991, respectively)	(48,213)	(45,200)	(40,715)
Balance at end of year	$941,775	852,956	816,604

See accompanying notes to consolidated financial statements.

CONSOLIDATED STATEMENTS OF CASH FLOWS — Willamette Industries

Years ended December 31, 1993, 1992 and 1991 (dollar amounts in thousands)

	1993	1992	1991
Cash flows from operating activities:			
Net earnings	$137,032	81,552	45,809
Adjustments to reconcile net earnings to net cash provided by operating activities:			
Net change in accounting standards	(26,364)	—	—
Depreciation	166,088	146,032	128,027
Cost of fee timber harvested	21,611	22,650	17,722
Other amortization	6,503	5,102	5,509
Increase in deferred income taxes	32,810	11,697	7,120
Changes in working capital items (net of acquisitions):			
Accounts receivable	(24,365)	(7,413)	14,425
Inventories	(20,367)	(8,929)	(15,557)
Prepaid expenses and timber deposits	(7,018)	(4,959)	6,508
Accounts payable and accrued expenses	8,444	11,019	(13,673)
Federal and state taxes on income	4,274	3,804	(8,308)
Net cash provided by operating activities	298,648	260,555	187,582
Cash flows from investing activities:			
Proceeds from sale of Bohemia's California assets	—	—	82,768
Proceeds from sale of equipment	6,988	7,002	1,837
Expenditures for property, plant and equipment	(361,488)	(337,032)	(224,129)
Expenditures for timber and timberlands, net	(18,295)	(23,649)	(14,074)
Expenditures for roads and reforestation	(7,081)	(6,492)	(6,170)
Acquisitions, net of cash acquired	-	(89,292)	(123,207)
Other	(10,719)	3,166	(1,415)
Net cash used in investing activities	(390,595)	(446,297)	(284,390)
Cash flows from financing activities:			
Debt borrowing	388,929	190,259	230,900
Proceeds from sale of capital stock	4,073	134,016	1,927
Cash dividends paid	(48,213)	(45,200)	(40,715)
Payment on debt	(252,333)	(86,509)	(114,170)
Net cash provided by financing activities	92,456	192,566	77,942
Net increase (decrease) in cash	509	6,824	(18,866)
Cash at beginning of year	9,034	2,210	21,076
Cash at end of year	$ 9,543	9,034	2,210
Supplemental disclosures of cash flow information:			
Cash paid during the year for:			
Interest (net of amount capitalized)	$ 65,183	62,998	58,592
Income taxes	$ 41,416	32,399	28,568

See accompanying notes to consolidated financial statements.

EXHIBIT 17-3   APPROXIMATING CASH FLOW FROM OPERATIONS (continued)

CONSOLIDATED STATEMENTS OF INCOME — Pinnacle West Capital Corporation

Year Ended December 31,

(Dollars in Thousands, Except Per Share Amounts)	1993	1992	1991
Operating Revenues			
Electric	$ 1,686,290	$ 1,669,679	$ 1,515,289
Provision for rate refund (Note 3)	—	—	(53,436)
Real estate	32,248	19,959	12,697
Total	1,718,538	1,689,638	1,474,550
Fuel Expenses			
Fuel for electric generation	231,434	230,194	223,983
Purchased power	69,112	57,007	49,788
Total	300,546	287,201	273,771
Operating Expenses			
Utility operations and maintenance	401,216	390,512	401,736
Real estate operations	38,220	27,309	25,482
Depreciation and amortization	223,558	220,076	219,010
Taxes other than income taxes (Note 10)	222,345	217,063	215,541
Palo Verde cost deferral (Notes 1 and 3)	—	—	(70,886)
Disallowed Palo Verde cost (Note 3)	—	—	577,145
Total	885,339	854,960	1,368,028
Operating Income (Loss)	532,653	547,477	(167,249)
Other Income (Deductions)			
Allowance for equity funds used during construction (Note 1)	2,326	3,103	3,902
Palo Verde cost deferral (Notes 1 and 3)	—	—	63,068
Palo Verde accretion income (Note 3)	74,880	67,421	5,306
Interest on long-term debt	(245,961)	(272,240)	(316,282)
Other interest	(16,505)	(12,718)	(16,447)
Allowance for borrowed funds used during construction (Note 1)	4,153	4,492	6,636
Preferred stock dividend requirements of APS	(30,840)	(32,452)	(33,404)
Other—net	(2,282)	(13,045)	(31,463)
Total	(214,229)	(255,439)	(318,684)
Income (Loss) From Continuing Operations Before Income Taxes	318,424	292,038	(485,933)
Income Tax Expense (Benefit) (Note 4)	148,446	141,598	(145,616)
Income (Loss) From Continuing Operations	169,978	150,440	(340,317)
Income From Discontinued Operations (Note 2)	—	6,000	153,455
Cumulative Effect of Change in Accounting for Income Taxes (Note 4)	19,252	—	—
Net Income (Loss)	$ 189,230	$ 156,440	$ (186,862)
Average Common Shares Outstanding	87,241,899	87,044,180	86,937,052
Earnings (Loss) Per Average Common Share Outstanding			
Continuing operations	$ 1.95	$ 1.73	$ (3.91)
Discontinued operations	—	0.07	1.76
Accounting change	0.22	—	—
Total	$ 2.17	$ 1.80	$ (2.15)
Dividends Declared Per Share	$ 0.20	$ —	$ —

See Notes to Consolidated Financial Statements.

CONSOLIDATED STATEMENTS OF CASH FLOWS —
Pinnacle West Capital Corporation

Year Ended December 31,

(Thousands of Dollars)	1993	1992	1991
(NOTE 1)			
CASH FLOWS FROM OPERATING ACTIVITIES			
Income (loss) from continuing operations	$169,978	$ 150,440	$ (340,317)
Items not requiring cash			
Depreciation and amortization	258,562	259,637	268,153
Deferred income taxes—net	139,725	84,146	(128,863)
Palo Verde cost deferral (Notes 1 and 3)	—	—	(133,954)
Provision for rate refund—net (Note 3)	(21,374)	(21,374)	52,057
Disallowed Palo Verde costs (Note 3)	—	—	577,145
Palo Verde accretion income (Note 3)	(74,880)	(67,421)	(5,306)
Other—net	(168)	(1,829)	(4,235)
Changes in current assets and liabilities			
Accounts receivable—net	31,090	(31,715)	18,006
Accrued utility revenues	(8,839)	(7,055)	1,004
Materials, supplies and fossil fuel	2,252	5,094	(8,490)
Other current assets	(5,782)	2,042	(478)
Accounts payable	(27,196)	9,547	18,866
Accrued taxes	(21,391)	45,962	(18,902)
Accrued interest	(905)	(16,593)	(3,588)
Other current liabilities	(18,408)	(16,549)	3,364
Additions to real estate	(29,290)	(12,647)	(18,593)
Sales of real estate	21,396	14,622	7,787
Other—net	34,292	5,973	4,407
Net Cash Flow Provided By Operating Activities	449,062	402,280	288,063

	1993	1992	1991
CASH FLOWS FROM INVESTING ACTIVITIES			
Capital expenditures	(234,944)	(224,419)	(182,687)
Allowance for equity funds used during construction	2,326	3,103	3,902
Sale of property (Note 3)	89	5,480	233,875
Other—net	1,609	(6,555)	(2,630)
Net Cash Flow Provided By (Used For) Investing Activities	(230,920)	(222,391)	52,460
CASH FLOWS FROM FINANCING ACTIVITIES			
Issuance of long-term debt	535,893	649,165	485,844
Issuance of preferred stock	72,644	24,781	49,375
Short-term borrowings (repayments)	(47,000)	195,000	(159,000)
Dividends paid on common stock	(17,466)	—	—
Repayment of long-term debt	(711,241)	(1,109,181)	(593,252)
Repayment of preferred stock	(78,663)	(27,850)	(15,175)
Other—net	(8,108)	2,407	6,042
Net Cash Flow Used For Financing Activities	(253,941)	(265,678)	(226,166)
Net Cash Flow	(35,799)	(85,789)	114,357
Cash and Cash Equivalents at Beginning of Year	87,926	173,715	59,358
Cash and Cash Equivalents at End of Year	$ 52,127	$ 87,926	$ 173,715

See Notes to Consolidated Financial Statements.

Profits are an opinion, but cash is a fact 183

EXHIBIT 17-3   APPROXIMATING CASH FLOW FROM OPERATIONS (*continued*)

CONSOLIDATED STATEMENTS OF INCOME (LOSS) — Pilgrim's Pride Corporation and Subsidiaries

Years Ended

	October 2, 1993 (53 weeks)	September 26, 1992 (52 weeks)	September 28, 1991 (52 weeks)
Net sales	$887,843,000	$ 817,361,000	$786,651,000
Business interruption insurance	—	2,225,000	—
	887,843,000	819,586,000	786,651,000
Costs and expenses:			
Cost of sales	777,630,000	784,940,000	711,084,000
Selling, general and administrative	54,111,000	48,121,000	44,528,000
	831,741,000	833,061,000	755,612,000
OPERATING INCOME (LOSS)	56,102,000	(13,475,000)	31,039,000
Other expenses (income):			
Interest expense, net	25,719,000	22,502,000	19,777,000
Miscellaneous	(2,455,000)	(2,265,000)	(973,000)
Total other expenses, net	23,264,000	20,237,000	18,804,000
Income (loss) before income taxes and extraordinary charge	32,838,000	(33,712,000)	12,235,000
Income tax expense (benefit)	10,543,000	(4,048,000)	(59,000)
Net income (loss) before extraordinary charge	22,295,000	(29,664,000)	12,294,000
Extraordinary charge-early repayment of debt, net of tax	(1,286,000)	—	—
NET INCOME (LOSS)	$ 21,009,000	$ (29,664,000)	$ 12,294,000
Net income (loss) per common share before extraordinary charge	$.81	$(1.24)	$.54
Extraordinary charge per common share	(.05)	—	—
Net income (loss) per common share	$ .76	$(1.24)	$.54

See notes to consolidated financial statements.

CONSOLIDATED STATEMENTS OF CASH FLOWS —
Pilgrim's Pride Corporation and Subsidiaries

Years Ended

	October 2, 1993 (53 weeks)	September 26, 1992 (52 weeks)	September 28, 1991 (52 weeks)
Cash Flows From Operating Activities:			
Net income (loss)	$ 21,009,000	$ (29,664,000)	$ 12,294,000
Adjustments to reconcile net income (loss) to cash provided by (used in) operating activities:			
Depreciation and amortization	26,034,000	24,090,000	19,860,000
(Gain) loss on property disposals	(2,187,000)	(620,000)	173,000
Provision for doubtful accounts	2,124,000	1,045,000	882,000
Deferred income taxes	5,028,000	(5,382,000)	(2,436,000)
Extraordinary charge	1,904,000	—	—
Net income for the month ended September 28, 1991, excluded above due to the change in fiscal year of Mexican subsidiaries	—	931,000	—
Changes in operating assets and liabilities:			
Accounts and other receivables	(6,555,000)	(9,720,000)	(1,033,000)
Inventories	(2,366,000)	7,807,000	(16,974,000)
Prepaid expenses	4,175,000	(4,416,000)	3,207,000
Accounts payable and accrued expenses	(4,168,000)	14,598,000	3,989,000
Other	(28,000)	(242,000)	(99,000)
Net Cash Flows Provided by (Used in) Operating Activities	44,970,000	(1,573,000)	19,863,000
Investing Activities:			
Acquisitions of property, plant and equipment	(15,201,000)	(18,043,000)	(60,518,000)
Proceeds from property disposal	2,977,000	3,766,000	148,000
Other assets	713,000	(536,000)	1,056,000
Net Cash Used in Investing Activities	(11,511,000)	(14,813,000)	(59,314,000)
Financing Activities:			
Proceeds from notes payable to banks	28,419,000	163,629,000	210,500,000
Repayments on notes payable to banks	(81,398,000)	(156,150,000)	(197,850,000)
Proceeds from long-term debt	126,468,000	—	31,600,000
Payments on long-term debt	(106,302,000)	(11,502,000)	(8,346,000)
Cost of refinancing debt	(5,510,000)		
Extraordinary charge, cash items	(1,188,000)	—	—
Proceeds from leasing transaction	—	565,000	—
Net proceeds from sale of stock	—	29,923,000	—
Cash dividends paid	(828,000)	(1,355,000)	(1,355,000)
Cash Provided by (Used in) Financing Activities	(40,339,000)	25,110,000	34,549,000
Effect of exchange rate changes on cash and cash equivalents	(144,000)	(49,000)	99,000
Increase (decrease) in cash and cash equivalents	(7,024,000)	8,675,000	(4,803,000)
Cash and cash equivalents at beginning of year	11,550,000	2,875,000	7,678,000
Cash and cash equivalents at end of year	$ 4,526,000	$ 11,550,000	$ 2,875,000
Supplemental disclosure information:			
Cash paid during the year for:			
Interest (net of amount capitalized)	$ 23,015,000	$ 22,507,000	$ 20,983,000
Income taxes	$ 3,688,000	$ 1,455,000	$ 2,273,000

See notes to consolidated financial statements.

Profits are an opinion, but cash is a fact   185

EXHIBIT 17-3 APPROXIMATING CASH FLOW FROM OPERATIONS (*continued*)

CONSOLIDATED STATEMENTS OF INCOME AND RETAINED EARNINGS—
Portland General Corporation & Subsidaries

For the Years Ended December 31 (Thousands of Dollars)

	1992	1991	1990
Operating Revenues	$ 884,240	$ 889,935	$ 852,105
Operating Expenses			
Purchased power and fuel	222,127	226,264	201,272
Production and distribution	93,677	95,960	90,749
Maintenance	70,496	91,304	55,463
Administrative and other	112,010	124,174	105,423
Depreciation, decommissioning and amortization	98,706	112,567	90,523
Taxes other than income taxes	55,515	59,023	59,602
	652,531	709,292	603,032
Operating income before income taxes	231,709	180,643	249,073
Income taxes	67,235	44,005	72,616
Net operating income	164,474	136,638	176,457
Other Income (Deductions)			
Regulatory reserves—net of taxes ($14,153)	—	—	16,090
Loss from independent power— net of taxes $16,058,$531	—	(74,144)	(3,390)
Interest expense	(73,895)	(81,745)	(83,532)
Allowance for funds used during construction	2,769	2,049	1,757
Preferred dividend requirement—PGE	(12,636)	(12,913)	(13,073)
Other—net of income taxes	8,911	9,417	5,643
Income (loss) from continuing operations	89,623	(20,698)	99,952
Discontinued Operations			
Estimated loss on disposal of real estate operations, including provision for operating losses during the phase-out period	—	(29,169)	—
Net Income (loss)	$ 89,623	$ (49,867)	$ 99,952

Common Stock

Average shares outstanding	46,887,184	46,333,096	46,133,303
Earnings (loss) per average share			
Continuing operations	$ 1.93*	$ (0.43)*	$ 2.17
Estimated loss from disposal of real estate operations	—	(0.63)	—
Earnings (loss) per average share	$ 1.93*	$ (1.06)*	$ 2.17
Dividends declared per share	$ 1.20	$ 1.20	$ 1.20

*Includes $.02 for tax benefits from ESOP dividends.

Retained Earnings

Balance at beginning of year**	$ 19,635	$ 124,112	$ 79,292
Net income	89,623	(49,867)	99,952
ESOP tax benefit and preferred stock premium at redemption	(2,505)	992	230
	106,753	75,237	179,474
Dividends declared on common stock	56,272	55,602	55,362
Balance at end of year	$ 50,481	$ 19,635	$ 124,112

**Beginning balances are changed from prior reports due to the reclassification of the ESOP tax benefit from paid-in capital to retained earnings. The accompanying notes are an integral part of these statements.

CONSOLIDATED STATEMENTS OF CASH FLOWS—
Portland General Corporation & Subsidiaries

For the Years Ended December 31 (Thousands of Dollars)

	1992	1991	1990
Cash Provided By—			
OperationsNet income (loss)	$ 89,623	$ (49,867)	$ 99,952
Adjustments to reconcile net income (loss) to net cash provided by operations:			
Non-cash loss from independent power	—	83,493	—
Depreciation, decommissioning and amortization	109,884	115,285	103,117
WNP-3 exchange agreement amortization	5,658	6,231	(9,314)
Amortization of deferred charges	8,689	9,798	8,300
Regulatory reserves—net of tax	—	—	(16,090)
Deferred income taxes—net	26,480	1,200	43,199
Other non-cash revenues	(2,659)	(4,160)	(6,175)
(Increase) Decrease in receivables	(12,736)	(3,750)	(19,377)
(Increase) Decrease in inventories	(4,181)	751	(858)
Increase (Decrease) in payables	(6,231)	25,208	(360)
Other working capital items—net	7,020	(1,895)	102
Net assets of discontinued operations	(30,948)	34,751	13,557
Deferred charges	(23,540)	(15,435)	(24,159)
Miscellaneous—net	23,149	15,046	6,781
	190,208	216,656	198,675
Investing Activities			
Utility construction	(143,561)	(138,905)	(109,116)
Rentals received from leveraged leases	12,373	11,099	1,912
Nuclear decommissioning trust	(12,842)	(20,104)	—
Marketable securities—net	—	2,708	36,759
Advances to affiliates	—	(42,494)	(36,779)
Other	(9,964)	(16,851)	(11,326)
	(153,994)	(204,547)	(118,550)
Financing Activities			
Short-term borrowings—net	48,273	(22,701)	14,574
Long-term debt issued	123,000	178,016	120,700
Long-term debt retired	(143,902)	(119,004)	(99,306)
Nonrecourse borrowings for leveraged leases	—	—	4,020
Repayment of nonrecourse borrowings for leveraged leases	(11,215)	(10,304)	(7,270)
Preferred stock issued	30,000	—	—
Preferred stock retired	(31,225)	(1,800)	(1,800)
Common stock issued	9,753	6,585	408
Unearned compensation	—	—	(36,000)
Dividends paid	(56,230)	(55,564)	(64,164)
	(31,546)	(24,772)	(68,838)
Increase (Decrease) in cash and cash equivalents	4,668	(12,663)	11,287
Cash and cash equivalents at the beginning of period	2,021	14,684	3,397
Cash and cash equivalents at the end of period	$ 6,689	$ 2,021	$ 14,684

Supplemental Disclosure of Cash Flow Information

Cash paid during the year:

	1992	1991	1990
Interest	$ 72,535	$ 76,326	$ 82,334
Income taxes	22,241	23,560	18,462

The accompanying notes are an integral part of these statements.

Profits are an opinion, but cash is a fact   187

EXHIBIT 17-4 RECONCILIATION OF NET INCOME TO CASH FLOW FROM OPERATIONS

J.B. Hunt Transport Services, Inc. and Subsidiaries
(in thousands)

	1993
Net Earnings	$ 38,221
Depreciation, net of gain on disposition of equipment	83,210
	$121,431
Net cash provided by operating activities	121,427
Difference	$ 4
Percent	0%

United Missouri Bancshares, Inc.
(in thousands)

	1993
Net income	$ 41,119
Depreciation and amortization	19,222
	$ 60,341
Net cash provided by operating activities	60,521
Difference	$ 180
Percent	.3%

Union Electric Company
(in thousands)

	1992
Net income	$302,748
Depreciation and amortization	237,659
Amortization of nuclear fuel	47,816
	$588,223
Net cash provided by operating activities	591,011
Difference	$ 2,788
Percent	.5%

PHH Corporation and Subsidiaries
(in thousands)

	1993
Net income	$ 56,417
Depreciation	738,062
	$794,479
Net cash provided by operating activities	776,542
Difference	$ 17,937
Percent	2.3%

Texas Industries, Inc. and Subsidiaries
(in thousands)

	1993
Net income	$ 1,058
Depreciation, depletion, and amortization	49,799
	$ 50,857
Net cash provided by operations	49,361
Difference	$ 1,496
Percent	3.0%

Atmos Energy Corporation
(in thousands)

	1992
Net income	$ 10,031
Depreciation and amortization	17,500
	$ 27,531
Net cash provided by operating activities	28,589
Difference	$ 1,058
Percent	3.7%

Willamette Industries, Inc.
(in thousands)

	1993
Net earnings	$137,032
Depreciation and other amortization	172,591
	$309,623
Net cash provided by operating activities	298,648
Difference	$ 10,975
Percent	3.7%

Profits are an opinion, but cash is a fact

Pinnacle West Capital Corporation
(in thousands)

	1993
Income from continuing operations	$169,978
Depreciation and amortization	258,562
	$428,540
Net cash flow provided by operating activities	449,062
Difference	$ 20,522
Percent	4.6%

Pilgrim's Pride Corporation and Subsidiaries
(in thousands)

	1993
Net income	$ 21,009
Depreciation and amortization	26,034
	$ 47,043
Net cash flows provided by operating activities	44,970
Difference	$ 2,073
Percent	4.6%

Portland General Corporation & Subsidiaries
(in thousands)

	1992
Net income	$ 89,623
Depreciation, decommissioning, and amortization	109,884
	$199,507
Net cash provided by operations	190,208
Difference	$ 9,299
Percent	4.9%

Relative Ranges

0%	J.B. Hunt Transport Services, Inc. and Subsidiaries
.3%	United Missouri Bancshares, Inc.
.5%	Union Electric Company
2.3%	PHH Corporation and Subsidiaries
3.0%	Texas Industries, Inc. and Subsidiaries
3.7%	Atmos Energy Corporation
3.7%	Willamette Industries, Inc.
4.6%	Pinnacle West Capital Corporation
4.6%	Pilgrim's Pride Corporation and Subsidiaries
4.9%	Portland General Corporation & Subsidiaries

In Conclusion

Understanding and managing cash flows is important to every business. These are learned skills that use the same basic techniques in each company. As stated at the beginning of this chapter, operating managers in different industries are successful in many different ways, but good cash management operates the same in every company. This book tries to lay out the basics of good cash management. The rest is up to you.

18

THE STATEMENT OF CASH FLOWS: CASH FROM OPERATING ACTIVITIES

The preceding chapter points out that depreciation and amortization are operating expenses that do not require cash outflows each year. Therefore, depreciation and amortization are often added to net income to give a simple approximation of cash from operations. Also in the preceding chapter an income statement for Ametek is used to illustrate the calculation of this technique.

Although the technique is frequently used, it is not accurate. Perhaps worse still, it is not even inaccurate in a predictable way. We cannot say it is inaccurate because it gives an optimistic (too high), or a pessimistic (too low) estimate. Exhibit 18–1 lists cash from operations for a random sample of 50 Fortune 1,000 companies. Cash from operations is measured two ways: (1) as estimated from the income statement by adding back depreciation and amortization and (2) as calculated and presented in the statement of cash flows. Of these estimates, 25 are too high and 25 are too low.

For each company, we divided the difference between the two measures of cash flow by cash flow from operations, as shown in the statement of cash flows, to find the percentage difference between the two measures. Cash flows from operations estimated by adding depreciation and amortization expense to net income in our sample is off by an average difference of 92.28%, and as likely to be wrong on the high side as on the low side. For this reason, we recommend against any serious use of estimations made using this technique.

EXHIBIT 18–1 COMPARING ESTIMATES OF CASH FLOW FROM OPERATIONS WITH CASH FROM OPERATIONS IN THE STATEMENT OF CASH FLOW (000 OMITTED)

Company	Net Income (Loss)	Depreciation & Amortization	Cash Provided (Used) in Operations Estimated	Cash Flow Statement	Error Over (or Under)
Rockwell International Corp.	($1,036,000)	$558,100	($477,900)	$701,900	($1,179,800)
Greater New York Savings Bank	($14,658)	$2,586	($12,072)	$319,743	($331,815)
Great American Management	($49,800)	$51,900	$2,100	$20,100	($18,000)
Barnes Group, Inc.	$4,383	$23,094	$27,477	$19,642	$7,835
American Maize-Products	$13,011	$26,434	$39,445	$48,432	($8,987)
Data General Corporation	($60,479)	$96,524	$36,045	$74,631	($38,586)
La-Z-Boy Chair Company	$38,069	$14,014	$52,083	$28,085	$23,998
PacifiCare Health Systems	$43,590	$10,644	$54,234	$67,920	($13,686)
ACX Technologies	$12,982	$41,580	$54,562	$33,267	$21,295
Kellwood Company	$35,614	$25,113	$60,727	$67,577	($6,850)
The Valspar Corporation	$40,182	$20,621	$60,803	$57,121	$3,682
Danaher Corporation	$31,601	$37,105	$68,706	$72,908	($4,202)
Block Drug Company	$61,546	$11,659	$73,205	$45,674	$27,531
Reliance Electric	$26,000	$49,000	$75,000	$108,000	($33,000)
UJB Financial Corp.	$53,824	$22,181	$76,005	$1,324,522	($1,248,517)
Longs Drugs	$52,782	$33,241	$86,023	$114,163	($28,140)
McGraw-Hill, Inc.	$28,568	$74,319	$102,887	$251,086	($148,199)
Allmerica Financial	$104,400		$104,400	$37,800	$66,600
Centex Corporation	$85,162	$19,640	$104,802	($56,034)	$160,836
Compass Bancshares	$89,260	$26,237	$115,497	($6,304)	$121,801
Mercantile Bancorporation	$116,972	$24,496	$141,468	$227,131	($85,663)
Beverly Enterprises	$57,924	$86,127	$144,051	$130,877	$13,174
Signet Banking Corporation	$109,200	$35,178	$144,378	$640,888	($496,510)
First Alabama Bancshares	$112,045	$33,590	$145,635	$61,229	$84,406
Old Kent Financial Corporation	$127,902	$27,174	$155,076	$177,206	($22,130)
Consolidated Freightways	($3,656)	$166,917	$163,261	$131,779	$31,482

UtiliCorp United Inc.	$52,900	$131,100	$184,000	$175,800	$8,200
Kansas City Southern Industries	$90,500	$97,200	$187,700	$189,200	($1,500)
Ashland Oil, Inc.	($68,298)	$302,105	$233,807	$398,191	($164,384)
PaineWebber Group Inc.	$213,175	$29,156	$242,331	($397,880)	$640,211
Westvaco Corporation	$104,341	$194,994	$299,335	$240,459	$58,876
SYSCO Corporation	$201,807	$107,718	$309,525	$257,165	$52,360
Union Camp Corporation	$50,043	$261,518	$311,561	$418,420	($106,859)
Walgreen Company	$220,628	$92,109	$312,737	$337,858	($25,121)
CNA Financial Corp.	$267,523	$46,513	$314,036	$1,272,135	($958,099)
Safeco Corporation	$311,294	$31,928	$343,222	$664,577	($321,355)
Marsh & McLennan Companies	$263,700	$112,000	$375,700	$345,100	$30,600
Freeport-McMoRan Inc.	$187,811	$211,176	$398,987	$339,637	$59,350
FMC Corporation	$192,601	$236,633	$429,234	$375,137	$54,097
The Home Depot, Inc.	$362,863	$69,536	$432,399	$338,142	$94,257
R.R Donnelly & Sons	$234,659	$258,169	$492,828	$452,041	$40,787
H.J. Heinz Company	$396,313	$234,935	$631,248	$411,898	$219,350
General Public Utilities	$324,430	$362,536	$686,966	$596,052	$90,914
Norwest Corporation	$653,600	$194,800	$848,400	$389,400	$459,000
Wells Fargo & Company	$612,000	$266,000	$878,000	$1,533,000	($655,000)
Duke Power Company	$626,415	$657,068	$1,283,483	$1,333,635	($50,152)
Primerica Corporation	$1,187,800	$97,100	$1,284,900	$460,100	$824,800
NationsBank Corporation	$1,501,000	$352,000	$1,853,000	$2,137,000	($284,000)
Minnesota Mining and Mfg.	$1,263,000	$1,076,000	$2,339,000	$2,091,000	$248,000
American International Group	$1,938,773	$472,247	$2,411,020	$6,467,451	($4,046,431)

Operating Cash Flows: The Direct Method

Companies are required to include a statement of cash flows in their annual reports. There are two ways of determining and presenting cash flow from operating activities that are used in the statement of cash flows: the direct method and the indirect method.

The direct method is simple; it consists of operating cash flows grouped into major categories of receipts and payments, their net amount determining the net cash flow provided by or used in operations. The direct method, essentially a cash-basis income statement, takes the general form shown in Exhibit 18–2. Exhibit 18–3 shows the statement of cash flows from the annual report of a real company, MCI Communications. MCI uses the direct method.

EXHIBIT 18–2 STATEMENT OF OPERATING CASH FLOWS USING THE DIRECT METHOD— XYZ COMPANY

For the year ended December 31, FY2		
Cash collected from customers		$100,000
Less cash paid for expenses:		
For goods sold	$50,000	
For royalties	30,000	
For other operating costs	10,000	90,000
Net cash provided by operating activities		$10,000

Year ended December 31, *In millions*	1993	1992	1991
OPERATING ACTIVITIES			
Cash received from customers	$ 11,546	$ 10,328	$ 9,362
Cash paid to suppliers and employees	(9,097)	(8,154)	(7,597)
Taxes paid	(321)	(292)	(292)
Interest paid	(150)	(156)	(202)
CASH FROM OPERATING ACTIVITIES	1,978	1,726	1,271
INVESTING ACTIVITIES			
Cash outflow for communications system	(1,733)	(1,272)	(1,377)
Other, net	(26)	11	1
CASH USED FOR INVESTING ACTIVITIES	(1,759)	(1,261)	(1,376)
NET CASH FLOW BEFORE FINANCING ACTIVITIES	219	465	(105)
FINANCING ACTIVITIES			
Issuance of Senior Notes and other debt	756	481	527
Retirement of Senior Notes and other debt	(1,468)	(218)	(504)
Commercial paper and bank credit facility activity, net	(497)	(69)	(84)
Issuance of preferred stock	830		
Redemption of preferred stock		(400)	
Purchase of treasury stock	(198)	(180)	
Issuance of common stock for employee plans	319	168	79
Payment of dividends on common and preferred stock	(28)	(56)	(55)
CASH USED FOR FINANCING ACTIVITIES	(286)	(274)	(37)
Net (decrease) increase in cash and cash equivalents	(67)	191	(142)
Cash and cash equivalents at beginning of year	232	41	183
CASH AND CASH EQUIVALENTS AT END OF YEAR	$ 165	$ 232	$ 41

See accompanying Notes to Consolidated Financial Statements

EXHIBIT 18–4   PARTIAL FINANCIAL STATEMENTS— XYZ COMPANY

Income Statement
For the year ended December 31, FY2

Sales		$90,000
Cost of goods sold	$47,000	
Royalty expense	27,000	
Depreciation expense	4,000	
Other operating expenses	10,000	
Loss on sale of obsolete equipment	1,000	89,000
Net income		$ 1,000

Partial Balance Sheet
Current Assets and Current Liabilities
As of December 31, FY2

Current Assets:		Current Liabilities:	
Cash	$12,000	Accounts payable	$27,000
Accounts receivable	15,000	Royalties payable	10,000
Inventory	15,000		
Prepaid expenses	4,000		
Total	$56,000	Total	$37,000

Partial Balance Sheet
Current Assets and Current Liabilities
As of December 31, FY1

Current Assets:		Current Liabilities:	
Cash	$23,000	Accounts payable	$25,000
Accounts receivable	25,000	Royalties payable	13,000
Inventory	10,000		
Prepaid expenses	4,000		
Total	$52,000	Total	$38,000

The cash flows are determined from the revenue and expense amounts, adjusted for changes in related current assets or liabilities during the period. Cash collected from customers is determined by adjusting the sales revenue account for changes in accounts receivable.

The hypothetical XYZ Company is used to illustrate how the statement of cash flows is constructed. An income statement and partial balance sheet information for FY1 and FY2 are given in Exhibit 18–4. The process is described in the following paragraphs.

Cash Collected from Customers

XYZ Company has sales of $90,000, but accounts receivable decreased from $25,000 at the beginning of the year to $15,000 at the end of the year. XYZ must have collected the entire $90,000 sold, plus $10,000 from sales to customers last year.

Cash Collected from Customers

Sales	$ 90,000
Plus decrease in accounts receivable	10,000
Cash collected from customers	$100,000

Cash Paid for Goods Sold

Cash paid for goods sold is determined by adjusting the income statement amount for cost of goods sold, an expense, by the changes in both inventories and accounts payable. The logic follows: If the company sold only goods purchased in the current period for cash, cash flow would be equal to cost of goods sold. However, because XYZ increased inventories by $5,000, an additional $5,000 cash is spent. But, XYZ did not pay for all of its purchases. Accounts payable for inventory purchases last year were $25,000 at the beginning of the year (representing inventory purchases from the previous year) and $27,000 at year end. Thus, XYZ paid $2,000 ($27,000 − $25,000) less for inventory than it purchased.

Cash Paid for Goods Sold

Cost of goods sold	$47,000
Plus cash paid to increase inventory	5,000
Less reduction in cash paid by increasing accounts payable	(2,000)
Cash paid for goods sold	$50,000

Other Operating Cash Outflows

Other expenses can be converted to their cash flow equivalent in the same way. Royalties expense was $27,000 but XYZ also paid $3,000 to decrease royalties payable from $13,000 to $10,000.

Cash Paid for Royalties

Royalties expense	$27,000
Plus cash paid to decrease royalties payable	3,000
Cash paid for royalties	$30,000

Other operating expenses were $10,000. Prepaid operating expenses were $4,000 in both years FY1 and FY2. There were no operating expenses payable. Because there was no change in the current asset or liability accounts related to other operating expenses, we know that the cash paid was equal to the expense shown in the income statement.

Depreciation and Amortization: Direct Method

Cash is used to purchase a productive asset such as a plant or a delivery truck, but no cash is used when, year by year, the cost of the asset is expensed against earnings. Similarly, an intangible asset, such as a patent, is purchased for cash and amortized to expense over its useful life. Depreciation or amortization expense is only an allocation of an original cost to the period benefited. Therefore, depreciation and amortization are operating expenses that do not require operating cash outflows each year. There is no cash flow, so depreciation and amortization are not used in determining cash flow from operations using the direct method.

Gains and Losses

The amount of a gain or loss shown in the income statement does not show the amount (or even the direction) of the related cash flow. XYZ shows a $1,000 loss on the sale of obsolete equipment. First, this is not an operating activity. Most gains and losses are not operating activities and should not be in the part of the cash flow statement that shows cash flow from operations.

Second, the cash flow involved is not $1,000. The loss decreases earnings by $1,000, but what is the effect on cash flow? Not $1,000. The $1,000 loss resulted from selling obsolete equipment for $1,000 less than its book value. It could be that XYZ sold equipment with a book value of $11,000 for $10,000 cash, resulting in a loss of $1,000 and a cash inflow of $10,000. This cash inflow should appear as an investing activity cash inflow of $10,000 from the sale of obsolete equipment. Investing activities are discussed in Chapter 19.

Operating Cash Flows: The Indirect Method

When the indirect method is used to determine and show cash from operating activities in the statement of cash flows, accrual-based net income is adjusted for changes in the current asset and liability accounts to determine cash flows. This method does not determine the major categories of operating cash flows, such as the cash cost of goods sold or royalties.

Cash provided by operations is calculated by (1) adding to net income any changes in current asset or liability accounts that result in increases in cash from operations and (2) subtracting from net income any changes that result in decreases. The ways in which changes in the current accounts affect cash flow are shown in the following list:

Change in Account	Effect on Cash from Operations	Add (Subtract) to (from) Net Income (NI) to Determine Cash from Operations
Increase in current asset	Decrease in cash	Subtract from NI
Decrease in current asset	Increase in cash	Add to NI
Increase in current liability	Increase in cash	Add to NI
Decrease in current liability	Decrease in cash	Subtract from NI

The chart in Exhibit 18–5 works like this: If a current asset "Goes Down" or decreases (shown in the second column), that

EXHIBIT 18–5   THE EFFECT OF CHANGES IN THE CURRENT ACCOUNTS ON CASH FROM OPERATIONS

	Increase in Cash	Decrease in Cash
Current Asset	Goes Down	Goes Up
Current Liability	Goes Up	Goes Down

is an "Increase in Cash" (second column heading), as when receivables are collected. If, instead, the current liability "Goes Down," (third column), that results in a "Decrease in Cash" (third column heading), as when accounts payable are paid.

Depreciation and Amortization: Indirect Method

Because depreciation expense does not consume cash, it is added back to net income to determine cash from operating activities when the indirect method is used. For XYZ, depreciation for the year is $5,000. All XYZ's operating expenses used cash (in some amount), except depreciation. Depreciation expense required no cash, because the assets depreciated were not purchased in the current year. (Even then, cash would have been required for the assets' acquisition, not their depreciation.) If net income is to be adjusted to equal cash from operations, XYZ's $5,000 depreciation expense must be added back to net income.

Exhibit 18–6 shows the format for a determination of cash flow from operating activities for XYZ, using the indirect method. Exhibit 18–7 shows a determination of cash from operations for a real company, Marriott Corporation, using the indirect method.

EXHIBIT 18–6 OPERATING CASH FLOWS USING THE INDIRECT METHOD—XYZ COMPANY

Schedule of Operating Cash Flows
For the year ended December 31, FY2

Net income for FY2		$ 1,000
Plus:		
Depreciation	$ 4,000	
Loss on sale of equipment	1,000	
Increase in accounts payable	2,000	
Decrease in accounts receivable	10,000	17,000
Less:		
Increase in inventory	5,000	
Decrease royalties payable	3,000	(8,000)
Net cash provided by operating activities		$10,000

EXHIBIT 18–7 A STATEMENT OF CASH FLOWS USING THE DIRECT METHOD— MARRIOTT CORPORATION

CONSOLIDATED STATEMENT OF CASH FLOWS—
Marriott Corporation and Subsidiaries

Fiscal years ended January 1, 1993, January 3, 1992 and December 28, 1990

	1992	1991	1990
		(in millions)	
OPERATING ACTIVITIES			
Net income	$ 85	$ 82	$ 47
Adjustments to reconcile to cash from operations:			
Depreciation and amortization	284	272	208
Income taxes	(28)	27	18
Net restructuring charges	21	—	153
Proceeds from sales of timeshare notes receivable	41	83	—
Amortization of deferred income	(19)	(38)	(50)
Other	1	6	49
Working capital changes:			
Accounts receivable	(40)	88	(76)
Inventories	(16)	63	(22)
Other current assets	(14)	13	(5)
Accounts payable and accruals	106	(47)	63
Cash from continuing operations	421	549	385
Cash from (used in) discontinued operations	(11)	3	(10)
Cash from operations	410	552	375

	1992	1991	1990
INVESTING ACTIVITIES			
Proceeds from sales of assets	484	84	990
Less noncash proceeds	(97)	—	(15)
Cash received from sales of assets	387	84	975
Capital expenditures	(210)	(427)	(1,094)
Acquisitions	(47)	—	(118)
Other	(82)	(126)	(129)
Cash from (used in) investing activities	48	(469)	(366)
FINANCING ACTIVITIES			
Issuances of long-term and convertible subordinated debt	917	815	1,317
Issuance of convertible preferred stock	—	195	—
Issuances of common stock	7	3	24
Repayment of long-term debt	(1,179)	(1,316)	(846)
Purchases of treasury stock	—	—	(294)
Dividends paid	(41)	(27)	(27)
Cash from (used in) financing activities	(296)	(330)	174
INCREASE (DECREASE) IN CASH AND EQUIVALENTS	162	(247)	183
CASH AND EQUIVALENTS, beginning of year	163	410	227
CASH AND EQUIVALENTS, end of year	$ 325	$ 163	$ 410

See notes to consolidated financial statements.

19

THE STATEMENT OF CASH FLOWS: CASH FROM INVESTING AND FINANCING ACTIVITIES

From where, beside operations, can a company obtain cash? A company can issue more stock, borrow, or sell its productive assets (such as factory and equipment). These are the four general sources of cash. The general uses of cash are related to these general sources, with one addition. A company's operations can consume cash (instead of providing cash), plus the company may repurchase its stock, repay debt, buy productive assets and execute a fifth action, pay dividends. These general sources and uses of cash are shown in Exhibit 19–1.

A company is required to present its sources and uses of cash according to three classes of activities:

1. Operating activities

2. Investing activities

3. Financing activities

All the sources and uses listed in Exhibit 19–1 can be grouped into these three classes of activity.

EXHIBIT 19–1   GENERAL SOURCES AND USES OF CASH

Sources	Uses
Operations	Operations
Issue Stock	Reacquire Stock
Borrow	Repay Debt
Sell Assets	Buy Assets
	Pay Dividends

Operating Activities

Chapter 18 showed how accountants determine and display cash from operations in the statement of cash flows. Accountants use the phrase "associated with net income" to identify operating activities. "Associated with net income" means that the item is on the income statement. Generally, all cash flows that do not result from investing or financing activities result, by default, from operating activities. Operating cash flows include all items on the income statement except gains and losses, as explained in the preceding chapter.

All financing expenses (such as interest paid) and all investing costs (such as commissions) and investment income (such as dividends or interest received) are income statement items and, as such, are operating cash flows. All income taxes paid are operating cash flows.

Investing Activities

For the purpose of categorizing cash flows, investing for the short term is an operating activity. Investing for the long term in noncurrent investments is, for cash flow purposes, an investing activity. Investing activities consume cash when long-term investments are acquired, and provide cash when they are sold. The sources of cash classified as investing activities are:

Selling long-term assets (inventory sales are operating activities)

Selling or collecting loans (as a creditor)

Selling an investment in stock

The uses of cash classified as investing activities are:

Purchasing long-term-assets (inventory purchases are operating activities)

Becoming a creditor (lending money or purchasing a loan)

Purchasing stock as an investment

Financing Activities

Most of the transactions a company has with its stockholders and long-term creditors are financing activities. Financing activities provide long-term capital. The two sources of cash from financing activities are:

Issuing stock

Borrowing long term (short-term borrowing is an operating activity)

There are only three uses of cash classified as financing activities:

Reacquiring a company's own stock

Repaying loans (including capitalized leases)

Paying cash dividends

The cash cost of the capital provided by stockholders is paid as dividends. Dividends are distributions of retained earnings, not income statement items. Dividends are financing uses of cash. The cash cost of the capital provided by creditors is paid as interest. Interest payments are income statement items and, as such, are operating cash flows.

Noncash Investing and Financing Activities

Some investing and financing activities do not involve cash but still affect the company's financial position. Consider, for example, a company that issues shares of stock worth $100,000 in exchange for land to use as a building site. The issuance of stock is a financing activity that ordinarily provides cash, and the purchase of land is an investing activity that ordinarily consumes cash. If financial statement readers are to be fully informed, both activities must appear in the statement of cash flows.

But when the stock is exchanged for land, cash is not affected and neither activity is shown in the statement of cash flows. To avoid misleading financial statement readers, accountants are required to show noncash investing and financing activities in a supplementary schedule to the statement of cash flows or in the notes to the financial statements.

Additional examples of noncash investing and financing activities include (all items listed are noncurrent):

Trading assets for other assets

Issuing debt to retire other debt

Acquiring assets by issuing stock or debt (including capital leases)

Exchanging assets for debt or stock

Issuing stock in exchange for debt

Issuing debt in exchange for stock

Issuing stock to retire other stock (common for preferred, or the reverse)

Preparing a Statement of Cash Flows

A statement of cash flows can be prepared by looking at all the changes in balance sheet accounts, not just at the current assets and liabilities, included in the preceding chapter. If any asset increases during the year, cash is consumed (as when an asset is purchased for cash). If any asset is reduced during the year, cash is increased (as when obsolete equipment is sold). The reverse is true for liabilities and owners' equity account balances. If a liability or owners' equity account balance is increased during the year, cash is increased (as when the company borrows or owners invest). If one of these accounts is reduced, cash is reduced (as when loans are repaid or dividends are distributed).

These facts are summarized in Exhibit 19–2, which is an expansion of the Exhibit 18–5, showing current assets and liabilities, in the preceding chapter.

EXHIBIT 19–2   THE EFFECT OF CHANGES IN THE ACCOUNTS ON CASH FLOWS

	Increase in Cash	Decrease in cash
Asset	Goes Down	Goes Up
Liability or Owners' Equity	Goes Up	Goes Down

Sources and Uses Worksheet

Because a statement of cash flows can be prepared by looking at all changes in the balance sheet accounts, a simple statement of cash flows can be constructed using worksheets such as those shown in Exhibits 19–3 and 19–4. In our illustration, The XYZ Company, used as an example in Chapter 18, is used here as well. The preceding chapter dealt with operating cash flows and used the balances in current asset and liability accounts. The same current account balances, shown in Exhibit 18–4, are used in the worksheet in Exhibit 19–3.

Several items on the worksheet require explanation. First, the decrease in cash from $23,000 to $12,000 is a decrease in cash and (per Exhibit 19–2) a source of cash on the worksheet. In reality, it is this $11,000 change in cash with which the statement of cash flows must reconcile. The only way to conceptualize this is to think of the decrease in the cash account as a source, perhaps, of "spendable" cash to the company managers.

Moreover, it was explained in Chapter 18 that equipment with a book value of $11,000 was sold for $10,000, a $1,000 loss. Let the historical cost of the obsolete equipment be $20,000 and the accumulated depreciation be $9,000. Then the beginning and ending balances of plant and equipment can be reconciled as follows:

	Plant and Equipment	Accumulated Depreciation
Beginning balance	$60,000	$14,000
Less obsolete equipment sold	(20,000)	(9,000)
Plus depreciation expense		4,000
Plus purchase	50,000	
Ending balance	$90,000	$ 9,000

From this reconciliation, we see that XYZ had a $50,000 investing cash outflow to purchase equipment. How did we know XYZ purchased $50,000 in plant and equipment? There must have been a purchase, otherwise the beginning and ending balances do not reconcile. In real life, we would be able to confirm this purchase by examining a document of some sort; here, we accept it.

Exhibit 19–5 uses the information from the worksheet and the preceding information on plant and equipment sales and purchases to prepare a statement of cash flows for XYZ. Exhibits 18–3 and 18–7 show the statement of cash flows for two real companies, MCI Communications and Marriott Corporation, as they appeared in annual reports.

EXHIBIT 19–3 THE SOURCE AND USES OF CASH WORKSHEET—XYZ COMPANY

	Beginning Balance Sheet FY1	Ending Balance Sheet FY2	Source of Cash	Use of Cash
Cash	$23,000	$12,000	$11,000	
Accounts Receivable	25,000	15,000	10,000	
Inventory	10,000	15,000		$5,000
Prepaid Expenses	4,000	4,000		
Plant and Equipment	60,000	90,000		30,000
Accumulated Depreciation	(14,000)	(9,000)		5,000
Other Assets	5,000	3,000	2,000	
Accounts Payable	25,000	27,000	2,000	
Royalties Payable	13,000	10,000		3,000
Mortgage Payable	44,000	61,000	17,000	
Owners' Equity	31,000	32,000	1,000 (income)	
Total			$43,000	$43,000

EXHIBIT 19–4 THE SOURCES AND USES OF CASH WORKSHEET—XYZ COMPANY

	Beginning Balance Sheet FY1	Ending Balance Sheet FY2	Source of Cash	Use of Cash
Cash	$23,000	$12,000	$11,000	
Accounts Receivable	25,000	15,000	10,000	
Inventory	10,000	15,000		$5,000
Prepaid Expenses	4,000	4,000		
Plant and Equipment	60,000	90,000	20,000 (item sold)	50,000 (purchase)
Accumulated Depreciation	(14,000)	(9,000)	4,000 (expense)	9,000 (item sold)
Other Assets	5,000	3,000	2,000	
Accounts Payable	25,000	27,000	2,000	
Royalties Payable	13,000	10,000		3,000
Mortgage Payable	44,000	61,000	17,000	
Owners' Equity	31,000	32,000	1,000 (income)	
Total			$67,000	$67,000

EXHIBIT 19–5 STATEMENT OF CASH FLOWS— XYZ COMPANY

For the year ended December 31, FY2

Operating Activities:			
Net income for FY2			$ 1,000
Plus:			
Depreciation	$4,000		
Loss on sale of equipment	1,000		
Increase in accounts payable	2,000		
Decrease in accounts receivable	10,000	17,000	
Less:			
Increase in inventory	5,000		
Decrease royalties payable	3,000	(8,000)	
Net cash provided by operating activities			$10,000
Investing Activities:			
Sale of plant and equipment	10,000		
Sale of other assets	2,000		
Purchase of plant and equipment	(50,000)		
Cash used by investing activities			(38,000)
Financing Activities:			
Increase in mortgage payable	17,000		
Cash provided by financing activities			17,000
Decrease in cash and cash equivalents			11,000
Cash and cash equivalents, beginning of the year			23,000
Cash and cash equivalents, end of the year			$12,000

Statements of Cash Flow for International Companies

Most large companies publish consolidated financial statements that contain the financial statements of the company and its subsidiaries, often located around the world. In the annual report, the financial statements of these different companies are combined as if they were all one company (which, in essence, they are). Before the financial statements of a foreign subsidiary can be combined with those of its stateside parent, the foreign currency financial statements must be translated into U.S. dollars.

Often, exchange rate fluctuations (changes in the values of the foreign and U.S. currencies) create a difference between the translated values of a subsidiary's net assets and its stockholders' equity that requires an adjustment (a gain or loss) to make assets equal liabilities plus owners' equity. This adjustment is called a foreign-currency translation adjustment, and the cumulative amount necessary over the years is reported in the stockholders' equity section of the balance sheet.

The translation adjustment arises because some of a company's accounts are translated at current exchange rates and other accounts are translated at historical exchange rates. Consider the simple example illustrated by the cash flows of a hypothetical subsidiary in Wayoff Land.

The currency units in Wayoff are called "Wayoffs," abbreviated as "Wfs." Our subsidiary begins the year with cash of 1,000 Wfs, collects 2,000 Wfs when the exchange rate is 10 Wfs per $1 U.S., and pays 2,000 Wfs when the exchange rate is 12 Wfs per $1 U.S. The exchange rate at the beginning of the year is 8, and at end of the year 14 Wfs per $1 U.S. Our subsidiary's cash flows, converted to U.S. dollar equivalents, are as follows.

	Wfs $\times$	Rate	=	U.S. $
Beginning of year	1,000	8		8,000
Collection	+2,000	10		+20,000
Payment	−2,000	12		−24,000
End of year	1,000	14		14,000

But something is wrong. In U.S. dollars, the flows do not explain the growth in cash from $8,000 to $14,000. Reconciling the beginning balance and the flows to the ending balance requires a $10,000 "fudge" factor. That $10,000 fudge is the foreign-currency translation adjustment.

Beginning of year	$ 8,000
Collection	+20,000
Payment	−24,000
Subtotal	$ 4,000
Foreign-currency translation adjustment	10,000
End of year	$14,000

Translation adjustments are accumulated and disclosed as a component of stockholders' equity, normally between invested capital and retained earnings. The adjustment is reported as a component of stockholders' equity.

Exhibit 19–6 presents an illustration of the preparation and remeasurement of the Hypothetical Company, a wholly-owned subsidiary of a U.S. company. The exchange rates at the beginning and end of the year are 22 and 30, respectively. The average rate weighted by cash flows is 25. The only change in property and equipment is a sale when the exchange rate is 22. Dividends are paid when the exchange rate is 27. All other changes in account balances are translated using the average exchange rate weighted by cash flows.

The translation adjustment of $37,000 is due to exchange rate changes. If a different measure of the weighted average exchange rate were used, the equipment sold on a different date, or dividends paid on a different date, the cash flows and translation adjustment (but not the change in cash) might be different.

Hypothetical Company
Statement of Cash Flows
For the year ended December 31, 19XX

Operating Activities:	Local Currency	Exchange Rate	Reporting Currency
Net Income	H4,000	25	$100,000
Adjustments to reconcile net income to cash provided by operating activities:			
Depreciation	1,000	25	25,000
Changes in operating assets and liabilities:			
Decrease in accounts receivable	1,000	25	25,000
Increase in inventory	(1,600)	25	(40,000)
Increase in accounts payable	400	25	10,000
Cash provided by operating activities	4,800		120,000
Investing Activities:			
Sale of equipment	2,000	22	44,000
Cash provided by investing activities	2,000		44,000
Financing Activities:			
Repayment of mortgage payable	(4,000)	25	(100,000)
Payment of dividends	(1,000)	27	(27,000)
Cash used in financing activities	(5,000)		(127,000)
Effect of exchange rate changes on cash	NA		37,000
Increase in cash or cash equivalents	1,800		74,000
Cash and cash equivalents, beginning of year	2,000	20	40,000
Cash and cash equivalents, end of year	H3,800	14	$114,000

Exchange rates used:
1. Beginning of year   20
2. At time equipment was sold   22
3. At time dividends were paid   27
4. Weighted average rate   25
5. End of year   30

20

COMPARATIVE ANALYSIS OF THE STATEMENT OF CASH FLOWS

The purpose of cash flow analysis is to make judgments about the future. An analyst might want to know whether the company will be able to repay a six-month bank loan or whether earnings and dividend payments will continue to grow. In making these judgments, we use historical information and assume, unless there is information to the contrary, that historical trends will, for the most part, continue.

Users look for signs that the future will be different from the past. A strike might result in lost sales. A company's primary product could become obsolete, or a competitor might develop a vastly superior product. An analyst also assesses whether management is operating the company efficiently and effectively. Good management is a critical factor if the company is to be successful. Therefore, financial statement analysis focuses not only on financial and quantitative information, but on nonfinancial and qualitative information as well.

In addition to information found in the financial statements, other sources of information include the financial press (such as *The Wall Street Journal*), reports to the Securities and Exchange Commission, and business service publications (such as *Value Line*). This chapter focuses on financial and quantitative information in the company's statement of cash flows. We apply two types of comparative analysis to the statement of cash flows of Lubrizol Corporation to highlight significant relationships and trends. These techniques are called horizontal analysis and vertical analysis.

Horizontal Analysis

Horizontal analysis focuses on the changes in information from period to period. This type of analysis can tell us whether a company's sales, gross profit, expenses, and net income are increasing or decreasing over time, as well as what the change was for each item for each year. Horizontal analysis also reveals whether cash (or any other financial statement item) has increased or decreased over a particular period of time. The dollar change from one period to the next in an individual account may not adequately explain a change. The percentage change increases the user's understanding of the significance and nature of the change in that account.

There are two steps involved in performing horizontal analysis: (1) compute the dollar amount of the change from the base year to the year against which you are making the comparison, and (2) divide the dollar amount of the change by the base year amount.

Comparative financial statements present a company's financial statements for two or more successive periods and are used in horizontal analysis. Exhibit 20–1 contains the comparative statements of cash flows for Lubrizol Corporation for 1992, 1991, and 1990. The company uses the direct method to present its statements of cash flows and includes a reconcilia-

tion of net income to net cash provided by (used for) operating activities in the footnotes to the financial statements. (Note 9 also includes supplemental cash flow information using the indirect method to arrive at "net cash provided by operating activities.") We use these statements to illustrate horizontal analysis. Exhibits 20–2 and 20–3 present the horizontal analysis of the statement of cash flows of the Lubrizol Corporation.

Base-Year-To-Date Approach

Exhibit 20–2 uses 1991 as the base year, with the base amount (for 1991) presented as 100%. The 1992 amounts are then expressed as a percentage of the 1991 amounts. This is called a base-year-to-date approach and is most appropriate for a horizontal analysis involving three or more years.

Year-To-Year Approach

In contrast to the base-year-to-date approach, Exhibit 20–3 presents the same information in a different format: only the increase or decrease from 1991 to 1992 is expressed as a per-

EXHIBIT 20–1 CONSOLIDATED STATEMENTS OF CASH FLOWS—THE LUBRIZOL CORPORATION

THE LUBRIZOL CORPORATION CONSOLIDATED STATEMENTS OF CASH FLOWS

(In Thousands of Dollars)	Year Ended December 31		
	1992	1991	1990
Cash provided from (used for):			
Operating activities:			
Received from customers	$1,549,848	$1,480,776	$1,395,667
Paid to suppliers and employees	(1,361,971)	(1,265,058)	(1,206,060)
Income taxes paid	(62,576)	(55,116)	(87,713)
Interest and dividends received	12,071	9,960	10,181
Interest paid	(5,245)	(7,129)	(6,058)
Tax refund received, including interest		20,418	
Other—net	3,036	8,266	8,302
Total operating activities	135,163	192,117	114,319
Investing activities:			
Proceeds from sale of investments	8,512		105,843
Capital expenditures	(95,814)	(82,398)	(77,407)
Investments in non-consolidated companies	(2,402)	(751)	(6,690)
Acquisitions—net of cash acquired		(392)	(8,134)
Other—net	1,541	3,589	1,912
Total investing activities	(88,163)	(79,952)	15,524
Financing activities:			
Short-term borrowing (repayment)	(3,837)	2,587	3,240
Long-term borrowing	3,690	18,400	34
Long-term repayment	(20,000)	(18,660)	
Dividends paid	(55,883)	(53,322)	(52,257)
Common shares purchased, net of options exercised	(19,235)	(10,327)	(86,980)
Total financing activities	(95,265)	(61,322)	(135,963)
Effect of exchange rate changes on cash	(1,289)	(796)	579
Net increase (decrease) in cash and short-term investments	(49,554)	50,047	(5,541)
Cash and short-term investments at the beginning of year	126,147	76,100	81,641
Cash and short-term investments at the end of year	$ 76,593	$ 126,147	$ 76,100

The accompanying notes to financial statements are an integral part of these statements.

Note 9—Supplemental Cash Flow Information

The company generally invests its excess cash in short-term investments with various banks and financial institutions. Short-term investments are cash equivalents as they are part of the cash management activities of the company and are comprised primarily of investments having maturities of less than three months.

The following is a reconciliation of net income to net cash provided by (used for) operating activities:

	1992	1991	1990
Net income	$124,646	$123,659	$190,046
Depreciation and amortization	62,013	59,473	59,529
Deferred income taxes	(37)	(2,716)	3,749
Distributed (undistributed) earnings of non-consolidated companies	2,792	(3,743)	(4,178)
Write-down of assets			14,734
Gain on sales of investments	(6,484)		(101,921)
Change in current assets and liabilities:			
Receivables	(2,400)	4,470	(57,034)
Inventories	(30,807)	(14,187)	(32,244)
Accounts payable and accrued expenses	(13,693)	1,780	39,716
Other current assets	(316)	15,304	(2,146)
Increase in non-current liabilities	714	1,554	4,126
Other items—net	(1,265)	6,523	(58)
Net cash provided by operating activities	$135,163	$192,117	$114,319

continued

In 1990, net cash provided by operating activities is after deducting $31.2 million of income taxes paid resulting from the gain on sale of Genentech, the proceeds from which are included in investing activities.

As described in Note 16, substantially all of the net assets of the Agribusiness segment totaling $88.7 million plus consideration of $4.6 million were transferred or exchanged for $39.4 million of Mycogen preferred stock, 2,294,590 shares of Mycogen common stock with a carrying value of $13.1 million and a 49 percent interest in a joint venture (partnership) with a carrying value of $40.8 million.

centage of the 1991 amount. This is called a year-to-year approach and is used in analyzing a financial statement for only two periods.

The same results are obtained from Exhibits 20–2 and 20–3 as long as only two periods are examined. For example, cash received from customers increased by 4.7% in Exhibit 20–3. In Exhibit 20–2 the 1992 amount is expressed as an increase of 104.7% of the 1991 amount. Similarly, in Exhibit 20–2 cash and short-term investments at the end of 1992 are 60.7% of the amount at the end of 1991. And in Exhibit 20–3 the change in cash and short-term investments is shown as decreasing by 39.3% (100.0% – 60.7%). The advantage of the base-year-to-date approach over the year-to-year approach is that it allows the user to analyze the relative changes over an extended period of time.

Both exhibits show a correct form of horizontal analysis; they are included here to apprise the reader of these alternate forms.

Exhibit 20–3 shows that cash from operating activities decreased by approximately $57.0 million during 1992. This

decrease was primarily the result of a $27.8 million increase in payments to suppliers and employees (net of the increase in receipts from customers), a $7.5 million increase in tax payments, and $20.4 million in tax refunds received in 1991.

Lubrizol spent $88.2 million in 1992 for investing activities, as compared with approximately $80.0 million in 1991. Increased capital expenditures were partially offset by the proceeds from the sale of investments and other cash from investing activities.

Concerning financing activities, we see that these net outflows were approximately $34.0 million more in 1992 than in 1991. The company repurchased a significantly larger number of shares of its common stock in 1992 than it did in 1991. Dividend payments ($56.9 million) and debt repayment ($23.8 million) also help explain the increase in financing outflows of cash. In addition, the company's short-term and long-term debt borrowings were reduced in 1992.

The company's annual report provides an explanation for the decrease in cash in 1992. It shows that the company's working capital requirements, capital expenditures, dividends, and share repurchases were financed from three sources: internally generated funds, cash and short-term investments on hand at the beginning of the year, and short-term borrowings to meet seasonal needs. As a result of these activities, cash and short-term investments decreased by $49.6 million in 1992.

The company's investments in nonconsolidated companies went from $0.75 million in cash outflows in 1991 to $2.4 million in outflows in 1992. This is the largest percentage increase or decrease in cash flows for 1992 (increase of 219.8%). However, the absolute dollar amount of the increase

EXHIBIT 20–2   HORIZONTAL ANALYSIS OF THE STATEMENTS OF CASH FLOWS— THE LUBRIZOL CORPORATION

(In Thousands of Dollars)

	Year Ended December 31			
	1992	%	1991	%
Cash provided from (used for):				
Operating activities:				
Received from customers	$1,549,848	104.7%	$1,480,776	100.0%
Paid to suppliers and employees	(1,362,971)	107.7	(1,265,058)	100.0
Income taxes paid	(62,576)	113.5	(55,116)	100.0
Interest and dividends received	12,071	121.2	9,960	100.0
Interest paid	(5,245)	73.6	(7,129)	100.0
Tax refund received, including interest		0.0	20,418	100.0
Other—net	3,036	36.7	8,266	100.0
Total operating activities	$ 135,163	70.4%	$ 192,117	100.0%
Investing activities:				
Proceeds from sale of investments	8,512	*		
Capital expenditures	(95,814)	116.3	(82,398)	100.0
Investments in nonconsolidated companies	(2,402)	319.8	(751)	100.0
Acquisitions—net of cash acquired		0.0	(392)	100.0
Other—net	1,541	42.9	3,589	100.0
Total investing activities	$ (88,163)	110.3%	$ (79,952)	100.0%
Financing activities:				
Short-term borrowing (repayment)	(3,837)	**	2,587	100.0
Long-term borrowing	3,690	20.1	18,400	100.0
Long-term repayment	(20,000)	107.2	(18,660)	100.0
Dividends paid	(55,883)	104.8	(53,322)	100.0
Common shares purchased— net of options exercised	(19,235)	186.3	(10,327)	100.0
Total financing activities	$ (95,265)	155.4%	$ (61,322)	100.0%
Effect of exchange rate changes on cash	(1,289)	161.9	(796)	100.0
Net increase (decrease) in cash and short-term investments	(49,554)	**	50,047	100.0
Cash and short-term investments at the beginning of year	126,147	165.8	76,100	100.0
Cash and short-term investments at the end of year	$ 76,593	60.7%	$ 126,147	100.0%

*Mathematically, you cannot calculate a percentage change if the base year is zero.

**When a negative amount appears in the base year and a positive amount in the following year, or vice versa, no percentage change can be meaningfully computed.

EXHIBIT 20–3   HORIZONTAL ANALYSIS OF THE STATEMENTS OF CASH FLOWS— THE LUBRIZOL CORPORATION

| | (In thousands of dollars) Year Ended December 31 | | | |
	1992	1991	Increase/ (Decrease)	%
Cash provided from (used for):				
Operating activities:				
Received from customers	$1,549,848	$1,480,776	$ 69,072	4.7%
Paid to suppliers and employees	(1,362,971)	(1,265,058)	96,913	7.7
Income taxes paid	(62,576)	(55,116)	7,460	13.5
Interest and dividends received	12,071	9,960	2,111	21.2
Interest paid	(5,245)	(7,129)	(1,884)	(26.4)
Tax refund received, including interest		20,418	(20,418)	(100.0)
Other—net	3,036	8,266	(5,230)	(63.3)
Total operating activities	$ 135,163	$ 192,117	$ (56,954)	29.6%
Investing activities:				
Proceeds from sale of investments	8,512		8,512	*
Capital expenditures	(95,814)	(82,398)	13,416	16.3
Investments in nonconsolidated companies	(2,402)	(751)	1,651	219.8
Acquisitions—net of cash acquired		(392)	(392)	(100.0)
Other—net	1,541	3,589	(2,048)	(57.1)
Total investing activities	$ (88,163)	$ (79,952)	$ 8,211	10.3%

	1992	1991	Increase/ (Decrease)	%
Financing activities:				
Short-term borrowing (repayment)	(3,837)	2,587	(6,424)	**
Long-term borrowing	3,690	18,400	(14,710)	(79.9)
Long-term repayment	(20,000)	(18,660)	1,340	7.2
Dividends paid	(55,883)	(53,322)	2,561	4.8
Common shares purchased— net of options exercised	(19,235)	(10,327)	8,908	86.3
Total financing activities	$ (95,265)	$ (61,322)	$ 33,943	55.4%
Effect of exchange rate changes on cash	(1,289)	(796)	493	61.9
Net increase (decrease) in cash and short-term investments	(49,554)	50,047	(99,601)	**
Cash and short-term investments at the beginning of year	126,147	76,100	50,047	65.8
Cash and short-term investments at the end of year	$ 76,593	$ 126,147	$(49,554)	(30.9%)

*Mathematically, you cannot calculate a percentage change if the base year is zero.

**When a negative amount appears in the base year and a positive amount in the following year, or vice versa, no percentage change can be meaningfully computed.

is only $1.65 million. In contrast, receipts from customers increased by only 4.7%, an increase of $69.1 million. A user must remember that percentage changes are best viewed from the perspective of the item's relative importance.

Trend Analysis

Trend analysis is a form of horizontal analysis that uses comparative financial statements for more than two successive periods. A user selects a base year and compares other years with the base year. Trend analysis of financial statements over several time periods is useful for two reasons. The analysis (1) discloses changes occurring over time and (2) provides information as to the direction in which a company is moving. Trends are important. Comparing only one year with another highlights unusual differences, but these differences may not be part of a significant pattern. Moreover, small changes that seem insignificant in viewing only two years might be seen as part of a significant trend when several years are examined together. Users of financial statements are generally interested in an increasing or decreasing trend in sales, net income, assets, or cash flows.

Exhibit 20–4 is an excerpt from the three-year summary of cash flows from operating activities in the annual report of the Lubrizol Corporation.

We compute trend percentages for the data in Exhibit 20–4 using 1990 as the base year. Trend percentages for the years 1990, 1991, and 1992 are presented in Exhibit 20–5.

It is apparent that cash received from customers has risen steadily, along with payments to suppliers and employees. We cannot tell whether the increases are attributable to increased revenues and expenses or to changes in collection and/or payment policies.

Comparing Exhibits 20–2 and 20–5, we see that the percentage changes are not the same, because we are comparing a two-year period (Exhibit 20–2) with a three-year period (Exhibit 20–5) and each has a different base year. The base-year-to-date approach for two years shown in Exhibit 20–2 has the advantage of highlighting year-to-year changes, but it does not provide for understanding relative changes over time. Because different years are used as bases, the changes from year to year cannot be added to arrive at a cumulative change. This is why the "base-year-to-date" method for more than two periods is used. We start with the base year and compare cumulative results from later years with the base year to determine cumulative percentage changes. This is the approach used in Exhibit 20–5.

Trend analysis is not limited to cash flow items; it can be used for any item in the financial statements. Keep in mind that although a percentage change in an item in one year might appear important, the change should be viewed both in terms of absolute dollars and in its relationship to other items in the financial statements.

EXHIBIT 20-4   THREE-YEAR SUMMARY OF CASH FLOW FROM OPERATIONS—THE LUBRIZOL CORPORATION

THE LUBRIZOL CORPORATION CONSOLIDATED STATEMENTS OF CASH FLOWS

(In Thousands of Dollars)	Year Ended December 31		
	1992	1991	1990
Cash provided from (used for):			
Operating activities:			
Received from customers	$1,549,848	$1,480,776	$1,395,667
Paid to suppliers and employees	(1,361,971)	(1,265,058)	(1,206,060)
Income taxes paid	(62,576)	(55,116)	(87,713)
Interest and dividends received	12,071	9,960	10,181
Interest paid	(5,245)	(7,129)	(6,058)
Tax refund received, including interest		20,418	
Other—net	3,036	8,266	8,302
Total operating activities	135,163	192,117	114,319
Investing activities:			
Proceeds from sale of investments	8,512		105,843
Capital expenditures	(95,814)	(82,398)	(77,407)
Investments in non-consolidated companies	(2,402)	(751)	(6,690)
Acquisitions—net of cash acquired		(392)	(8,134)
Other—net	1,541	3,589	1,912
Total investing activities	(88,163)	(79,952)	15,524
Financing activities:			
Short-term borrowing (repayment)	(3,837)	2,587	3,240
Long-term borrowing	3,690	18,400	34
Long-term repayment	(20,000)	(18,660)	
Dividends paid	(55,883)	(53,322)	(52,257)
Common shares purchased, net of options exercised	(19,235)	(10,327)	(86,980)
Total financing activities	(95,265)	(61,322)	(135,963)
Effect of exchange rate changes on cash	(1,289)	(796)	579
Net increase (decrease) in cash and short-term investments	(49,554)	50,047	(5,541)
Cash and short-term investments at the beginning of year	126,147	76,100	81,641
Cash and short-term investments at the end of year	$ 76,593	$ 126,147	$ 76,100

The accompanying notes to financial statements are an integral part of these statements.

EXHIBIT 20-5   TREND ANALYSIS OF CASH FLOW FROM OPERATIONS—THE LUBRIZOL CORPORATION

	Year Ended December 31		
	1992	1991	1990
Cash provided from (used for):			
Operating activities:			
Received from customers	111%	106%	100%
Paid to suppliers and employees	113	105	100
Income taxes paid	71	63	100
Interest and dividends received	119	98	100
Interest paid	87	118	100
Tax refund received, including interest	—	*	-0-
Other—net	37	100	100
Total operating activities	118%	168%	100%

*Mathematically, you cannot calculate a percentage change if the base year is zero.

Vertical Analysis

Horizontal analysis focuses on the dollar and percentage changes in the financial statement items over time. In contrast, vertical analysis focuses on the financial relationships in the financial statements of a single period. Exhibit 20–6 presents a vertical analysis of the statement of cash flows from the annual report of Lubrizol Corporation. We have used the supplemental cash flow information in Lubrizol's 1992 annual report, from Note 9 (our Exhibit 20–1).

As a general rule, a vertical analysis of an income statement presents the income statement item dollar amount and its percentage. Each of the percentages are calculated by dividing the income statement amounts by the net sales figure for that year. This results in the sum of all the items equalling 100%. The percentage of each financial statement item denotes the relative significance of that item in the determination of net income. Each expense is shown as a percentage by which it decreases net sales.

Sometimes users examine the percentage of certain expenses to sales to compare the company with a benchmark, such as a target set by management or the average values for an industry. These benchmarks are usually found in industry trade association publications. Company managers find this type of comparison especially useful in assessing the performance of the company relative to its competitors.

A vertical analysis of the balance sheet expresses each balance sheet amount as a percentage of total assets or of total liabilities plus stockholders' equity. Again, users examine the relative components of assets, liabilities, and stockholders' equity based on these percentages as compared with some target or with industry averages.

Exhibit 20–6 expresses each item in the statement of cash flows as a percentage of the total inflows of cash and short-term investments from all sources for 1991 and 1992. Because short-term investments are near-cash items, the company combines them with cash in its balance sheet and statement of cash flows. Total net inflows of cash and short-term investments were $148,906,000 and $216,693,000 in 1992 and 1991, respectively. These amounts can be verified by summing the cash inflows from operating activities and investing and financing activities.

By examining Exhibit 20–6, we see that cash inflows from operating activities have increased from 88.7% of total cash inflows in 1991 to 90.8% in 1992. This is a good sign. We see however, that net investing activities accounted for almost

EXHIBIT 20–6 VERTICAL ANALYSIS OF THE STATEMENTS OF CASH FLOWS— THE LUBRIZOL CORPORATION

(In thousands of dollars)

Cash provided from (used for):	1992	%**	1991	%
Operating activities:				
Net income	$ 124,646	83.7%	$ 123,659	57.1%
Noncash items included in net income:				
Depreciation and amortization	62,013	41.6	59,473	27.4
Deferred income taxes	(37)	(0.0)	(2,716)	(1.3)
Distributed (undistributed) earnings of nonconsolidated companies	2,792	1.9	(3,743)	(1.7)
Gain on sales of investments	(6,484)	(4.4)		
Changes in current assets and liabilities:				
Receivables	(2,400)	(1.6)	4,470	40.7
Inventories	(30,807)	(20.7)	(14,187)	(6.5)
Accounts payable and accrued expenses	(13,693)	(9.2)	1,780	0.8
Other current assets	(316)	(0.2)	15,304	7.1
Increase in noncurrent liabilities	714	0.5	1,554	0.7
Other items—net	(1,265)	(0.8)	6,523	3.0
Total operating activities	$ 135,163	90.8%	$ 192,117	88.7%
Investing activities:				
Proceeds from sale of investments	8,512	5.7		
Capital expenditures	(95,814)	(64.3)	(82,398)	(38.0)
Investments in nonconsolidated companies	(2,402)	(1.6)	(751)	(0.3)
Acquisitions—net of cash acquired			(392)	(0.2)
Other—net	1,541	1.0	3,589	1.6
Total investing activities	$ (88,163)	(59.2)%	$ (79,952)	(36.9)%
Financing activities:				
Short-term borrowing (repayment)	(3,837)	(2.6)	2,587	1.2
Long-term borrowing	3,690	2.5	18,400	8.5
Long-term repayment	(20,000)	(13.5)	(18,660)	(8.6)
Dividends paid	(55,883)	(37.5)	(53,322)	(24.6)
Common shares purchased—net of options exercised	(19,235)	(12.9)	(10,327)	(4.8)
Total financing activities	$ (95,265)	(64.0)	$ (61,322)	(28.3)%
Effect of exchange rate changes on cash	(1,289)	(0.9)	(796)	(0.4)
Net increase (decrease) in cash and short-term investments	(49,554)	(33.3)%	50,047	23.1%
Cash and short-term investments at the beginning of year	126,147		76,100	
Cash and short-term investments at the end of year	$ 76,593		$ 126,147	

**Common-size percentages are based on total cash inflows from all sources. In 1992 the percentages are reconciled to 100% by summing:

Operating Activities	+	Sale of Investments	+	Other	+	Short- and Long-Term Borrowings	=	Total Cash Inflows
90.8%	+	5.7%	+	1.0%	+	2.5%	=	100.0%
$135,163	+	$8,512	+	$1,541	+	$3,690	=	$148,906

60% of total cash inflows. The primary investing activities were capital expenditures. Capital expenditures were significantly higher in 1992 than in 1991 as a percentage of cash inflows. Recall that the company indicated in Note 9 to the annual report that capital expenditures were financed by the beginning balance of cash and short-term investments and internally generated funds.

Finally, our vertical analysis corroborates our horizontal analysis in showing that cash outflows from financing activities were used to repurchase the company's stock, pay dividends, and reduce debt. Each of these items was a significantly higher percentage of cash inflow in 1992 than in 1991. Moreover, all of these items reduce cash and correlate with the overall decrease in cash and short-term investments for the year. One conclusion is that, unlike what happened in 1991, cash flows from operations were unable to support the net investing and financing activities. This is not a good sign.

Further analysis may include comparisons with prior periods' statements of cash flow for Lubrizol, or with companies within its industry. This extension may indicate other areas requiring further investigation.

Horizontal analysis highlights changes in an item over time. Vertical analysis discloses the relationship between a statement item and a base item. In our examples we use both techniques, because no one technique gives a complete picture of Lubrizol's statements of cash flows.

Common-Size Financial Statements

One type of vertical analysis uses financial statements that contain only percentages. Each component of the financial statement is shown as a percentage of some amount of some common item in the statement. Statements of this type are called *common-size* financial statements.

Common-size financial statements differ from statements prepared for vertical analysis, in that common-size financial statements contain only percentages, not dollar amounts. All figures on a common-size balance sheet are percentages of total assets or total liabilities plus stockholders' equity. On a common-size income statement the items are percentages of net sales. In the statement of cash flows each item is a percentage of the increase or decrease in cash inflows for the year (as was similarly shown in Exhibit 20–6). This type of presentation is "common-size" because the items always sum to 100%.

Common-size statements give the user a better understanding of the relationship between a particular item and sales (on the income statement), or between an item and total assets or total liabilities plus stockholders' equity (on the balance sheet), or the item and the change in cash (on the statement of cash flows). Such statements can give the reader a better under-

standing than can be gained by merely looking at absolute dollar amounts. The information can be compared with industry averages to assess a company's standing in its industry.

Common-size financial statements also allow comparisons to be made between companies of different sizes. For example, because General Motors Corporation is much larger than Chrysler Corporation, comparison is difficult. However, if the financial statements of each company are modified to common-size, changes in the relative size of the components of the financial statements become apparent. These changes might be missed if only absolute dollar amounts are examined. For example, a company's sales may increase, providing a positive signal, but if gross margin decreased or selling, general, and administrative expenses increased as a percentage of sales, the benefit of additional sales may be lost. Common-size financial statements reveal both types of change.

Exhibit 20–7 displays the common-size consolidated statements of cash flows for 1991 and 1992 for Lubrizol Corporation. The statements differ from those in Exhibit 20–6 only in that the dollar amounts are omitted.

EXHIBIT 20–7   COMMON-SIZE STATEMENTS OF CASH FLOWS—THE LUBRIZOL CORPORATION

(In thousands of dollars)
Year Ended December 31

	1992	1991
Cash provided from (used for):		
Operating activities:	**	**
Net income	83.7%	57.1%
Noncash items included in net income:		
Depreciation and amortization	41.6	27.4
Deferred income taxes	(0.0)	(1.3)
Distributed (undistributed) earnings of nonconsolidated companies	1.9	(1.7)
Gain on sales of investments	(4.4)	
Changes in assets and liabilities:		
Receivables	(1.6)	2.1
Inventories	(20.7)	(6.5)
Accounts payable and accrued expenses	(9.2)	0.8
Other current assets	(0.2)	7.1
Increase in noncurrent liabilities	0.5	0.7
Other items—net	(0.8)	3.0
Total operating activities	90.8%	88.7%
Investing activities:		
Proceeds from sale of investments	5.7	
Capital expenditures	(64.3)	(38.0)
Investments in nonconsolidated companies	(1.6)	(0.3)
Acquisitions—net of cash acquired		(0.2)
Other—net	1.0	1.6
Total investing activities	(59.2)%	(36.9)%
Financing activities:		
Short-term borrowing (repayment)	(2.6)	1.2
Long-term borrowing	2.5	8.5
Long-term repayment	(13.5)	(8.6)
Dividends paid	(37.5)	(24.6)
Common shares purchased—net of options exercised	(12.9)	(4.8)
Total financing activities	(64.0)%	(28.3)%
Effect of exchange rate changes on cash	(0.9)	(0.4)
Net increase (decrease) in cash and short-term investments	(33.3)%	23.1%

**Common size percentages are based on total cash inflows from all sources. In 1992 and 1991 the percentages are reconciled to 100% by summing:

	Operating Activities	+	Sale of Investments	+	Other	+	Long-Term Borrowings	=	Total Cash Inflows
1992	90.8%	+	5.7%	+	1.0%	+	2.5%	=	100.0%
1991	88.7%	+	–0–	+	1.6%	+	9.7%	=	100.0%

21

RATIO ANALYSIS OF THE STATEMENT OF CASH FLOWS

Cash flow is the lifeblood of every business. A company survives by ensuring that its cash receipts and cash payments are efficiently and effectively managed. When lenders and suppliers analyze cash flow, they focus on repayment, knowing that their claims can be satisfied only with cash. Stockholders and potential investors, interested in return on investment, also assess the adequacy of cash.

To aid in analyzing cash flow, the accounting profession requires that companies issue a statement of cash flows in their annual reports. The profession suggests that the primary purpose of the statement of cash flows is to provide relevant and timely information regarding a company's cash receipts and payments. The statement can then be used by investors, creditors, and others to assess (1) a company's ability to generate positive future net cash flows, (2) the company's ability to pay its debts and make dividend payments, (3) what causes the difference between reported net income and net cash inflow, and (4) the effects on the company's financial condition of both its cash and noncash investing and financing activities.

This chapter deals with cash flow ratios that can assist in these assessments. That is not to say that ratio analysis of the accrual-based income statement and balance sheet are not important. The cash flow ratios presented in this chapter should be used in conjunction with traditional income statement and balance sheet ratios to corroborate the overall financial strength or weakness of a company. All the ratios we discuss examine the statement of cash flows, the income statement, and the balance sheet. Our list of ratios is not all-inclusive. A user could construct other cash flow ratios that would be appropriate for analyzing a company's cash position.

Ratio Analysis Techniques

There are many aspects to financial statement and cash flow analysis. For example, Chapter 18 discusses comparative analysis. However, the calculation and interpretation of ratios is one of the most prevalent tools used in financial statement and cash flow analysis. Ratios in and of themselves tell very little, unless they are compared with benchmarks or norms. When compared with norms, their informational benefit is greatly enhanced. Common benchmarks include average industry ratios and values for the same company in previous years.

There are three areas of interest to users of a statement of cash flows that deserve attention: (1) liquidity and solvency, (2) capital expenditures and investing, and (3) cash flow returns. These areas form the basis for classifying ratios in this chapter. Liquidity is the ability to pay short-term liabilities, and solvency refers to the ability to meet long-term obligations. The capital expenditures and investing ratios provide signals as to the company's ability to maintain its investment in capital assets. The cash flow return ratios complement the accrual-based profitability measures, such as return on sales and return on investment.

As we begin our discussion of cash flow ratio analysis, remember that computing ratios is only a starting point in analyzing a company. Ratios do not give answers, but they do often provide indications as to what might be expected. However, ratios often give conflicting signals. For example, if a company has excess cash, it is better able to pay its liabilities. Yet, having excess cash is not necessarily good, because cash in a checking account earns little or no return. The company might increase earnings if it invested its excess cash. This type of contradiction is found wherever ratios are used.

Our discussion of cash flow ratios uses the financial statements of the Lubrizol Corporation. Lubrizol's statements of cash flows are analyzed using comparative analysis in Chapter 20. Exhibits 21–1, 21–2, and 21–3 are the statements of cash flows, income statements, and balance sheets for the company.

EXHIBIT 21-1   STATEMENTS OF CASH FLOWS— THE LUBRIZOL CORPORATION

THE LUBRIZOL CORPORATION CONSOLIDATED STATEMENTS OF CASH FLOWS

	Year Ended December 31		
(In Thousands of Dollars) Cash provided from (used for):	1992	1991	1990
Operating activities:			
Received from customers	$1,549,848	$1,480,776	$1,395,667
Paid to suppliers and employees	(1,361,971)	(1,265,058)	(1,206,060)
Income taxes paid	(62,576)	(55,116)	(87,713)
Interest and dividends received	12,071	9,960	10,181
Interest paid	(5,245)	(7,129)	(6,058)
Tax refund received, including interest		20,418	
Other—net	3,036	8,266	8,302
Total operating activities	135,163	192,117	114,319
Investing activities:			
Proceeds from sales of investments	8,512		105,843
Capital expenditures	(95,814)	(82,398)	(77,407)
Investments in non-consolidated companies	(2,402)	(751)	(6,690)
Acquisitions—net of cash acquired		(392)	(8,134)
Other—net	1,541	3,589	1,912
Total investing activities	(88,163)	(79,952)	15,524
Financing activities:			
Short-term borrowing (repayment)	(3,837)	2,587	3,240
Long-term borrowing	3,690	18,400	34
Long-term repayment	(20,000)	(18,660)	
Dividends paid	(55,883)	(53,322)	(52,257)
Common shares purchased, net of options exercised	(19,235)	(10,327)	(86,980)
Total financing activities	(95,265)	(61,322)	(135,963)
Effect of exchange rate changes on cash	(1,289)	(796)	579
Net increase (decrease) in cash and short-term investments	(49,554)	50,047	(5,541)
Cash and short-term investments at the beginning of year	126,147	76,100	81,641
Cash and short-term investments at the end of year	$ 76,593	$ 126,147	$ 76,100

The accompanying notes to financial statements are an integral part of these statements.

EXHIBIT 21–2   STATEMENTS OF INCOME—THE LUBRIZOL CORPORATION

THE LUBRIZOL CORPORATION CONSOLIDATED STATEMENTS OF INCOME

Year Ended December 31

(In Thousands of Dollars Except Per Share Data)	1992	1991	1990
Net sales	$1,544,670	$1,467,901	$1,444,758
Royalties and other revenues	7,578	8,405	7,943
Total revenues	1,552,248	1,476,306	1,452,701
Cost of sales	1,054,376	992,275	1,006,341
Selling and administrative expenses	181,326	172,418	157,953
Research, testing and development expenses	154,762	143,983	124,097
Total cost and expenses	1,390,464	1,308,676	1,288,391
Gain on sale of Genentech			101,921
Other income—net	11,905	9,500	504
Interest income	7,070	8,748	10,526
Interest expense	(3,615)	(7,738)	(6,049)
Income before income taxes	177,144	178,140	271,212
Provision for income taxes	52,498	54,481	81,166
Net income	$ 124,646	$ 123,659	$ 190,046
Net income per share	$1.81	$1.79	$2.67

The accompanying notes to financial statements are an integral part of these statements.

CONSOLIDATED BALANCE SHEETS THE LUBRIZOL CORPORATION

(In Thousands of Dollars)	December 31 1992	1991
Assets		
Cash and short-term investments	$ 76,593	$ 126,147
Receivables	221,094	240,382
Inventories	272,418	306,993
Other	20,911	28,049
Total current assets	591,016	701,571
Property and equipment—at cost	958,692	962,261
Less accumulated depreciation	583,105	582,231
Property—net	375,587	380,030
Investments in non-consolidated companies	139,660	52,441
Intangible and other assets	20,857	37,641
TOTAL	$1,127,120	$1,171,683

Liabilities and Shareholders' Equity	1992	1991
Short-term debt	$ 25,140	$ 32,801
Accounts payable	105,237	126,140
Income taxes and other current liabilities	75,871	103,221
Total current liabilities	206,248	262,162
Long-term debt	23,258	34,982
Non-current liabilities	41,217	41,979
Deferred income taxes	37,035	38,094
Total liabilities	307,758	377,217
Common shares without par value— Outstanding 68,450,586 shares in 1992 and 69,031,464 shares in 1991	80,274	77,423
Retained earnings	759,906	713,229
Accumulated translation adjustment	(20,818)	3,814
Total shareholders' equity	819,362	794,466
TOTAL	$1,127,120	$1,171,683

The accompanying notes to financial statements are an integral part of these statements.

Liquidity Ratios

Liquidity refers to the company's ability to repay its short-term debts as they come due. Common ratios relating to liquidity are the current ratio, the quick (acid-test) ratio, and accounts receivable and inventory turnover. These ratios are discussed in Chapter 2. Although these ratios can be helpful in measuring a company's liquidity, they may give a distorted picture. This can occur if the balances used to calculate the ratios do not represent the balances carried during the year—which can happen if the year-end account balances used in the ratios are unusually large or small as compared with balances maintained the rest of the year.

Current Cash Debt Coverage

The ratio of *cash flow from operations* (CFO) to average current liabilities attempts to overcome the aforementioned problem, because it compares amounts over a period of time rather than considering a balance at a point in time.

$$\text{Current Cash Debt Coverage} = \frac{\text{CFO}}{\text{Average Current Liabilities}}$$

Average current liabilities is computed by taking the beginning balance plus the ending balance in the current liabilities and dividing by 2.

$$1992: \frac{\$135,163}{(\$206,248 + \$262,162)/2} = 57.7\%$$

Lubrizol's current cash debt coverage is approximately 58%, which is a good sign, since current research suggests that the ratio should be about 40% (or more) for a company.

Cash Dividend Coverage

The cash dividend coverage ratio provides evidence about a company's ability to meet current dividend payments with cash flows from operations. The ratio is expressed as cash flow from operations divided by total dividend payments. This ratio can be modified to reflect dividend payments to all stockholders or only to common stockholders. To reflect coverage only to common stockholders, preferred dividends are subtracted from the numerator and the denominator is common stock dividends.

$$\text{Cash Dividend Coverage} = \frac{\text{CFO}}{\text{Dividends Paid}}$$

$$1992: \frac{\$135,163}{\$55,883} = 2.4 \text{ times} \qquad 1991: \frac{\$192,117}{\$53,322} = 3.6 \text{ times}$$

Solvency Ratios

Solvency refers to a company's ability to meet both its short-term and long-term obligations. For decades solvency has been measured by the debt ratio and the times interest earned ratio. But now two cash flow ratios have been developed that measure solvency: the ratio of CFO to the company's average total liabilities, and CFO (before interest and taxes) divided by interest paid.

Cash Long-Term Debt Coverage

Several analysts believe the traditional debt ratio (debt divided by total assets) overlooks the differing degrees of liquidity for assets that will be used to repay the company's debt. The cash long-term debt coverage ratio overcomes that limitation by focusing directly on cash. All things being equal, the higher the ratio the better. Current literature suggests that 20% is a reasonable measure for this ratio. Lubrizol's ratio is almost double this benchmark.

$$\text{Cash Long-Term Debt Coverage} = \frac{\text{CFO}}{\text{Average Total Liabilities}}$$

$$1992: \frac{\$135,163}{(\$307,758 + \$377,217)/2} = 39.5\%$$

An alternative form of this ratio reduces cash flow from operations by total dividend payments, resulting in "retained" operating cash flows as the numerator. The rationale is that reducing the numerator by dividend payments results in a better measure of the amount of cash available for reinvestment.

Cash Interest Coverage

The times interest earned ratio normally is calculated by taking income before interest and taxes and dividing that amount by interest expense. A better measure of interest coverage is CFO (plus interest paid and taxes paid) divided by interest actually paid rather than interest expense. This is a more pragmatic approach, because interest is paid in cash and reduces cash from operations. We use taxes actually paid rather than the taxes accrued as an expense in the numerator.

$$\text{Cash Interest Coverage} = \frac{\text{CFO} + \text{Interest Paid} + \text{Taxes Paid}}{\text{Interest Paid}}$$

Lubrizol's cash interest coverage has increased slightly from 1991 to 1992. Without knowing the industry average we cannot determine what the ratio should be; however, all things being equal, the higher the ratio the better.

$$1992: \frac{\$135,163 + \$5,245 + \$62,576}{\$5,245} = 38.7 \text{ times}$$

$$1991: \frac{\$192,117 + \$7,129 + \$55,116}{\$7,129} = 35.7 \text{ times}$$

Capital Expenditures and Investing Ratios

To be successful and competitive a company must meet all of its obligations. In addition, a company must maintain its existing capital assets and finance expenditures to increase that asset base. To determine whether the company can cover these expenditures, several new ratios have been developed.

Capital Acquisitions Ratio

The capital acquisitions ratio reveals whether a company can currently pay for its capital expenditures. Again, we subtract dividends paid from CFO to approximate the amount of cash retained by the company and available for reinvestment.

$$\text{Capital Acquisitions} = \frac{\text{CFO} - \text{Total Dividends Paid}}{\text{Capital Expenditures}}$$

Lubrizol's capital acquisitions ratio has declined significantly in 1992 because of a reduction in CFO. This is cause for concern.

$$1992: \frac{\$135,163 - \$55,883}{\$95,814} = 82.7\%$$

$$1991: \frac{\$192,117 - \$53,322}{\$82,398} = 168.4\%$$

Investment/CFO Plus Finance Ratio

A user can assess how investments are financed by comparing net cash flows from investing activities to net cash flows from operating and financing activities. One new ratio that does this is net cash flows from investing activities divided by net cash flows from financing activities.

$$\text{Investment/CFO} + \text{Finance} = \frac{\text{Net Cash Flows for Investing (CFI)}}{\text{Net Cash Flows from Operations and Financing Activities}}$$

$$1992: \frac{\$88,163}{\$135,163 + (\$95,265)} = 221.0\%$$

$$1991: \frac{\$79,952}{\$192,117 + (\$61,322)} = 61.1\%$$

In evaluating this ratio, keep in mind that a lower ratio indicates that a lower percentage of investment is financed by operating and financing activities—a good sign. Because Lubrizol's ratio has tripled in one year, there is cause for concern. As in evaluating most other ratios, we might want to examine this ratio over a number of years to see what the trend has been.

Operations/Investment Ratio

To assess a company's potential for funding expansion from internally generated funds, we compute the ratio of cash flow from operations to cash flow from investing activities. All things being equal, the higher the ratio, the less the company must rely on external financing.

$$\text{Operations/Investment} = \frac{\text{CFO}}{\text{CFI}}$$

$$1992: \frac{\$135,163}{\$88,163} = 153.3\% \qquad 1991: \frac{\$192,117}{\$79,952} = 240.3\%$$

Lubrizol's CFO as a percentage of investing activities has declined from 1991 to 1992 primarily as a result of its decrease in cash flow from operations.

Cash Reinvestment Ratio

The cash reinvestment ratio compares the cash flow retained for reinvestment with the gross amount of noncurrent assets plus working capital. This ratio is a useful measure of the percentage of the cash flow available to be used to replace existing assets and provide for expansion. Again, all things being equal, the greater the reinvestment, the greater is the expectation that CFO will increase. A reinvestment ratio between 7 and 11 is reasonable. Lubrizol's reinvestment ratio was within this range in 1991 but has declined in 1992.

$$\text{Cash Reinvestment} = \frac{\text{CFO} - \text{Dividends Paid}}{\text{Noncurrent Assets (gross)} + \text{Working Capital}}$$

$$1992: \frac{\$135,163 - \$55,883}{\$958,692 + \$139,660 + \$20,857 + (\$591,016 - \$206,248)} = 5.3\%$$

$$1991: \frac{\$192,117 - \$53,322 =}{\$962,261 + \$52,441 + \$37,641 + (\$701,571 - \$262,162)} = 9.3\%$$

Cash Flow Return Ratios

As stated earlier, cash flow ratios are counterparts to accrual-based ratios, which are expressed in the general form:

$$\text{Return on Investment} = \frac{\text{Income}}{\text{Investment}}$$

Cash flow returns on investment can be computed in the same manner as accrual-based profitability measures.

Overall Cash Flow Ratio

The overall cash flow ratio measures the extent to which internally generated CFO supplies the cash required for investing and financing activities.

$$\text{Overall Cash Flow Ratio} = \frac{\text{CFO}}{\text{Financing} + \text{Investing Cash Outflows}}$$

$$1992: \frac{\$135,163}{[(\$88,163) + (\$95,265)]} = 73.7\%$$

$$1991: \frac{\$192,117}{[(\$79,952) + (\$61,322)]} = 136.0\%$$

The Lubrizol Corporation's cash flow from operations was more than the cash needed for financing and investing activities in 1991 but declined substantially in 1992.

Cash Return on Sales Ratio

Cash return on sales is a measure similar to the traditional return on sales (net income divided by sales). This ratio and the ratio of CFO to net income seeks to determine whether the company's sales and net income are matched by its cash flows.

$$\text{Cash Return on Sales} = \frac{\text{CFO}}{\text{Sales}}$$

Cash return on sales is sometimes called *cash flow margin* and measures the percentage of cash flow per dollar of sales (or any type of revenue). This ratio measures the ability of the company to translate dollars of sales (or revenue) into cash, and the higher the ratio the better.

$$1992: \frac{\$135,163}{\$1,544,670} = 8.7\% \qquad 1991: \frac{\$192,117}{\$1,467,901} = 13.1\%$$

The company's ability to turn sales dollars into cash has declined, even though its sales increased by slightly 5%. Further study is necessary to determine the cause of the decline.

Cash Flow to Net Income Ratio

The cash flow to net income ratio is calculated as:

$$\text{Cash Flow to Net Income} = \frac{\text{CFO}}{\text{Net Income}}$$

$$1992: \frac{\$135,163}{\$124,646} = 108.4\% \qquad 1991: \frac{\$192,117}{\$123,659} = 155.4\%$$

Not surprisingly, even though net income increased slightly, CFO declined from more than one and one-half times of net income to just more than one times net income. For the Lubrizol Corporation, total revenue could have been used instead of sales. The inclusion of royalties and other revenues in the denominator would have moderately reduced the ratios for 1991 and 1992.

Quality of Sales Ratio

Among the assessments analysts must make in examining the statement of cash flows is a determination of the reasons for differences between net income and cash receipts and payments. This assessment is the basis for evaluating the quality of earnings. One measure of this difference is the quality of sales, calculated as:

$$\text{Quality of Sales} = \frac{\text{Cash from Sales}}{\text{Sales}}$$

Cash collections from customers (cash from sales) is available only if a company prepares its statement of cash flows using the direct method. Lubrizol uses the direct method, and its ratios for 1992 and 1991 are:

$$1992: \frac{\$1,549,848}{\$1,544,670} = 100.3\% \qquad 1991: \frac{\$1,480,776}{\$1,467,901} = 100.9\%$$

There is not much difference between sales and cash received from customers for Lubrizol in both 1991 and 1992, indicating high quality of earnings.

Quality of Income Ratio

When a company does not use the direct method in presenting its statement of cash flows, the quality of earnings can be examined by using the quality of income ratio.

$$\text{Quality of Income} = \frac{\text{CFO}}{\text{Operating Income}}$$

$$1992: \frac{\$135,163}{\$180,759} = 74.7\% \qquad 1991: \frac{\$192,117}{\$185,878} = 103.3\%$$

Note: Operating income is the same as income before interest and taxes, which in most cases is the same as net income plus interest expense and income taxes. For 1992, operating income is $180,759 ($124,646 + $3,615 + $52,498); and for 1991, $185,878 ($123,659 + $54,481 + $7,738).

The ratio provides information about the difference between accrual-based income and cash flow from operations. Lubrizol's ratio has substantially declined in 1992.

Cash Return on Assets Ratio

Cash return on investment ratios can also be useful in evaluating company performance. Cash return on total assets is the counterpart to return on total investment ratio and is calculated as:

$$\text{Cash Return on Assets} = \frac{\text{CFO Before Interest Paid and Taxes Paid}}{\text{Average Total Assets}}$$

$$1992: \frac{\$135,163 + \$5,245 + \$62,576}{(\$1,127,120 + \$1,171,683)/2} = 17.7\%$$

This ratio would have to be compared with an industry average and with previous periods to determine whether there is a strong correlation between cash returns and investment.

Cash Return on Stockholders' Equity Ratio

The cash return on stockholders' equity reveals whether the company is able to generate a sufficient cash return for stockholders. The ratio is calculated as:

$$\text{Cash Return on Stockholders' Equity} = \frac{\text{CFO}}{\text{Average Stockholders' Equity}}$$

$$1992: \frac{\$135,163}{(\$819,362 + \$794,466)/2} = 16.8\%$$

Cash Flow per Share Ratio

Although the accounting profession prohibits the presentation of cash flow per share in the financial statements, analysts normally do calculate this ratio. The ratio is useful in tracking changes in cash flows over time. A comparison can also be made with the accrual-based ratios, such as earnings per share, dividend yield, and the payout ratio.

$$\text{Cash Flow per Share} = \frac{\text{CFO} - \text{Preferred Dividends}}{\text{Average Number of Shares of Common Stock Outstanding}}$$

$$1992: \frac{\$135,163 - \$0}{(\$68,451 + \$69,031)/2} = \$1.97$$

Ratio analysis must be used with care. Ratios provide information only in the context of a comparison. They can be interpreted only in comparison with past ratios of the same company, with ratios of other companies in the same industry, or with some predetermined norm. The reader should realize that in using ratios containing accrual-based amounts, different accounting methods such as LIFO and FIFO, or sum-of-the-years'-digits depreciation and straight-line depreciation, can cause similar firms to show quite different ratios. Exhibit 21–4 provides a summary of the cash flow ratios.

EXHIBIT 21–4   SUMMARY OF CASH FLOW RATIOS

LIQUIDITY AND SOLVENCY

$$\text{Current Cash Debt Coverage} = \frac{\text{CFO}}{\text{Average Current Liabilities}}$$

$$\text{Cash Dividend Coverage} = \frac{\text{CFO}}{\text{Dividends Paid}}$$

$$\text{Cash Long-Term Debt Coverage} = \frac{\text{CFO}}{\text{Average Total Liabilities}}$$

$$\text{Cash Interest Coverage} = \frac{\text{CFO + Interest Paid + Taxes Paid}}{\text{Interest Paid}}$$

CAPITAL EXPENDITURES AND INVESTING

$$\text{Capital Acquisitions} = \frac{\text{CFO + Total Dividends Paid}}{\text{Capital Expenditures}}$$

$$\text{Investment/CFO + Finance} = \frac{\text{Net Cash Flows for Investing (CFI)}}{\text{Net Cash Flows from Operations and Financing Activities}}$$

$$\text{Operations/Investment} = \frac{\text{CFO}}{\text{CFI}}$$

$$\text{Cash Reinvestment} = \frac{\text{CFO} - \text{Dividends Paid}}{\text{Noncurrent Assets (Gross) + Working Capital}}$$

CASH FLOW RETURN

$$\text{Overall Cash Flow Ratio} = \frac{\text{CFO}}{\text{Financing + Investing Cash Outflows}}$$

$$\text{Cash Return on Sales} = \frac{\text{CFO}}{\text{Sales}}$$

$$\text{Cash Flow to Net Income} = \frac{\text{CFO}}{\text{Net Income}}$$

$$\text{Quality of Sales} = \frac{\text{Cash from Sales}}{\text{Sales}}$$

$$\text{Quality of Income} = \frac{\text{CFO}}{\text{Operating Income}}$$

$$\text{Cash Return on Assets} = \frac{\text{CFO Before Interest Paid and Taxes Paid}}{\text{Average Total Assets}}$$

$$\text{Cash Return on Stockholders' Equity} = \frac{\text{CFO}}{\text{Average Stockholders' Equity}}$$

$$\text{Cash Flow per Share} = \frac{\text{CFO} - \text{Preferred Dividends}}{\text{Average Number of Shares of Common Stock Outstanding}}$$

INDEX

Note: Numbers in **boldface** indicate those pages where terms are defined.

About the Authors

Franklin J. Plewa, Jr., is Professor of Accounting at Idaho State University and the recipient of honors and awards for both teaching and research. He is the author of many books and articles, and is coauthor with George T. Friedlob of *Keys to Improving Your Return on Investment (ROI)* and *Financial and Business Statements.*

George T. Friedlob is Professor and Institute of Internal Auditors Research Foundation Faculty Fellow in the School of Accountancy at Clemson University. He has received numerous academic and professional awards and is the author of a wide variety of professional publications.